SPACE

The Next
Business Frontier

SPACE

The Next Business Frontier

LOU DOBBS

with HP Newquist

Pocket Books / ibooks
New York
www.ibooksinc.com
An Original Publication of Pocket Books, and ibooks, Inc.,
a Division of Simon & Schuster, Inc.

SPACE
c o m

A Space.com Book

To my wife, Debi, and my kids, Chance, Jason, Heather and Hillary, who are first in all things.

—LD

This book is dedicated, collectively, to Trini, Madeline and Katherine. Quite simply, I couldn't have done it without them.

—HPN

An Original Publication of ibooks, inc.
and Pocket Books, a division of Simon & Schuster

Pocket Books, a division of Simon & Schuster, Inc.
1230 Avenue of the Americas, New York, NY 10020

Cover Design: Mike Rivilis and j.vita
Editor: Howard Zimmerman

Space.com
120 West 45th Street
New York, NY 10036
(212) 703-5800
www.space.com

ibooks, inc.
24 West 25th Street
New York, NY 10010
www.ibooksinc.com
ISBN 0-7434-2389-5

First Printing October 2001

10 9 8 7 6 5 4 3 2 1

Printed in the U.S.A.

ACKNOWLEDGEMENTS

Special thanks to my collaborator, Harvey Newquist, whose unwavering focus, diligence, talent and dedication to space made this project possible. My gratitude also to my agent, Wayne Kabak of William Morris, my attorney Robert Zeller, good friends both, to Simon & Schuster, and to Byron Preiss, who oversaw this project from conception to completion. In addition, I want to thank my friends, colleagues and fellow space enthusiasts at Space.com. To board members Neil Armstrong, John Higginbotham, Donald Marron, Jack Williams, Jack Wyant, William Helman and Ray Rothrock, whose bright mind, constant enthusiasm and support makes us all better. To Fred Abatemarco, Andrew Chaikin, Lon Rains and all the people of Space News and Starry Night. The important work you do is making a critical difference in raising public awareness of space. To Jamie Kellner, Walter Isaacson, Phil Kent, Ken Jautz and everyone at CNN for their support. To Ted Turner, Reese Schonfeld and Burt Reinhardt for their friendship and counsel and a lot of laughs along the way. To my personal space heroes, mentors and friends, Neil, General Thomas Stafford and Captain Eugene Cernan. And to all of the heroes of the space community. Your imagination, achievements and courage are the foundation of our boundless future.

—LD

A book of this scope is never written in isolation. Facts, figures, perspectives, and varied viewpoints came from meetings, phone calls, emails, and casual conversations with hundreds of individuals across the country. First, thanks must go to Lou Dobbs, whose passion for space and business drove this book from conception to printed reality. His desire to make the business of space accessible to everyone—and to create a stage for serious discussion of the economics of space—set the tone for this book from the outset. And through the frenzy of the year 2001 (a veritable "space odyssey"), he always made this project both enjoyable and vital. When the frontiers of space commerce finally open, much of the credit will be his. My gratitude and appreciation also go to those individuals who provided assistance, information, and insight during the writing of this book. Foremost among them are Tucker Greco, Fred Abatemarco, Lon Rains, the staff of Space.com, Tim Carlson, John Higginbotham, Dr. George Mueller, Eddie Newquist, Arlene Forman, and Dr. Dale Webb. Respite, assistance, and good humor was provided by my parents, brothers and sisters (and their families), Lynne Carlson and family, Sammy Cemo and family, Rich Maloof and Pete Prown, and Michael S. Johnson. Finally, honorable mention must be given to Howard Zimmerman. His editorial and structural input made this book a far better work than it would have been had he not taken an active, fervent, and immensely personal interest. He was there every step of the way.

—HPN

CONTENTS

CONTENTS

INTRODUCTION

If asked to define the hottest technology on the planet, any man-on-the-street would undoubtedly say "the Internet." Of course, the odds are high that that same man on the street had no idea that the Internet even existed just five years ago.

Such is the pace of technology change, which today drives the evolution and dynamism of commerce. E-commerce—as business on the Internet is known—has dominated the hearts and minds of investors, technologists, and the business community since 1996, and will continue to do so for the next two or three years. This is because e-commerce has managed to both change the way business is done and push computer technology to its limits. One can even argue that e-commerce has changed business and technology forever.

Yet in the next decade, a new form of commerce and a new level of technology will compete with the Internet for the attention span, and dollars, of this very same business community.

Space.

Yes, space. The next—and perhaps the last—frontier for man and man's endeavors, is just past the bounds of gravity. It is more than the metaphysical frontier, more than just breaking the chains of this mortal coil. For wherever man goes, he takes with him the structures and support of his environment and his culture. This is a fact of life when new frontiers are broached. And with any frontier, there are always new opportunities that avail themselves and new businesses that grow up to help support the move into that frontier.

In the frontier of space we will create entirely new forms of technology, new forms of manufacturing, new forms of recreation, and even new materials. The creation of these entities and pursuits will lead to a whole new world of commerce built on doing business in space. Call it space commerce, or better yet, s-commerce.

Space commerce is not new. In fact, there is an entire industry already devoted to conducting "space business," from the launching of GPS satellites to the providing of launch insurance. The overall space business has already grown to over $100 billion in 2001 and shows no signs of abating. The number of satellites for telecommunication systems—the bread and butter of s-commerce—is expected to increase by more than one thousand in the next decade. (Source: Teal Group, cited in report by Keith Calhoun-Senghor, Director, Office of Air & Space Commercialization Technology Administration, U.S. Department of Commerce, before the Senate Committee on Commerce, Science, and Transportation Subcommittee on Science, Technology and Space, March 5, 1998, http://www. prospace.org/issues/SpaceCommerce/030598deptofspacecommerce.htm). And that's just maintaining the status quo. There is so much more to s-commerce than what we've done so far.

What have we done so far? Well, for better or worse—and you'll see which we think is what later in the book—we all think of only one organization when discussing our space efforts to date: NASA. The National Aeronautics and Space Administration did a fabulous job of getting America into space on short notice. With President John F. Kennedy's edict—and funded with nearly one percent of the country's Gross National Product—the agency accomplished things never before thought possible in time frames thought to be totally impossible. But outside of its Moon legacy, what have we as a populace come away with from NASA's ongoing legacy? More specifically, what long-term commercial results were derived from NASA's investment? Here are the four that most people rattle off: teflon, Tang, velcro, and space food sticks. These are nice cultural icons, but hardly the technological benefits one would expect from a program that has taken billions of dollars out of the economy every year for the past 40 years. (In fact, teflon, Tang, and velcro had all been commercially available prior to the start of the space program. So while NASA may have been an early adopter, it certainly wasn't responsible for the most famous spinoffs associated with it.)

To be fair, NASA was never set up to be a commercial endeavor. Its goals and mission were lofty in the era of the Cold War: to show that the United States could get a man into outer space and then put him on the Moon and, just as important, get him back safely. And perhaps most important, do it before the Communists did. With the achievement of this goal in 1969, NASA validated its existence, but in the ensuing three decades little from NASA has crept back into the public sector, let alone the public consciousness. Since then, it has been the occasional notable or newsworthy event (Mars Pathfinder, sending John Glenn back into space) that has kept NASA in the news.

But still, billions and billions of dollars with little product or commercial effect? It seems ludicrous. Any other modern endeavor that did not return vast sums in either dollar value or practical technology back to the industry would have been shut down faster than you can say "Abort liftoff."

Actually, there have been significant commercial gains that

have come out of NASA, but they have been due to the efforts of private organizations and entrepreneurs who have wrested the technology out of the space agency's hands. Artificial intelligence software programs, manufacturing technology, materials processing and handling—all of these and more have been spun off from space-program technology through the efforts of commercial enterprise. Other technologies run the gamut from the routine to the really exciting. These include uses in water and air monitoring, medical analysis, portable X-ray machines, noise abatement, solar heating, clean-room technology, art preservation, and on to cameras and sports simulators. The list goes on and on.

With this in mind, it is important to point out that NASA does exist as a "space business" unto itself: there are thousands of companies, research institutions, and academic centers doing business with NASA every year—competing for and working on more than 60,000 individual contracts (which doesn't even count the contracts that come in with a value of less than $25,000—we can add thousands more to this list at that level). The reluctance of NASA to pursue commercial benefit does not diminish the value and potential of space. Indeed, it points out that with a different structure, a different paradigm, space could be, and should be, a source of vast commercial opportunity and wealth for those willing to cross its borders. And those people and companies will be the last pioneers from our planet.

Where We're Going, and Who's Going First

This is not the world of science fiction. We are not talking about venturing into other galaxies or the nether regions of our universe. We are talking about conducting business in a space where man currently deploys telescopes and satellites, within eyesight of the oceans and landmasses that make up Earth. This is not only near space, it is viable space. As of the beginning of the year 2001, 397 different people have flown in space, representing 29 different nations. This is no longer an exclusive club—enough people have circled our sphere to populate a small town.

Venturing into space doesn't require any leap of faith, simply because we are already there—with the regular launches of the space shuttle, with the planned constructs for the space station, and with the ever growing number of satellites that we put into orbit around our planet every year.

The thought that "it's so far away" (a common refrain from naysayers) is really not applicable. The distances are not overwhelming when put into context. Satellites are sent into geosynchronous transfer orbit at just over 22,000 miles out—not even a tenth of the way to the moon. And the space shuttle currently operates at a maximum distance of 320 nautical miles above the Earth, or about the distance from downtown Phoenix to Los Angeles. Eventually, as technology allows us to reach further into space and out to the other planets and their satellites, we will be able to conduct business that involves the materials and conditions found on those worlds.

The technology for getting into space is now fairly commonplace. In addition to NASA, several other national organizations regularly launch rockets into space, although not with people aboard. Dozens of private and consortium-based companies also launch vehicles through our atmosphere for the purpose of placing satellites into position above the Earth. Fully one-quarter of those launches now belong to France's Arianespace, a company that is getting significantly more commercial bookings with each passing year. Even Russia—the former foe whose successes lit the spark for the NASA program—has realized the importance of s-commerce and has created Energia, a private space business that began with plans to salvage the now-gone Mir space station for commercial use. The company attracted a huge amount of media attention for its plans to partner with the wildly popular CBS TV show *Survivor* to send a winning contestant into space. And even though Mir was deorbited into the South Pacific on March 23, 2001, the Russians gave millionaire businessman Dennis Tito a spot on board their next flight to the International Space Station—for the hefty fee of $20 million.

Yes, there have been both success stories and abysmal failures. Like any new venture, this is bound to happen. When the first European explorers decided to traverse the Atlantic Ocean—backed by investment capital—many of them were aware that they would never make it, or make it back. And once they reached the far lands, they had to chart out a whole new world and learn to adapt to new environments. Back on the shores of Europe, many wished that they too could venture to the new lands, while still others prophesied nothing but doom and disaster for those setting sail to the west.

Once the "new lands" were settled, the explorers and pioneers created living environments, businesses, manufacturing plants, transportation routes, and a host of other entities that had never existed there before. It took time, but ultimately all of these thrived. Companies like Lockheed Martin have thrived in space by providing services that both NASA and the private sector want. On the other hand, Iridium, the satellite communications venture, failed dismally by not giving customers the kinds of phones and services they demanded. After vaporizing $5 billion in funding, Iridium was going to have to bring its 66 satellites out of orbit, giving a decade's worth of investors the lackluster joy of seeing the sky light up—when their investments re-entered the atmosphere as decommissioned and useless hulks of metal. This fireworks display was narrowly averted in March 2001 when a group of investors bought Iridium's assets and began targeting industrial and maritime organizations.

But for all the horror stories—and remember, there are still countless numbers of rotting Spanish galleons and English clippers scattered across the bottom of the Atlantic—there is a hugely successful space business that actually forms the underpinnings of modern commerce. No satellites and no space business means no Internet, no global cell phones, no uninterrupted real-time stock quotations and trading. And no rockets means no satellites. Our technological underpinnings, whether we know it or not—or whether we want to admit it or not—rely on us being in space. And going forward, we'll never be there less—we can only be there more.

The coming endeavors will be part of New Space, a place that holds the promise once offered to Europeans by the New World. It represents a departure from Old Space, where getting there was all that mattered, and the costs be damned. It didn't necessarily matter what we found (although it was hoped that something of value would be there) and it didn't matter that there would be any return on investment. Research and exploration for their own sake were noble properties of Old Space and the Old World.

Once you're there, however, the priorities change. Finding something is one thing, doing something with it another thing altogether—and that is what will mark the divide between Old and New Space. The frontiers of New Space present the same scenarios that were met by New World explorers, with one significant difference. We have already done much of the research and exploration of the space that we will occupy. Four decades of space flights and centuries of celestial observation and analysis have taught us more about the space above our heads than people knew about the lands across the ocean. Military missions, space science and earth science missions, all of them have provided us with the pieces we need for moving aggressively into the space business. Our maps are drawn and we know the requirements for provisions. We are ready.

Will every project be a success story that bolsters all subsequent projects? No, but that has never been the case in any venture, be it business or explorative, that man has undertaken. Pioneers, as the saying goes, are identifiable by the fact that you find them laying face down in the mud with arrows in their backs. As we shall see in subsequent chapters, venturing into new businesses, and new worlds, has its perils, and we need to plan for them.

When We Get There

Our historical relationship with space has been limited to exploration, communication, and military projects. Exploration speaks for itself and includes everything from the Mars Pathfinder to the Hubble Telescope. Our communication networks on the ground are enabled via the use of satellites, and the military orbits both its "eye in the sky" and "switchboards in the sky" for a vast number of activities from photography to mapping to communications.

Our everyday world is becoming more dependent upon space commerce than we can imagine. The ubiquity of cell phones and pagers is made possible only through an intricate network of satellites that pass digital signals from one location to another across the face of the globe. The occasional failure of these satellites results in communication downtime that is felt by every user who relies on the constant ability to communicate from any place at any time. The Internet, too, is fueled by satellite links that allow web pages to pop up on a user's computer screen in near real-time. GPS systems, now becoming popular in rental cars and high-end retail vehicles, depend exclusively on "space business" to help people track where they are here on Earth.

But what of the next generation of space projects—using space for a myriad of commercial ventures? It appears that we've tackled the easy ones, unmanned satellites that relay information from various points around the globe. The next generation of space work will take a different tack. For one, we will begin to explore the processing and use of materials in micro-gravity and low gravity states. What we know about most of the materials we work with and use is based on how these materials behave when affected by gravity. Right now there is no way to learn much about them without gravity as a factor— unless we take them into space. Then we can investigate and capitalize upon new forms of growing crystals, separating and purifying, mixing, solidifying, and processing liquids. Tests on Skylab demonstrated that more uniform and flaw-free crystals could be grown in space. Does this have s-commerce applications? It sure does, if the crystals are silicon. And the benefits of observing materials without having to support them—another gravitational drawback—are countless. The allure of micro-gravity chemical refineries, manufacturing facilities, and chemical laboratories just scratches the surface of the potential of space.

There is also the bastard child of space business—tourism. Long scoffed at by serious space explorers, space tourism could actually become one of the driving financial forces of s-commerce. One only need look at the parallels on Earth: many states, such as Arizona, Hawaii, and Florida, derive significant chunks of their revenue from tourist dollars. Indeed, tourism could be considered their main industry. The lens of mystery and awe through which we have viewed space almost guarantees that it will be a major tourist attraction. Cost will certainly be an early factor, but as with all businesses, once the cost of delivery comes down, the potential will manifest itself in ways ranging from orbiting hotels and hospices for the terminally ill to quick trips around the world in sub-stratospheric vehicles. Both America and Russia have shown that people can spend minimal periods in space without harmful effects, and the allure of being in space is sure to attract those who will spend thousands (or tens and hundreds of thousands) of dollars for the opportunity to make that once-in-a-lifetime flight.

Who's Taking the Risks

The way that NASA has operated has been exclusionary. Those with personal or corporate interest in space have been left to watch from the sidelines, with an occasional shot at getting a project on board the shuttle. That's about it. As we enter the millennium, with commercial launches becoming more frequent, the opportunity to expand the scope of these flights becomes possible with the use of new capital, especially from the investment community. While many of the players in the space program have their own commercial strategies underway, there is also ample opportunity for new companies and startups to enter the space business. As mentioned earlier, there are a host of industries that are going to have to work together to make s-commerce a reality, from financiers to fuel providers.

There are plenty of companies, and countries, anxious to dive deeply into s-commerce. Already, a multinational consortium headed by Boeing has created Sea Launch, an endeavor to send satellites skyward from an equatorially located floating platform in the Pacific Ocean. Countries as diverse as Australia, Brazil, and French Guyana are capitalizing on their proximity to the equator, setting up launch sites for commercial use, and building new business infrastructures in the process. There are also numerous entities, from private companies like Bigelow Aerospace and Rotary Rockets to multinational consortiums, like the International Space Station group, that are working on getting more business—and more of us—into space. The money for these projects is coming from numerous sources: venture capitalists, government coalitions, established corporations, wealthy benefactors with a fondness for space, entrepreneurial businessmen and women, and even ex-astronauts. Each has a purpose in mind: cargo transportation and delivery, tourism, satellite repair, manufacturing, chemistry, entertainment, and even colonization. And each has plans to make a profit from its enterprise.

It is business of this sort that NASA has no business getting involved in. NASA was severely upbraided in March 2000 for conducting an increasing number of "faster, better, cheaper" space missions that resulted in catastrophic failures during 1999. Its own review board pointed out that the organization was structured to focus on long-term and large projects, and that it has failed at trying to reinvent itself as a "commodity" supplier. Well, surprise, surprise. A government agency shows that it isn't equipped to be the low-cost provider. So who—historically—does that mantle fall to? The commercial sector, of course.

The uninformed have scoffed at the prospect of a non-government entity making space business work. They can make this argument because most people don't realize that the four space shuttles, while owned by NASA, are actually operated and maintained by a company called United Space Alliance, popularly known as USA. What is USA? It's a joint venture between Lockheed Martin and Boeing, and it controls almost every aspect of the shuttle program—and has done so since 1996. And that's just the government-sponsored part of it. Lockheed is working on its own to develop a reusable launch vehicle (RLV) for commercial purposes called the VentureStar, and has built a prototype of this vehicle called the X-33. The thousands of other contractors who do work for NASA are perfectly capable of selling their products into the commercial sector—as soon as the demand is there.

As with any enterprise, demand will drive down cost. The cost of today's commercial launch services range as provided by Boeing, Loral, and others weighs in at about $10,000 per

pound of payload. With its huge adminstration and infrastructure, NASA's shuttle launch costs are estimated to be more than
double that—with a per launch cost of approximately $350 mil-
lion. A large part of this latter number has to do with the requisite resources that need to be in place at all times—not just
during actual launches. It takes years to create a launch program, not to mention the costs associated with individual payloads. The actual development costs for those launch programs
are traditionally counted in the billions of dollars, and it's not
always an easy amount to cough up—or swallow. The European
Space Agency's first Ariane 5 launch was ten years and $7 bil-
lion in the making, and it all went up in smoke—literally—at 39
seconds into the launch. That was painful, but it didn't stop the
program.

All s-commerce companies are looking to bring the cost of
getting into space way down. Foremost among the industry-
wide projects is the creation of an RLV. When commercial
launch services companies such as Lockheed Martin and Boeing
launch a rocket, they throw the whole thing away as each component or stage is used up. This waste is enough to make the
average taxpayer want to view space from the cheap confines
of his back porch, and makes the average payload cost between
$15,000 and $20,000 per pound of payload. But private entrepreneurs are looking at ways to reuse rocket components and
bring payload costs down to around $1,000 per pound. That
makes the entire business much more attractive, and certainly
more affordable. Plus, it won't be coming out of anybody's
paycheck.

At the same time, industry is developing launch vehicles
that are designed from the outset to meet the needs of commercial customers. Current launchers are based primarily on Intercontinental Ballistic Missile (ICBM) designs that incorporated
extreme edge-of-the-envelope specifications. Vehicles that are

created specifically to deliver payloads will change the nature of launch and delivery costs.

So the s-commerce road is paved, as it were. It's only a matter of time until the road attracts adventurous travelers who see its potential for reaping business rewards and creating wealth. After that, it will be so well-traveled that people will wonder what took us so long to get there.

The Road to New Space is just outside the door. Are you ready to go?

I

WHY SPACE?

S keptics will remain unconvinced and demand more
detailed answers to the obvious questions: Why should
we seriously look into the business of space? For that
matter, why bother with space at all?

The answers are simpler than they might initially appear.
First, as previously noted, space is currently a $100 billion busi-
ness worldwide. Billion, with a b. That's a huge marketplace,
especially given that most people think of space business as
nothing more than NASA shuttle launches. Three-quarters of
that total, or just over $60 billion, is based in the United States.
At that size, space dwarfs the combined U.S. movie business ($8
billion in receipts) and the broadcast business ($30 billion) and
is about the same size as the domestic pharmaceutical business
($98 billion) (Source: Plunkett Research 2000). This qualifies as
a respectable size—no, make that a phenomenal size—for an
industry that doesn't sell directly to the retail consumer. And
it's just about to take off.

For the answer to the second question—"why space at all?"—
we actually need to reverse our focus. Instead of looking at the
nighttime sky, we need to look internally at what drives us as a

species and as individuals. From the first moment that humans could get an intellectual grasp on their immediate surroundings, they have explored the realms beyond their immediate boundaries. Many of homo sapien's first discoveries were driven by the constant need for self-preservation—finding better places in which to survive. Perhaps this began with chasing animals over a hill into the next valley and finding fresh water, or stumbling onto superior hunting grounds while trying to escape a storm. These discoveries are recognizable as results of fortunate accidents driven by biological need. This same need explains the mass human migrations that occur today in areas as diverse as Afghanistan, Mozambique, India, and Sudan—people leaving drought-stricken areas or escaping the ravages of flood.

The really big discoveries have not always been driven by the need for better shelter or better food supplies, however. While these certainly motivated the agrarians and hunter-gatherers of early and prehistory, the development of industrial societies, such as 16th-century Spain and 17th-century Britain, gave us the ability to undertake huge ventures that were not survival-oriented. The discovery of "new worlds," whether those worlds were across the ocean or out to the farthest reaches of a contiguous land mass, was driven by the need to explore and to experience places that were beyond the familiar and the comfortable. They involved an incredible amount of planning and risk, both physically and financially, but the rewards were often greater than those associated with the ventures could have expected. New climates, more comfortable places to live, unique flora and fauna, and ultimately new ways to live were benefits of these adventures. After settling in, the economic result was new sources of business: agriculture, manufacturing, mining, shipping, etc. The benefits of a new economic resource were capitalized upon not only by the explorers, but also by those who stayed behind and identified the profit potential of these discoveries.

The impetus for this type of exploration was neither need nor mandate. No one forced Columbus, Vasco Da Gama, Henry Hudson, or the hundreds of other documented adventurers to sail off past the horizon. Rather, these men set out on trips that were generally considered foolhardy and ran against the prevailing wisdom of the scientists, geographers, politicians, and financiers of their time. Those backers that supported these men, financially and politically, ultimately found that their backing was worth taking the contrarian position.

What motivated these explorers? Financial reward was certainly a prime component, but it doesn't explain it all. Rarely do people embark on the kinds of adventure that have a high probability of ending in death simply for financial reward. There are larger issues at stake here, and they are the issues that have driven the most courageous of humankind to seek something new and exhilarating beyond the realm of our known environs. It cannot be rationalized, nor can it be taught. It is simply an innate part of us; a need to know and a need to discover. In this way, that drive can be considered a biological need. Moving, seeking, exploring—it all may be part of a biological imperative that comes with being able to think about our place in this world. The ability to mull this over and reflect on it is crucial to exploration. For it appears that when we've come to recognize and be comfortable with our immediate "world," we instinctively look to the mysterious and possibly wonderful opportunities the next world may offer.

In other words, it's quite possible that the idea that "the grass is always greener" is hardwired into our DNA.

While we might consider this a biological imperative, others have called it a moral and social imperative: the need and even the intellectual requirement that accompanies the responsibility of being thinking beings. Either way, it leads us on to ever new explorations and new worlds. And, quite frankly, in the grand scheme of exploration, space *is* the ultimate new destination—the ultimate underdeveloped territory. Yes, there are individual destinations within space, beginning with the Moon and extending on to nearby worlds and even out to the Asteroid Belt. But citing individual destinations is secondary to being able to have the permanent and routine ability to break the bonds of gravity. That makes space the ultimate adventure.

When we are regularly able to venture into space, we will begin an entirely new phase of human history, of our evolution, and our understanding of ourselves. It will restart the human adventure from a new beginning. Once we commit to being in space, we will create stepping stones that allow us to reach progressively further out and away from our home planet.

This is all well and good, you might think. It certainly makes a nice plot for a TV series or a sci-fi movie. So what's the point? Space is, well, space. Space is basically empty. This is true as a dictionary and even academic definition, but from a business perspective, space itself is not what's interesting. Space is the environment, the place where business can be conducted in the same way that oceans are the environments upon which we conduct intercontinental transport, deserts are the places where we drill, and cities are where we build our factories. Space is the environment, and it is a business environment with a potential unlike any we have known before.

What and Where Is Our Space

Let's look at space. There are myriad definitions as to where space begins, from 62 miles above the Earth's surface (the point at which aerodynamic principles cease to apply to objects in flight because of the thinness of the atmosphere) to 240 miles (the scientifically defined starting point of space at the end of our atmosphere, technically known as the exosphere), where the pull of gravity is quite small. However, relative to operating in space, we will begin with 103 miles up, which is the minimum altitude at which a satellite can be kept in orbit. This is known as low-Earth orbit, and objects orbiting here—including satellites and the space shuttle crews—have to be traveling at approximately 17,500 miles per hour to stay aloft. This is an incredibly fast rate of speed. By way of comparison, a bullet shot from a high-powered rifle can briefly reach speeds of 1,800 miles per hour. The Concorde and various jet fighters reach cruising speeds of over 1,300 miles per hour. Most of us can't even imagine moving faster than that. Yet we're conducting business in space at more than ten times this speed every day. So much for unimaginable being associated with impossible.

The Russian spacecraft Mir orbited at 235 miles above the Earth, which is considered a low-Earth orbit. This is only a fraction of the distance we go in order to keep our satellites aloft for any length of time. The majority of satellites currently in space are placed in what is known as geostationary or geosynchronous orbit. This is the orbit in which satellites can hold a fixed—or geostationary (geographically stationary)—position above a specific point because the satellite is travelling at the same speed at which the Earth rotates. This happens at an altitude of 22,300 miles above the Earth, usually at a point along the equator, which provides line of sight transmission to all but the most extreme northern and southern latitudes.

Twenty-two thousand three hundred miles is almost the length of the Earth's equator, only straight up. And it's an environment unlike any we find here on terra firma. Beginning with low-Earth orbit, 103 miles up, temperatures are within a few degrees of absolute zero (-459 Fahrenheit), although the temperatures in the thermosphere, just above this space, are around 1,000 degrees. At 22,300 miles up, absolute zero is an absolute given. Earth still has a gravitational pull at these distances—although greatly reduced the further out we go—so low-Earth orbiting objects are actually in a continual state of free-fall balanced by forward momentum that creates weightlessness.

The Economic Upside

Space, as an environment, sounds pretty miserable. Of course, the shore of North America, with harsh winters, rocky soil, icy waters, strange animals and insects, was replete with its share of miserable descriptions in the 16th and 17th centuries. The same can be said for the conditions that the Chinese found in what is now Mongolia in the 2nd century B.C.E., or what Romans found in Northern Europe in the 1st century A.D. But the possibilities inherent in this "miserable space" are more abundant than anything that was found on this continent. It's hard to do in retrospect, but one should consider the economic impact that resulted from the initial investments in a few eager sea-faring explorers, their crews, and their equipment. Given what colonization and the resulting cultures and economies produced (you could put the entire U.S. economy since the early 1500s into this category), it seems like an obvious win in hindsight, but it wasn't at the time. As is true now, it was government (in the form of monarchies) that funded the initial European explorations that led to the profitable exploration of the New World. That paradigm is quite acceptable—right up until the time that government tries to stand in the way of opening exploration and exploitation to the capital markets and private industry. That's when government involvement in exploration borders on the egregious. It's something we'll explore at length in the next chapter.

Once again, we're looking at a global business that currently accounts for $100 billion annually. During 1999, the Federal Aviation Administration estimated that $61.3 billion of that went into the U.S. economy, only two years after private space business revenues surpassed those of government. So the money is not all going to NASA (which is still funded exclusively by taxpayer dollars), it's going into the private sector. Where exactly does it go?

According to the FAA's Office of Commercial Space Transportation, which licenses commercial U.S. space launches (yes, there is such an office), that $61 billion sum includes goods, services, and more than half a million workers in the space industry. Satellite and ground-equipment manufacturing were responsible for $30.9 billion or half the total, with $8.9 billion in earnings, and 270,448 jobs. Right behind that, the satellite-services business contributed $25.8 billion, with an attendant $6.1 billion in earnings and 186,954 jobs. That number means that there are more people in the satellite-services business than are employed in some of the world's largest companies, including Sony, Hewlett-Packard, and Philip Morris. Further down the scale, distribution and transportation of materials was responsible for just under a billion dollars in activity, with $874 million, earnings of $265.8 million, and 8,506 employees. Remote sensing, one of the most crucial areas of space business, brought in $235.9 million while employing 2,820 people and racking up $85.2 million in earnings.

Now we get to the interesting part. Right in the middle of these figures is the business of manufacturing launch vehicles, meaning the creation of individual rockets and boosters, and "provision of launch services." Despite its role in getting other businesses into space (such as the satellite business), the launch vehicle business brought in $3.5 billion, employing 28,617 and earning $1.07 billion. A significant amount by most measures, but paltry in relation to this overall report. In fact, the launch vehicle industry contributed only six percent of the total economic activity generated by the commercial space industry. It should be obvious to most, and it is to the FAA, that the launch business serves as an "enabler" for the other businesses cited above.

What if these launch vehicle figures were larger? They would be if we had more options and more cost-effective launch vehicles, and if transportation into space were available to more customers. With minimal extrapolation, we would expect to see more use of launch vehicles, and even larger numbers in the other categories. The FAA itself predicts that the future could bring more satellite-oriented businesses, such as faster Internet delivery and satellite-oriented agricultural services. Transportation of overnight packages, cargo, and even humans (the FAA study mentions spaceports) would dramatically increase the overall space industry. That doesn't even include energy and manufacturing opportunities.

As it is, the FAA points out that space business also affects and involves traditional terrestrial businesses ranging from textile and mill products to supplier industries and interstate ground transport. These include such diverse suppliers as steel mills, garment manufacturers, rail and truck hauling, electronic equipment manufacturers, etc. As a $100 billion business, the activity generated by space affects not only direct suppliers and contractors but goes all the way back to mining and refining.

The New Businesses

When we get into space more regularly, there will be a host of new industries we can create, investigate, and nurture. We'll be looking at all that space has to offer in the following chapters, but here is an overview of some of the conditions of space that make it attractive to both new and existing business.

We'll start with materials. On Earth, materials are affected to varying degrees by gravity and air. This has an effect on everything from the silicon that is used for computer chips and the

steel that forms the skeleton of skyscrapers to concrete manufacturing and the molding of plastic objects. This leads to a
wide variety of processes that must be employed to adjust and
compensate for the presence of air and gravity. In space, materials processing is mostly free of these two constraints (which, in
some cases, are severe obstacles). Starting with micro-gravity,
we eliminate two conditions that occur naturally in all materials processing: convection (hot air rises, cool air sinks) and sedimentation (heavier particles fall to the bottom). Where can we
apply these potential benefits of a space environment to materials processing? Primarily in areas of mixing, separation, crystal growth, and solidification: computer chips, pharmaceuticals,
alloys and composites, etc.

Mixing is about as ubiquitous a process as we have. Almost
every manufactured item you buy has been through a mixing
process of some sort (with the notable exception of precious
gems and metals), whether it is coffee (water and beans) or a
computer (mixed plastic, silicon composition, various metals).
Mixtures must be precise (think of making a cake or a cocktail)
in order to achieve the appropriate end result. This requires that
adjustments be made for density, anticipated sedimentation,
rate of cooling, and a host of other factors. For fragile or
volatile mixing, space provides an environment where density
is not a factor because materials neither rise to the top nor fall
to the bottom. Cooling, which results in layering, is also eliminated from the equation since the top, bottom, and middle of a
cooling object can be controlled without regard to convection.
Fluid processing, such as the mixing, separation, handling, and
movement of liquids, would also benefit from a micro-gravity
environment.

Separation, which incorporates the purity of a material, is
also better handled in space due to reduced gravity. When a
material, especially liquid or solid, can be suspended away from

surrounding components (such as similar materials or the container itself) there is an increase in the purity of the processed material. When this separation is achieved, a material can be treated more directly and more uniformly in temperature-controlled processes. It's almost like making things without worrying about getting them dirty by touching them or having to hurry and mold them before they cool down or settle.

Solidification is what happens when a material, such as liquid plastic or molten metal, is molded and then allowed—over time—to harden into a desired shape and product. Because of the rate of this change, and often the attendant cooling, there are stages at which parts of the product are in different states; the hotter ones being closer to liquid and the cooler ones becoming solid. Minimizing this state change throughout the object can elevate its uniformity and its quality.

Crystal growth is one of the most talked about aspects of materials processing in space, in part because there have been some initial successes starting way back with SkyLab. Crystals on earth invariably have defects due to the way atoms settle into position as the crystal grows. Both gravity and heat play a role in this. The growth of crystals is constrained in specific directions due to gravity, as is the growth of most materials. However, as crystals grow, they go through intense heat/cooling states as they go from liquid to solid formation. The resulting solid cools rapidly, and the process repeats with bursts of heat during each "growth spurt." The results are such that crystals are banded at these stages of growth (like rings on a tree) and thus not uniform. By gaining control of the heat/cooling phases in space, purer crystalline structures can be created for the development of higher quality microchips and pharmaceuticals.

The creation of "near-perfect" products, such as "zero-defect" ball bearings, would have ramifications far beyond the simple manufacture of more uniform product units. Take the small metal spheres that are found in almost every piece of machinery you can name. On Earth, the manufacturing of ball bearings is affected by gravity, which keeps the bearings from being perfectly round and smooth. A perfect ball bearing, or as close to perfect as we can measure, could potentially reduce friction and wear by a sizable degree, yielding better performance of products and potentially higher profits.

Which industries benefit from these potential space opportunities? Almost every industry you can think of, from biochemical and bioengineering to chemicals and pharmaceuticals on to synthetic minerals and component manufacturing and all the way to agricultural breeding. Does this mean we should do all our manufacturing in space? No. In fact, the bulk of manufacturing that we do on Earth is handled just fine as it is. However, as we utilize increasingly more exotic technologies in the electronics and biotech fields, we may find that space provides far greater returns than Earth-based manufacturing can. Just as Henry Ford's pioneering use of the assembly line for automobile manufacturing fundamentally changed the way that most manufacturing was done in other industries, the need to be creative and entrepreneurial in space may present us with production solutions never before thought of.

Energy

This is one of the least understood areas of space research and thus the space business. After all, if we're generating energy anywhere from a few hundred to tens of thousands of miles up, how do we make use of it here on Earth? Once again, that's where technology and entrepreneurship come in. As far back as 1968, discussion began about transmitting solar power from space back to Earth. The concept is similar in practice to solar panel fields currently in use in Southern California and other arid climates around the world. Construct similar fields—covering miles of space—and place them in a geostationary orbit. Link the solar panels together to generate power, and convert it to microwave energy. This power is then beamed back to Earth just as satellite signals are, except in this case they are sent to receiving antennas that route them to an electric power grid. (After the past year's worth of energy news coming out of California, we're all familiar with electric power grids.)

Satellites already use solar power to generate their own electricity for transmission. Converting this same power to usable microwave energy would involve collecting substantially larger amounts of power and then managing the strength of the transmission to maintain control of the energy (keep in mind that this is the same energy that powers microwave ovens, and it needs to be handled carefully). Receiving stations could be placed almost anywhere on the planet as long as they are linked to a usable grid. The solar panel fields would collect sunlight 24 hours a day (with minimal downtime during equinox periods when the fields would be in the Earth's shadow), use no moving parts, and require no other fuel source for transmission. And the power is available as long as the Sun keeps shining, meaning as long as we can imagine.

There are other forms of energy generation and transmission that are being investigated. Using reflectors, we could direct sunlight to areas that are lacking it, affecting the pattern of crop growth and lighting darkened regions. Directing sunshine to rain-soaked or flooded farmland could salvage potential crop loss. Directing this same light to a disaster area or the site of a rescue effort could allow for around the clock work in situations that are often called off because of darkness and nightfall.

The Russians attempted to do this with the 83-foot wide solar mirror called Znamya, which would have directed a 5-mile wide strip of sunlight across the Northern Hemisphere in

February 1999. The mirror, launched from Mir, failed to deploy properly, but the interest it garnered, and the discussions that it opened up, are worth pursuing.

Transport

In our business world, the words "overnight it" and "FedEx" are as common and essential as pens and paper clips. It is so routine now that we can barely remember a time before overnight delivery, although Federal Express didn't begin service until 1973, not even 30 years ago. Just as overnight continental delivery has become a huge business where no one thought there was one, suborbital transportation of everything from mails to fragile and time-sensitive materials could result in overnight intercontinental delivery and same business day continental delivery. Supersonic jets can already cross the North American continent in less than three hours; the speeds that can be reached in suborbital space would reduce this to a delivery time measured in minutes. We can already envision the slogan for these carriers: "When it absolutely positively has to be there yesterday."

There are people who like and/or need to be transported quickly. The success of the Concorde, which charged a hefty premium for shaving hours off of intercontinental flights, proves that delivery time has a price that many consider to be worth paying. Part of the attraction of the Concorde was its supersonic allure, flying higher and faster than regular jetliners. If we go higher into the sky, and even into very low-orbital space, next-generation transport to global destinations could make the speed of the Concorde seem pedestrian and passe.

Tourism

This is at once the most obvious and yet the most daunting of space businesses. Unlike overnight documents or satellites, which are impervious to the physical rigors of space, humans present another story. Your legal papers don't care how cold it is or how fast they're traveling or in what kind of comfort. The same cannot be said of the human body or mind.

Many of us would be willing to spend huge sums of money to venture into space, even near-Earth space. It is not uncommon to hear people say that they would spend their life savings for a shot at going into space, or claim that they would give up all their future vacations for a single trip past the atmosphere. And these aren't for lengthy trips lasting days or weeks; these are for quick shots up to get a real look back at our Earth as a big blue marble through a window seat. Shoot them up, get them back.

Of course, the stumbling block is "get them back." There are safety issues, coupled with comfort factors, that are at the core of any space tourist venture. We've always been good at shooting things into space and leaving them there, as the more than 5,000 satellites currently orbiting the planet can attest to. It's only recently that we've gotten good at sending people into orbit and bringing them back on a regular basis. But we've done it successfully.

Who has done this? NASA and the governmental space agencies. Yet to show how much those agencies value their ability to control who goes up and back in space, take the case of Dennis Tito. An avowed space junkie and former NASA rocket scientist, millionaire financier Tito offered to pay his way into space, was summarily turned down by NASA, then cut a quick deal with the Russians for a trip with their cosmonauts to *their* part of International Space Station. It all went without a hitch. The Russians got their $20 million and Tito got the ride of his lifetime. It added up to good business and good publicity for the Russian space program.

NASA's response? To cry foul. The NASA bureaucrats claim

that the Russians had no business letting Tito ride along, what-ever the cost. That said, what business did NASA have sending John Glenn back into space as a 65-year-old former astronaut and current retiree? Sure, it was good PR, and it did the soul good to see a national hero return to space. What were the tan-gible benefits for the immediate future of space activity? None. Nil. Zip. And guess what? The American taxpayers paid Glenn's way back into space. At least Tito was willing to pay for the trip himself.

To add a bit of insult to this bureaucratic injury, NASA cosponsored a study with the Space Transport Association in 1997 that said that space tourism could be a $10-20 billion business within the next few decades. Again, that's billion with a "b."

NASA has proven that people can get up into space for both long and short periods of time and return safely. If we can ensure that safety for more people (within the bounds of a cer-tain level of acceptable risk) using commercial tourist flights, why shouldn't we? The line has already formed and people are willing to pay. Talk about a market chomping at the bit. And unlike the vast majority of initial Internet businesses, there is a bottom line and a tangible benefit. Everybody involved wins.

The Cross-business Benefit

In addition to its potential for individual business, space is also the ultimate business challenge. In order to succeed, it will require not only the vast array of administrative and manage-rial skills that go into running all good businesses, but it will incorporate many of the advanced technologies that are being developed and refined daily. This includes artificial intelligence, nanotechnology, cellular automata, data mining, neural net-works, agent technology and more. Thus, while getting into space and making it viable is something of a technology in and

of itself, it incorporates almost the entire spectrum of technological development from the past century, from engine technology and propulsion to medical monitoring and databases.
Business conducted in space becomes the perfect amalgamation
of man's creative business efforts.

Space business also provides a feedback loop that is inherently development-oriented. As we press further into space and
confront new challenges, we will develop new solutions, systems, and technologies to make space more efficient and accessible. These technologies will in turn be used in more traditional
areas of business here on Earth. In the introduction, we mentioned velcro and teflon as two of the only recognizable commercial benefits of the space program since its inception (even
though the program merely popularized them rather than generated their invention). Of course, recognized benefits and actual
accomplishments are two different things. When we take a deep
look at the technological advances and viable products the
business sector has managed to pry out of the hands of NASA,
we find that space has served as the mother of invention for
hundreds of products that we use every day. It has spawned
huge businesses and even new industries: large database technology, composite materials, solar power, contamination con-
tainment, filtration, digital imagery, global mapping, protective
gear and clothing, sensors, laser implementation, packaging
materiel, health and patient monitoring, medical imaging, sound
modification, hazard control, virtual simulators, inventory control, cameras, optics, data visualization, warning systems,
weather forecasting, land management and large-area surveying,
portable appliances, prepared foods . . . and on and on. All of this
with little publicity and little effort on the part of the government
to get this technology into the commercial sector.

The impact of technologies and business practices that were
developed for or in conjunction with the space program is

impossible to overstate. The current healthy condition of numerous industries—computer, energy, medical, transportation, telecommunications, precision manufacturing, to name a few—owes much of its advance and success over the past two decades to technology that came out of the space program. The Apollo program alone helped drive the development of smaller computers—both for monitoring and onboard use—at a time when computers barely squeezed into entire rooms. Materials that we now take for granted, especially high-impact plastics and durable fabrics, are also direct descendants of space programs. In the same vein, the current space shuttle and ISS programs are pushing us into new realms like nanotechnology. Research has already begun into the possible development of molecular-sized machines that can maintain and repair equipment suffering from metal stress fatigue as well as creating airborne "scrubbers" that remove pollutants from the recycled air in the space station. All at a level that is invisible to the naked eye. Sound improbable? Sandia Labs already has working molecular machines. It's only a matter of time before they find their way into commercial applications.

As we push our space industries further, there will be similar terrestrial benefit. Much of it is ready for development given the right business acumen and market conditions. Business acumen is in the hands of entrepreneurs, investors, and business managers. Market conditions are something else altogether, as we'll see in the following chapter.

The First Steps to Space Success

What will make for successful space businesses? While each aspect of space business is different—there are different sets of requirements and parameters for transport than there are for, say, remote sensing—there are a list of factors that apply to the entire undertaking of establishing space businesses.

First of all, space as an environment is very predictable. The nature of space is fairly well understood, and the risk of operating there can be minimized with thorough advance planning, testing, and learning from history. Exhaustive testing contributed to Lockheed Martin's successes with the Viking Landers and the Mars Pathfinder, as did heightened cooperation and communication between corporate partners. Companies such as Boeing and Lockheed also have had a high degree of space success due to their ability to work well—and closely—with NASA partners such as the Jet Propulsion Laboratory and the Johnson Space Center. Knowing the goals, the operating procedures, and the limits takes a huge amount of initial risk out of any space project.

For all its predictability, though, space is also incredibly hostile, which makes it unforgiving of mistakes. Lax management of a project on the ground can rarely be overcome once a project is in space. For instance, the Mars Climate Orbiter was doomed to failure when its various contractors neglected to convert a series of measurements from American standard to metric. The Hubble telescope was launched with a lens ground to the wrong specifications—an oversight that seemed to doom the project. Its permanent myopia—and potential uselessness—was avoided thanks to some "reconstructive eye surgery" on the part of shuttle astronauts. Still, it was a mistake that should not have occurred.

Paying attention to history is crucial to making any venture work, on land and in space. There is a 40-year long list of "lessons learned" that need to be adhered to in order to escape the failures that have scrapped space projects ranging from Apollo missions to the Iridium satellite project and the Mars Polar Lander. This history and the value of practical experience demonstrate that space business is not much different from terrestrial business. But the unique context of space and its nascency require that businesses consider the myriad factors that make space ventures both potentially lucrative and potentially dangerous. The factors that will lead companies to success include:

- Identifying a profit-generating product. We need only to look at the scores of failed websites that have come crashing down since the beginning of 2001 to realize that "figuring out how to make a profit as we go along" doesn't play out well over the long term. Space businesses have to start with viable business plans that plot a course toward product or service development and lead to a goal of strong revenues and, ultimately, profits. Selling energy and transport services would appear to be viable businesses; giving away free space rides would not.

- Being market-driven. If there is no demand for a product, there will be no revenues. It may sound intriguing to put a global cell phone network in space, but not if it requires that users carry around a new cell phone that weighs more than a canned ham. Serving the market will be a hallmark of good space businesses.

- Avoiding technology for technology's sake. Technology-driven companies often develop radically new and useful technologies, but they are rarely the ones that capitalize on them. Artificial intelligence (AI) companies in the 1980s and 1990s created the first computer programs that appeared to think and learn, but users had no idea what to do with them. Every one of those AI companies is out of business, but their technology has been incorporated into everything from word processing applications and databases to Internet browsers by companies like Microsoft, IBM, and Oracle. These latter companies are market-driven but use technology to maintain a competitive advantage in their markets. The distinction is a fine one but of paramount importance.

- An Earth-based analog. Creating an entirely new business out of thin air, or space as the case may be, is almost as bad as creating a business just for technology's sake. Using a current profit-oriented business model, such as transport, will allow big thinkers and adventurous investors to extrapolate the market conditions into a space-based model. Then a determination of worthwhile or worthless can be made by asking two questions: "Does the business work well on Earth?" and "Will it work equally well or better in space?" If the answer to both questions is "yes," you're looking at a good idea. If the answer to either question is "no," then you should run—don't walk—to the nearest exit. Don't look back.

- Scalability. The product or service that a space business is offering must scale well, meaning that it should be profitable within a small number of launches. At the same time, operation costs must decline as the business ramps up. In this way, the business can "scale up" in terms of revenues and profits while "scaling down" in terms of costs and administration. If the infrastructure is too costly, there will never be any return on investment. And if the market isn't interested, there won't be any revenues or further investment anyway.

It should be apparent that all of these factors are interrelated, and they will be integrated in the creation of any space business. There are other success factors that we'll explore later, such as concerns over weight (and its cost relative to launch), the actual cost of launch, and markets served.

The Pitfalls of Space
(Where No One Can Hear You Scream)

Even when companies incorporate the above listed traits into their businesses, getting into space will not be easy. A number of business obstacles exist in the form of pre-existing conditions, including the lowest cost/lowest risk mentality of government customers (Department of Defense and NASA), long lead times for new initiatives (Iridium was 10 years in the making), drawing from a pool of talent that is currently entrenched in labs and academia, and the overriding fact that major innovation in the space industry requires major infusions of capital.

In addition, it is a given that some space businesses will be created for all the wrong reasons or with all the wrong traits. There are plenty of warning signs to look out for when evaluating space businesses, many of which are the converse of the above list of attributes. A list of even more egregious qualities to note includes:

- First to market with a new technology (a corollary to being technology-driven).
- Dependence on government funding, support, or facilities. The government is free to change its mind any time it likes, as we saw over the course of 2001 with its numerous NASA project cancellations. No matter how good the product or service, a space business that has all its eggs in a government basket is asking for trouble.
- Relying on the "space" label. "Space-age technology" as a term may have helped to sell frozen dinners and quadrophonic stereo systems in the 1970s and 80s, but no one's dancing to that tune anymore. The "space" tag works when people physically get to go into space,

but they don't care if their semiconductors are made
there or if their overnight packages fly there. Identifying or linking a product or service with space is little
more than hype, and hype is to be avoided at all costs.

Consider all of the above as benchmarks that indicate early
stage "dos" and "don'ts" when looking at or starting a space
business. It's like reviewing the profit and earnings statement of
an established company on terra firma. Are there space-ori-
ented companies that have successfully adhered to the former
list while avoiding the pitfalls of the latter? Certainly Boeing,
one of the premier aerospace companies in the world with sales
of over $51 billion, has routinely shown that it can compete in
the space arena. Its successful development of shuttle components and its Delta launch services, combined with work on
expendable launch vehicles (ELVs) and the ISS, make Boeing a
case study for successful space businesses. It is a company with
diversified yet focused businesses; commercial aircraft, military
aircraft and missiles, and space and communications. You can
see how all these are related. To ensure its business longevity,
Boeing has done business the way any successful company
should. It has numerous partners (financial, development, contracting); it has shown that it understands the difference
between market-driven and technology-driven (its airplane
division is a testament to this); it acquires companies that
enhance its expertise (Hughes' overall satellite communications
business, Autometric's geospatial imaging business, and others
in 2000); and it has longstanding customers in the U.S. space
business.

Being a diversified corporate giant is not a prerequisite for
space business success. In the following chapters we'll look at
dozens of companies in various industries—companies like
Analytical Graphics, SeaLaunch, and XM Satellite Radio—that

have a vested interest in making space a viable platform for business. Many of these companies are poised to take advantage of space in an explosive way when space business becomes as unfettered as terrestrial business.

How we go about establishing that business equality will determine just how soon we can get business into space and how successful it will be when we get there. And the way we go about it is by taking a hard and critical look at "them that brought us to the dance"—NASA.

2

HOW WE GOT HERE/NASA

In order to understand what the business of space is today, and what it will become, we have to see where it has been. In essence, we need to look at how we got to where we are.

Rest assured, this is not a history of the space program. There are hundreds of books and thousands of articles that review man's legacy in space. They range from those that praise the single-minded and unwavering dedication of NASA and its people on to ego- and legacy-shattering tomes that decry NASA as a budget-driven bureaucracy that cares little for the interests of the nation or its constituency. The grit and gristle of those stories, while fascinating, must be found elsewhere.

The dichotomy of the space program's history, though, is quite real. There are two paths that the business of space has taken, oftentimes simultaneously. One is quite literally bright and shining, replete with heroes and incredible tales of triumph over adversity. The other is, well, a bit tarnished. Perhaps even dark—fraught with the mindless and mind-numbing obstacles that impede scores of government agencies, from petty politics to self-serving agendas. And those realities not only define the current state of the space industry, they will also serve as the blueprints for how we should proceed.

Not that we have a lot of history to cull from. Space as an environment—of any kind—has existed for less than 50 years. From prehistory right up until 1957 space was simply the beyond; not much more than an idea, a concept, and an expanse of exotic emptiness that was physically out of reach. Even well into the 20th century, it was the purview of science-fiction writers, movies, and the occasional earth-bound dreamer.

The Slow Evolution of Rocket Science

Of course, we have been propelling objects into the air—but not much further—for centuries. The first rockets were believed to have been created in the 13th century by the Chinese, who used them for fireworks that lit up the sky over the Imperial Court. The essential ingredient was gunpowder, a concoction whose explosive property the Chinese had learned to control and master. By the 14th century rockets had made their way to Europe, little evolved from their Asian origin. From that point forward, all the way to the 20th century, the nature and use of rockets changed not at all. Powered by powder, simple rockets were used to propel objects longer distances than could be achieved with slings, catapults, or other machinery. In this span of nearly 700 years, the basis and basics of rocket science remain virtually unchanged.

The idea of men actually using rocket science to venture into space was followed quickly in time by the development of the means by which to put him there. H. G. Wells and Jules Verne wrote stories about humans living in space and reaching out to extraterrestrial bodies. Although there had been several stories about space flight prior to the publication of the classic novel *From the Earth to the Moon,* Verne captured in an eerily prescient way the conical rockets that would become reality a hundred years after its publication in 1865. Of course, the novel used the idea of propulsion as it existed at the time: namely, gunpowder to fire the rocket out of a cannon, and Verne's rocket relied on the symmetry of an artillery shell. In 1897, H. G. Wells wrote *The War of the Worlds*, a novel dealing with the contact between man and aliens from another world. The insidious alien invasion of Wells' novel gave imagery and form to the possibility that there might be more beyond our planet's grasp than we ever imagined.

These early space novels were a direct inspiration to Robert Goddard, the acknowledged father of rocketry. Just two decades after *The War of the Worlds*, Goddard wrote a ground-breaking paper in 1919 entitled "A Method of Reaching Extreme Altitudes." It was Goddard's idea to replace the powder-driven blasts that propelled rockets skywards with a liquid propulsion system. Though there were other scientists exploring the idea of putting objects into space, such as Hermann Oberth of Germany and Konstantin Tsiolkovsky of Russia, it was Goddard who worked laboriously to make the idea of venturing into space a reality.

Goddard's first liquid-fueled rocket took off from a farmyard in Massachusetts on March 16, 1926. The flight lasted less than three seconds and reached an altitude of just under two hundred feet. A small step admittedly, but it served as a "proof of concept" event.

The weather conditions in Massachusetts were not conducive to Goddard's need for year-round experimentation, so he moved his lab to Roswell, New Mexico. Thus began the integration of rocket launches with favorable climate choices. In this case, it also began a long and storied history of Roswell's association with space and all of its manifestations, including missile testing, government research, and unfortunate aliens.

Goddard's work, funded privately by the Smithsonian Institution and the Guggenheim Fund, nonetheless provided the impetus for two decades of intense military rocket development. The Germans, under the guidance of Wernher von Braun (who acknowledged Goddard's influence), developed impressive rocketry that was used to lethal effect during World War II. Germany's work in refining rocket technology led to increased accuracy and increased distance of launches.

After the war, von Braun came to work in the United States and was installed in White Sands, New Mexico, not far from Goddard's original desert labs. During this time, in the decade after the war, von Braun worked on ever more advanced propulsion systems and even ventured to discuss the possibility that rockets could propel more than explosive warheads from one place to another and deep into the sky.

All of this changed on October 4, 1957. That was the date that the Soviet Union launched Sputnik 1. Perched atop a Russian missile, Sputnik was a small satellite that forever altered the perception of how launch vehicles could be used. The satellite was an object designed to stay in space and, just as importantly, not explode. To drive this latter point home, four months later the Russians launched Sputnik 2, which carried a passenger named Laika. This dog was the first living being purposely launched into space. Like Goddard's backyard rocket, it may seem trivial in retrospect, but it established the groundwork for all the space activity that has followed.

In between Sputnik 1 and 2, the United States hurried to launch its first satellite, Vanguard. Unfortunately, the ignition was literal. On December 6, 1957, the Vanguard and its launch vehicle crumpled in a ball of flame to the launch pad at Cape Canaveral as the live image made its way to U.S. televisions. A second effort, demanded by President Eisenhower, launched the Explorer satellite into orbit on January 31, 1958. Under the guidance of the U.S. Army and Wernher von Braun, the Explorer satellite, weighing only thirty pounds, signaled America's entrance into what would become known as the space race.

A Bona Fide Race

America made the race official with the passage of the National Aeronautics and Space Act in July 1958. The National Advisory Committee for Aeronautics (NACA), formed back in 1915, now became NASA, the National Aeronautics and Space Administration. From that moment, NASA became the public face of the space program, while the military continued its research and development under a veil of secrecy.

The seriousness of America's commitment to the space program and the resources accorded to NASA are a matter of record. Within two years of its founding, NASA had nearly 20,000 employees and crucial relationships with many of the aerospace contractors that had been developing launch systems for the military.

Shortly thereafter, the first satellites to monitor weather effect and relay communications were put into orbit. In July 1962, Telstar 1 was launched. Built by Bell Laboratories in conjunction with NASA, this satellite could transmit several hundred phone calls at a time. Telstar also heralded the era of satellite television transmission, and along with the Relay 1 satellite owned by RCA, it heralded a new era in broadcasting.

While this was all well and good from a sheer technological standpoint, and certainly ushered in the communications technology that would eventually allow for cell phones and the direct-to-home transmission, it was the desire to put a man in space that truly jump-started humanity's efforts to leave the planet.

In April 1961, the Soviet Union achieved something that until then had only been the stuff of science fiction. It put cosmonaut Yuri Gagarin in a tiny capsule atop a launch vehicle, which in turn propelled him into space and into Earth orbit.

Gagarin's short once-around flight, lasting all of an hour and 29 minutes, changed the way the entire world viewed space. This was not a dog or satellite circling the Earth—either of which could be considered expendable. This was a man who'd gone into space, venturing where no one had ventured before, and he had returned safely. Not only was this an act of individual heroism, it firmly established Russia as the country most willing to take the risks that would result in a claim of ownership of space.

After Gagarin's flight, it took President John F. Kennedy only one month to deliver his plan for putting America out front in the nascent space race. He committed America to putting a man on the Moon and returning him safely to Earth by the end of the 1960s. He also made it clear that the endeavor would be difficult and expensive. The primary goal of rocket scientists would no longer be to find a more accurate missile guidance systems for the various branches of the military. Instead it would be to create a complete system for launching men into space and returning them safely—within ten years.

In rapid succession, the U.S. unveiled the Mercury, Gemini, and Apollo programs. They each delivered increasing levels of success in manned space flight, but there is a key development point we need to keep in mind. Throughout all of this, as the individual capsules changed from the one-seater Mercury to the two-seater Gemini to the three-man Apollo, the launch vehicles changed only in size and effectiveness. They were, and still are, essentially launch vehicles based on the missile technology developed in postwar America during the 1950s and 60s. These rockets were never redesigned completely to deliver humans or even any other payload efficiently and cost-effectively into space. Rather, they were modified to fit the needs of their individual payloads. And during the course of each mission, they still served the same purpose that missiles have always served:

launch the payload into orbit, deliver the payload, then fall completely spent and useless back to Earth.

In fact, early human capsules and satellite payloads were kept as small as possible to meet the needs of the existing launch equipment. The two-seater Gemini capsule, for instance, had less room for its human cargo than the average two-seater sports car. Even Apollo, which held three people, was kept to an uncomfortably cramped size. It was critical to make the payload work with the launcher, and not necessarily the other way around. We'll see how this plays out as we discuss the modern needs of space business.

But back to the space race. The U.S. quickly launched six manned Mercury missions, ten Gemini missions, and four Apollo missions before sending Apollo 11 to land on the Moon and back in July of 1969. This eclipsed anything and everything that the Soviet Union had undertaken in the space race. It may have eclipsed anything man had ever done prior to that, period. Putting a man on the Moon had effectively established America as the primary driver of space research and space exploration.

Not coincidentally, NASA and its legion of contractors had become a virtual industry unto itself, involving more than 300,000 people and some 20,000 affiliated partners, companies, contractors, and subcontractors. Getting to the Moon had become big business.

Shockingly, once it had achieved its stated goal, the U.S. government opted not to make it an ongoing commitment. For three more years, encompassing six Apollo missions, Americans in decreasing numbers watched a dozen more men step on the Moon. After that, NASA called it a day. No more Moon missions.

Pulling Out of Space

Since December 1972, almost 30 years ago, there has not been a single manned mission to the Moon. Thirty years. That's an astounding thought considering that all of the achievements and accomplishments, and in fact the very idea of going to the Moon, all occurred in a ten-year span. All these years later, putting a man on the Moon still stands as a singular accomplishment in human history, yet it carries an air of "been there, done that." Nothing more to do. The giant leap for mankind ended up being our last step into outer space.

There are no fingers to be pointed. The American public's fascination with the program waned during the years that we extricated ourselves from Vietnam, fought a Cold War, entered into bold new realms of political scandal, and found ourselves heading into a recession. At the same time, NASA's budget was slashed by nearly two-thirds between the 1972 launch of Apollo 17 and 1979, the year that marked the tenth anniversary of the initial manned Moon landing. Outside of Skylab, the space station launched in 1973, and the Apollo-Soyuz orbital test projects in 1975, NASA's manned space missions came to a grinding halt. They stayed in terrestrial mode until the launch of the first space shuttle in 1981.

In the two decades since the creation of the shuttle program, with the notable exception of the *Challenger* disaster, NASA has rebuilt its reputation with large and cutting-edge research projects. These include the Hubble telescope, the NEAR Shoemaker mission, the Mars Pathfinder (one of those Apollo-like missions that showed the can-do quality and personal face of NASA), the early assembly of the International Space Station (ISS), the Galileo spacecraft, and dozens of other outer space missions. In addition, the Mars Global Surveyor, which continues to deliver spectacular images and mountains of data, has provided us with information that indicates Mars may have once been—and may yet be—a hospitable environment for life.

NASA has proven, in every one of these latter cases, that what it does best is push the envelope. Research, technological innovation, and exploration are NASA's claim to fame. And like every other organization or business worth its salt, it succeeds when it concentrates on what it does best.

Business vs. Bureaucracy

Speaking of business, where was the private sector during the glory years of NASA's Apollo program and its subsequent fall from Mount Olympus? In all honesty, after being pressed into national public service, business was sitting on the sidelines. The aerospace industry as it existed in the 1960s and 1970s, with companies like Hughes, Martin Marietta, Lockheed, Grumman, McDonnell Douglas, Boeing, Northrop, and others, was rounded up by NASA and the U.S. government to get the U.S. into space as quickly as possible. This certainly wasn't done for charity, but it was impressed upon all of these companies that the space program was a national priority and a matter of national pride, with repercussions that extended into the Cold War. It was a ploy that was necessary, and one that worked. If NASA had waited for market-driven development of technology to reach a point at which space travel was feasible, we might be using Russian satellites for our cell phone communication, or maybe still sending pets into orbit.

The aerospace companies did not see space as a business venture, although their dealings with NASA were strictly business. Space was considered a scientific realm, a place from which we could study the universe and humanity's origins, and promote the social good. Long-term business goals and economic spinoffs where not part of the equation. There simply was no reason: satellites were still an anomaly, good for a few intercontinental phone calls and maybe a live television feed now and then. Tourism? Not hardly. Only a tiny fraction of America's population had ever flown on an airplane by the early 1960s. And the venture capital market for new business investment, so incredibly robust in the last decade, was barely in existence forty years ago.

So NASA acted as the market leader. It was a lean, effective organization. It was driven, like most successful businesses, by a strong competitor, albeit a non-commercial one, in the form of the Soviet Union. It had a stated goal: to deliver a man to the Moon and return him safely. It produced results unthinkable in most business climates, including the current one. It was—and still is—staffed by people whose diehard dedication made venturing into space and conducting business there a reality. It was, in effect, a classically powered business machine. But it became, like many government agencies, abused and insular. NASA has frequently behaved as if its current mission is self-preservation and doing just enough to justify its existence. To a large degree, it reached this unenviable position by tightening its stranglehold on the space industry.

By way of comparison, look at the U.S. Post Office. Since Benjamin Franklin became the first Postmaster General in 1775, the Post Office had a lock on the delivery of the printed word between people and between businesses. No competition, no other options for consumers. It got bigger, it got bloated, it had a virtual monopoly on what we call mail delivery.

In 1973, along comes Federal Express, founded by Fred Smith two years before. A company built on the concept of overnight delivery, featuring a fleet of planes flying in and out of a single hub in Memphis, Tennessee. The venture was scoffed at, even by the grad school professor to whom Smith originally presented it. No one needed overnight delivery, and a business structured on the hub system in a market nobody cared about was doomed to fail.

In the thirty years since, scores of other overnight services have come into being. Even the Post Office now offers speeded up versions of its delivery. The market for overnight packages is huge, with companies such as UPS, DHL, and Airborne all competing for business. FedEx's annual revenues alone now exceed $20 billion dollars. But all the companies that deliver overnight mail combined do not deliver a fraction of what the Post Office does every day. That's because the Post Office has a value, and a high one at that. No other entity is currently equipped to deliver individual letters door-to-door at the current stamp price. That's a valuable service, and it results in the Post Office being paid to deliver 200 billion pieces of mail per year. In the physical delivery business, all these options make for valuable businesses and consumer choices. You want it overnight? Go to an overnight carrier. If it can wait a few days or you want it to get there cheaply, use the Post Office. At the end of the day, everyone wins.

This is an appropriate analogy for NASA. What is the space agency good at? Exploration, research, envelope pushing. What should it leave to others? The business of delivering scheduled payloads into space and the business of conducting space business; those endeavors that can be handled by other companies, many of whom already work with NASA on everything from launches to ground communications. What should NASA do, then? Get out of the services business and focus in the realm of research and exploration. And do it soon, for the benefit of the space industry as it attempts to move forward.

This is not a call for the dismantling of NASA. Far from it, in fact. NASA has a lot to recommend it, as has been pointed out above. But in order to achieve many of the business objectives set forth in this book, NASA has to change. And the U.S. government needs to rethink our space policy. There are some specific areas in which this needs to be done, and the discussion should begin now.

The Agency of Record

Before we look at the solutions, there are some very real problems with the way that NASA has overseen space activity in the past. For instance, as far back as 1985, it was reported that NASA was pricing shuttle launches at $38 million per flight, when in actuality the cost was more than $150 million per flight. At $38 million, no commercial entity could compete effectively, let alone profitably. Of course, NASA was operating at a substantial loss, but that didn't matter—the wolves of private enterprise were kept at bay. The taxpayers simply ate the difference.

Private companies were also kept from the party by a bizarre NASA codicil that allowed these companies to send launch vehicles into orbit, but not bring them back to Earth. The Space Commercialization Act of 1998 put an end to that, but it takes very little thought to understand the ramifications in terms of stunted research and development. If companies were only permitted to fly single-use or ELVs, why would they consider developing equipment that could be sent into space, deliver payloads and return? It's like drawing up plans for a 40-room mansion when you're only allowed to build on a one-sixteenth of an acre. There's no incentive to think big. In 1998, the launch companies were allowed to create reusable launch vehicles (RLVs), but by then the damage had been done. These private companies had spent too much time behind the eight ball and were years away from launching RLVs. The net result? A flurry of private activity in the last few years to create something that had been banned for the last thirty years. Think of where we'd be if they'd had thirty years to work on RLVs.

Private individuals have also been kept from space, but now that genie is out of the bottle. We've already talked about individuals and their interest in space with mention of the Dennis

Tito situation. NASA so opposed his payment to the Russians for a trip to the ISS that it physically barred him from entering the Johnson Space Center in March 2001 for training with cosmonauts. Yet, Tito had completed the cosmonaut training program and was supported by his fellow cosmonauts, who threatened to boycott the training if Tito was not allowed in. While NASA literally stopped Tito at the gate, the cosmonauts were eventually persuaded by their superiors to report for work. Once again, NASA bullied its way into dictating who goes into space and who does not, at least temporarily. It also brought NASA unwanted publicity as the Russians showed a solidarity with Tito, who had undergone 700 hours of training with them. And it gave Tito the opportunity to point out that NASA is facing $4 billion in cost overruns.

Senator Christopher Bond (R-Mo) even called Tito's trip an insult to the ISS, saying that "this trip demeans the overall purpose of the ISS as a world class laboratory in Earth orbit where astronauts can live and conduct research." (Source: Letter from Bond to NASA's Goldin, April 25, 2001). Senator Bond did not mention that NASA's canceling of the space habitation module and limiting the number of full-time crew to only three people had already cast doubt on the ability of the ISS to conduct any meaningful lab work.

Even while Tito was in space, during what would prove to be an extremely successful trip, NASA chief Goldin couldn't resists taking potshots at the venture. On May 2, 2001, Goldin told a House subcommittee that "The current situation has put an incredible stress on the men and women of NASA. They are dedicated to safety, and Mr. Tito does not realize the efforts of thousands of people in the United States and Russia that are working to protect his safety and the safety of everyone else, taking extraordinary means." He even claimed that the first priority of the ISS crew during this mission was to "baby-sit Mr.

Tito, to make sure nothing goes wrong, because safety is our number one priority." Goldin then made the ridiculous statement that the price of Tito's babysitting far exceeded what he used to pay for his own kids' babysitters. Finally, Goldin's name-calling reached its zenith when he made the following remark: "I'd like to make a contrast here, because there is an American patriot who understood how to do this. That gentleman's name is James Cameron, who approached me some six months ago and asked about going to space." For those who don't know, James Cameron is the director of movies such as *Aliens, Terminator,* and *Titanic.* James Cameron, however, doesn't quite qualify as an American patriot, primarily because he is Canadian.

This illustrates one man's problems in dealing with NASA's intransigence when it comes to getting to space. But what of companies that want to put themselves into space, metaphorically speaking? Shuttle launches are high-profile media events, especially with the recent work on the ISS. What if a company were willing to pay millions of dollars to brand a launch with its logo? Would it impact the mission? No. After all, it's only paint. But as media events such as the Super Bowl or "Survivor" or the last episode of "Seinfeld" show, a minute's worth of publicity is worth millions of dollars—and companies are willing to pay. Advertising is a $200 billion industry, one of the biggest businesses in the world. How much is a logo on the outside of a booster rocket or a shuttle worth? You can guess, but it would be fruitless. NASA bans advertising outright. Another source of revenue down the proverbial drain.

Unbeknownst to many, NASA has what it calls "Commercial Science Centers" or CSCs. These groups, which are essentially university labs working closely with NASA's various facilities such as Marshall Space Center, are charged with helping the private sector get commercially-oriented research programs aboard U.S. manned flights. Participants include Texas A&M University, Auburn University, University of Alabama, University of Maryland, University of Wisconsin, Kansas State, University of Colorado (known as BioServe Space Technologies), and others. When companies like Bristol Myers Squibb or Coca-Cola want to do microgravity research, they go through one of these 17 centers to prepare their experiments and make sure the appropriate tests are done on board either the shuttle or the ISS. Here again is a conundrum; corporations work with a public university-run consortium (typically not set up as profit-generating entities) to do business with an agency that spurns any appearance of commerciality. The irony is almost palpable.

What can we do to change this? As with our Post Office example, not to mention Amtrak and other service agencies, many contest that there is only one way to make NASA workable in the future: privatize it. This may sound extreme, but it is logical and makes good business sense. Yet putting the whole of NASA—lock, stock, and barrel—on the auction block would leave us without a national space program that could pursue research on behalf of numerous academic and government labs. It's more important to identify the ways that a space policy shift could benefit all those interested, from NASA to private companies to the government and private citizens.

NASA: Drawn and Quartered

The following are some basic changes that could result in a viable and even desirable role for NASA in the future.

Review and refine priorities. Looking at priorities means having NASA focus on core businesses, trimming the fat and strengthening fundamentals. It also means placing the agency's business and business prospects in the proper perspective. Under the first administration of the new millennium, U.S. space interests may well be weighted more toward military considerations than those of the civilian sector. If this is the case, NASA needs to make its strategic planning and decision-making for the next four years within that context and the likely constraints.

This may mean eliminating projects and initiatives that are nonessential or not commercially viable. In terms of the ISS, we have to be straightforward and candid about what is commercially viable and what requires government sponsorship in terms of exploration, scientific advancement, and fulfilling our responsibilities with our international partners. NASA has stated that it will probably abandon or scale back the Crew Return Vehicle (CRV) and habitation and propulsion modules of the ISS to save money. In the future, NASA may revisit these components of the ISS as "enhancements." This ignores the fact that the habitation module and CRV are essential to accommodating the full seven members of the ISS crew. If NASA's cuts will severely impair commercial enterprise in the long-term, we need to hear now and hear it loud, until the administration reconsiders. This is something that the space services and applications community has to step up to the plate on. If it is not willing to do that, let's move on.

On the other hand, we may find that certain nonessential or noncommercial programs run by NASA are indeed worth keeping. When we find this to be the case, NASA should hand these programs off to someone else. For example, the resources devoted by NASA to education programs. Why not turn over education initiatives to the Education Department? And environmental initiatives to the Department of Environmental Protection? If the government needs to be in near-Earth space, then it can contract launches out just as it contracts out other services. Military requirements and issues regarding national security could be returned to their respective agencies, such as the National Security Agency (NSA) or the Department of

Defense. Then NASA can spend its allocations on things that it does best. As much as people inside and outside of NASA might not like to hear it, NASA is not in the education business, nor is it in the environmental protection business. It is in the space research and exploration business. These other endeavors are nice, socially conscious offshoots, but let us not confuse them with the core business.

Once we put NASA under the microscope, and possibly the knife, we can restructure it. In business, after a restructuring is announced, a company's stock usually goes shooting up. Cutting fat and keeping the focus is universally applicable to both the public and the private sector. NASA could use a good dose of business overhaul to make it lean and effective—as it was thirty five years ago.

This doesn't mean abandoning ambitious goals. NASA can back-burner certain goals until the business fundamentals are back in order. Plenty of companies have put off expansion until they know that their foundation is as strong as possible. In the case of NASA, this applies specifically to exploration. As we discussed in the last chapter, we have a human need to explore new frontiers. From that comes a biological and perhaps even moral imperative to return to space, to go back to the Moon, to send a manned mission to Mars, and to explore farther beyond—for our sake and for future generations. But first, we need to strengthen NASA's balance sheets.

To that end, we should create an external entity to ensure that NASA hits its marks. In other words, set goals and achieve them. There's been a lot of talk about re-instituting a National Space Council, an advisory group last seen under the first Bush Administration and eliminated by the Clinton White House. Practically speaking, we should ratchet up the NSC by also setting up a board of directors. If we want to turn space into a business, let's run it like one. This board would include a

National Space Adviser, key members of Congress, academics, former astronauts or NASA scientists, a retired aerospace executive or two. NASA, and appropriate military defense leaders, should report to this board on a regular basis so that budget overruns are caught early on and addressed. In this way, NASA will be held accountable by an outside body that represents more than one viewpoint. This board could also help NASA create a timeline with specific benchmarks for handing over commercially viable operations to private enterprise. Significantly, this would include accountability for missed deadlines.

The Benefits of Change

Looked at from an incentive perspective, that's the stick. That's how we get NASA to run a tight and efficient ship. Along with all sticks, one must have a supply of carrots. Here's the carrot. NASA keeps its status as a government agency charged with overseeing space activity. It also hands its ever more costly space programs back to the industry, getting out from under its growing cost overruns. To this end, the reporting board would assist NASA in rallying members of the space industry and the public to build support in Congress for tax incentives for space businesses. This is necessary because ultimately, in order for NASA to open itself up to privatization, private industry must be primed and ready to take over the business. Furthermore, we would have NASA entirely rethink its existing relationship with business. Perhaps it should recuse itself entirely from being a pseudo-commercial partner and become a regulatory body that oversees a field of private competitors, much like the FAA oversees the commercial airline industry today. That means stepping back from the day-to-day space launches and partnership negotiations and letting business do its job. The immediate result would be to allow competition to drive down prices, and foster entrepreneurship that could create the next IBM or Microsoft or Cisco Systems.

Finally, make it easier to get into space. Space, like the airways and the roads used for interstate commerce, falls under myriad jurisdictions and requires lots of navigation through the various government agencies that oversee commerce, communications, transportation, and ultimately, NASA. Let's streamline the process for early investors and entrepreneurs to get the balls rolling and the gears meshing. A restructured NASA could be the conduit for a more benevolent business climate aimed towards space.

Of course, the prospect of increased business investment in light of such changes at NASA may be easier said than done. As we all know, private companies are reluctant to spend the huge amount of R&D money necessary to create new space businesses until they're sure there's a proven market. This is particularly true in the wake of the Iridium communications satellite disaster, which has frightened investors of every stripe. A lack of investment, however, means that NASA ends up shouldering the costs because there's no direct commercial competition (remember, NASA isn't racing the Russians anymore); market conditions don't apply. The result is that the price tag for doing business under NASA's aegis goes up—and up and up. Congress gets frustrated by cost escalation. Projects get cancelled, as happened in March 2001 when NASA scuttled plans to fund a new shuttle vehicle, the X-34. And then investors get scared. And partners back off. And we slip further into a "do nothing" mentality.

This cycle of cynicism and lackluster management must end. Everyone who has ever worked in the space industry, or dreamed about space as a kid, or dreams about space now as an adult, has experienced space's power and its limitless potential.

From satellite communications to remote sensing to GPS to the future space businesses of biomedical research, natural resource mining, and space tourism, we are just beginning to realize space's commercial possibilities. But because NASA hiccups, we consider all space activity to be gravely ill. It's as if the proverbial 500-pound gorilla has been cowed, so we should declare that the entire ape population is headed for extinction. This is why we need to take the considerations of "space business" away from NASA, or we are going to be forever guilty by association.

Once we've broken free of that, we are free to attend to the business at hand. Or businesses, as we'll see in the next chapter.

3

THE SATELLITE BUSINESS

The satellite industry has been having an impact on business for more than 30 years now. Industries as diverse as communications, entertainment, shipping, transport, and medicine have come to rely on this sector of the space business to improve their own efficiencies and increase revenues. And the market is growing as businesses such as satellite-based Internet access and direct-to-home television expand their offerings further into the consumer marketplace.

There have been impressive numbers for the satellite companies in the last decade. In 1999, for instance, revenues for satellite services alone were more than $30 billion, according to Futron Corporation (Bethesda, MD). This doesn't include launch services, ground systems, and manufacturing, which are considered a separate business area. In all, the entire satellite industry generated more than $60 billion in 1999.

In this chapter, we'll look at where all the activity is, and ultimately where it is headed.

Telecommunications

The oft-heard refrain that "business is going global" is a tired conceit. Business *is* global. Period. From corporate partnerships to online shopping, international barriers are in reality little more than lines on a map and currency preference. The Internet allows consumers in any part of the world to buy goods from other parts of the world with the simple click of a button. Recently created multinational corporations such as Daimler Chrysler and Credit Suisse First Bank operate with major divisions based in different countries, climates, cultures, and time zones. News and entertainment are beamed and broadcast in real time to U.S. living rooms from places as remote as the Philippines and Beirut. A Big Mac is a Big Mac is a Big Mac.

The impetus for this environment has been—and will continue to be—communication. Operating on a 24-hour-a-day business schedule would have been unthinkable even thirty years ago, before the advent of fax machines, improved international telephony, overnight delivery, and email. With considerations made for time zones, today's business professional can reasonably expect completion of same day business transactions between London and New York, or Los Angeles and Hong Kong. A century ago, conducting business between these locales was not a matter of hours but a matter of months—each way.

Today, we take all of this for granted, and as such, we expect that the communications business will simply expand to meet the demand as global business increases. Unfortunately, the telecommunications industry is still built on the same infrastructure that has supported it for the last century: ground wire. Improvements in technology, notably in the use of fiber optic cable and digital transmission, have taken telephony to new and impressive levels, but we're still relying primarily on lengths of wire running underground and underwater to ensure our communication. Whenever we want more connectivity, we've got to dig into the dirt.

We're not in this landlocked situation for lack of vision. The vision goes back, in all seriousness, to an unusual convergence of science fiction and science fact that occurred more than half a century ago. Arthur Clarke, the writer of such sci-fi classics as *2001: A Space Odyssey, Fountains of Paradise,* and *Childhood's End,* actually laid the theoretical groundwork for today's satellite network in 1945. It was then that he published a paper entitled "Extraterrestrial Relays," which was published in *Wireless World Magazine.* Clarke's paper proposed a network of three satellites that could be placed above the Earth's surface in geosynchronous orbit and relay communications to any point on the globe. Astoundingly, he did this more than a decade before a single satellite or any other orbital object had ever been launched.

While Clarke envisioned these satellites as working platforms with personnel on board (this was, after all, during World War II), it was the technology of his idea that eventually found its way into our modern satellite network. He precisely determined the altitude (22,300 miles), the position (geosynchronous above equatorial locations on Earth), and the concept (relaying of communications from the Earth to the satellite and back). Twelve years after the paper was published, Sputnik was launched, and Clarke's proposition was on its way to becoming reality. Today, more than fifty years later, our satellites by and large adhere to the ideas set forth by Clarke, and geosynchronous orbit is often referred to as "Clarke's Orbit."

In keeping with Clarke's vision, satellites were initially deployed for communications. Since the early 1960s, satellites have served as adjuncts to our wired world, primarily for intercontinental communication as well as picking up the phone slack during line breaks or high traffic periods. We've come a long way in that time: the first operative commercial telecom satellite, Telstar, launched in 1962, could handle only a few hundred phone transmissions at a time. The current iteration of Intelsat satellites, by way of comparison, can handle over 100,000 calls at a time. Makes for an impressive "backup" system, doesn't it?

And therein lies the crux of our telecom future: satellites are being used to back up our wired infrastructure. Being wired, however, denotes that we are indeed tethered to some form of cable, line, or fiber, almost as if we were chained to it. In many respects, this has been literally and figuratively the case. It was not so long ago that running around to find a pay phone was the only way to call the office from the airport, or to call home when the car broke down. Technology and astute business operations have changed that. Cell phones, beepers, pagers, and now instant Internet and email access are becoming ubiquitous because they free us from being tied to a land line, as it were.

Mobile—in the truest sense of the word—means the ability to engage in communications without regard to a fixed site or location. We're only at the beginning of this stage of going mobile. Being completely wireless is a certainty in the next few years. Ten years ago, no one would have predicted the ubiquity of cell phones. Today, it's unusual if a business person doesn't own one. The same goes for email. Checking it on the train, during a long lunch, or at the beach is no longer a frivolous desire; it is part of our business arsenal. Such has been the benefit of unshackling the professional businessperson from a desk, or worse yet, the local pay phone.

Mobile Satellite Communications

Mobile satellite communications will free us even further from land lines. Current cell phones connect over land, transmitting signals from cell tower to cell tower across the country as if your call were playing hopscotch across the land. But it is still primarily land based, which is why you can't use your standard issue cell phone to make intercontinental calls—the cell stations end at the coastline.

Cell phone connectivity is also an issue in areas where towers are undesirable and thus not erected, or in cities like New York where huge buildings serve as signal obstacles. When a cell phone transmits, its signal must be bounced over and around the curve of the Earth in order to go from one cell to the next, encountering uneven terrain such as mountains and steep grades. Cell signals, in effect, take the worm's view and not the bird's-eye view. A satellite transponder (the technical term for a combined receiver and transmitter) would alleviate this situation by having signals beamed up and back from space, as opposed to over the Earth's uneven surface. And since thousands of transponders, each handling a different frequency, can be loaded onto a given satellite, heavy phone traffic could be easily routed through them. Low-Earth orbit satellites (which we'll call LEOs from here on out) can act in the capacity of unobstructed transmission towers, with the difference being they're positioned between 250 and 500 miles up.

LEO satellites offer a different set of benefits than their geo-synchronous Earth orbit (GEO) counterparts. Because of their extreme altitude, GEOs create a quarter-second delay when fielding and returning most phone transmissions. This delay is annoying and unacceptable to most phone users but is quite acceptable when sending one-way broadcasts. GEOs also have coverage of one-half the globe at any given time, but they require that both the transmitter and receiver be situated in line-of-sight, meaning that they have a direct and unobstructed "view" of the satellite. This isn't always possible, especially in urban areas and in locations where the position of the GEO may be too shallow relative to the ground to establish a direct link.

LEOs, which are much closer to the Earth and usually arranged in constellations, have near-instantaneous phone transmission and don't require line-of-sight situation. They don't have the same coverage areas (footprints) as GEOs since they are closer to specific terrestrial regions, so they rely on more signal "hand-offs" to gain wide-area coverage. LEOs are also better suited to Earth surface observation, especially for detailed mapping and monitoring land movement. Of course, there is a compromise position, which is medium-Earth orbits, or MEOs, that have an altitude above several hundred miles on up to several thousand miles. GPS satellites are MEOs, and their altitude allows them to have a greater footprint with smaller constellations.

LEO satellites can supply service to remote locales, especially underdeveloped or developing areas and nations where there is no Earth-based cell infrastructure. And before anyone defends the wide-area coverage of cellular, consider this: 80 percent of the world's landmass is not covered by cell service. And in many of those areas, there just isn't enough infrastructure or even population density to justify the investment by phone companies.

Satellites are already in use for non-land based communication services, such as in-flight airplane phones and shipboard calls. This service has been available for nearly two decades to the shipping and transport business. It began in earnest with the introduction of INMARSAT, a global satellite consortium that initiated service in 1982. Originally called the International Maritime Satellite Organization, INMARSAT was funded jointly by participating nations (a sure way to minimize capital risks) and has since been privatized. It now has business offices in London and Dubai. It has nine geostationary satellites that transmit and receive a wide variety of voice and data signals to its more than 150,000 terminals. The company claims that its users—journalists and broadcasters, health teams and disaster relief workers, land transport fleet operators, airlines, airline passengers and air traffic controllers, government workers, national emergency and civil defense agencies, and heads of state—use the service for everything from faxes, email, compressed video, and videoconferencing to telephone calls and telemedicine. As a private company, INMARSAT is aggressive; in 1999 it introduced a communications system called the Global Area Network that can be linked to a laptop for transmission anywhere in the world. It also had total revenues of $406.2 million with a profit of $119.4 million and saw its customer base grow by 32 percent over the previous year.

In addition to the need to stay in contact with other corporate locations and suppliers—or even loved ones in the case of ocean-based employees—remote businesses also are often in high risk zones and require a means for requesting help in times of emergency. Many of them utilize the Search And Rescue Satellite System (known as SARSAT), a distress system that expedites the search for, and aid to, ships or aircraft that are in need of assistance—an important feature when these craft are operating away from radar or land-based voice communications. With a simple transmitter, vessels can be in constant contact via satellite with authorities or rescue services should they become stricken.

Since businesses are built on people, this is a hugely important use of satellite networks. But the applications of mobile satellite communications are not restricted to human contact. A huge number of businesses utilize autonomous systems for remote monitoring and analysis—without the aid of human operators or supervisors. Industries that conduct and monitor business outside of urban and suburban areas, such as mining, forestry, highway construction, water power generation, interstate transport, and others have already benefited from having access to satellite communications for these non-personnel systems. The petroleum industry, for example, monitors remote pipeline activity by analyzing satellite signals that receive system data. Analysts can reply with control and change instructions to areas situated far from human habitat: think of the thousands of miles of the Alaskan Pipeline that travel across areas of North America, or the Gulf of Mexico pipes that run through the Mississippi bayou.

These are high-end business-to-business communications. Providing anytime/anywhere service as it applies to the consumer, though, is still a nascent business. The ill-fated, and recently resurrected, Iridium project was designed for bringing this type of point-to-point communication to individuals. Iridium was based on a great concept but suffered from poor execution. Launching 66 LEO satellites at an altitude of 485 miles, the original Iridium plan was to provide anytime/anywhere service to cell users anywhere in the world. It launched all of its car-sized satellites within 12 months, using launch services from the U.S., Russia, and China. Like a space-based cell network, calls could be handed off from satellite to satellite, ensuring true global coverage.

Launched in November 1998, Iridium embodied all the potential of satellite communications. However, its decade-long road to providing global phone service was marred by technical glitches, such as a phone that cost more than $3,000 and weighed as much as a Stephen King novel. It was also beset by the quick deployment of competitive regional and national cell phone services. Led by Motorola, the $5 billion dollar project was slow to accomplish anything, including a subscriber base of potential users that balked at using its unwieldy and expensive phones. In short, its planning and marketing were less than stellar—a bad sign in any business. In 2000, Iridium declared bankruptcy and planned to let its entire network of satellites drop into the atmosphere and die a fiery death.

Iridium was rescued in April 2001 for the firesale price of $25 million—about one-third to one-half the cost of an average satellite. Its new owners are repositioning the company as a service for the types of industrial customers listed above. The new Iridium, funded largely by investors from Brazil, Australia, and Saudi Arabia, has also introduced Motorola handsets that sell for less than $1,000. It plans to charge less than $1.50 per minute—a far cry from the roughly $7 per minute charged by the old Iridium. Long-time satellite giant Boeing is managing the Iridium satellite network, and now there is a marketing focus to its business. The perfect customers now have been identified: those industries clamoring for bandwidth. A simple oversight on the part of the initial administrators, but one that brought the company down the first time. As a new enterprise, privately held Iridium Satellite LLC has already lined up a $72 million deal with the Pentagon to provide unlimited airtime for up to 20,000 subscribers, and the company is actively courting other federal agencies. It sees mining, forestry, maritime, and even crisis response and humanitarian relief organizations as its potential customers.

Iridium's change of fortune will bring attention back around to the satellite communications business, especially competitors like Globalstar Communications. Offering global mobile communications since March 2000, Globalstar's technology and infrastructure are newer than Iridium's. One potential marketing and economic advantage that Globalstar has over Iridium is that it provides a land-based cell phone service (via service partners) that kicks in when the mobile user is in a coverage area, reducing per call costs whenever possible.

Globalstar is not without its own problems. Its primary backer, Loral Space & Communications, ran into financial trouble in 2000 (much of it related to Globalstar's cost-intensive startup) and has stated that it will focus largely on the development and construction of satellites going forward. Still, the demand for Iridium and Globalstar-style services is there. Making the service eminently desirable and affordable is going to be critical to keeping this company and others like it aloft.

Satellite companies originally formed by government fiat have found that keeping pace with market conditions and changing customer demographics requires them to change. In many cases, like INMARSAT, this means transmogrifying from a government consortium into a private enterprise. A perfect example of this is Intelsat, the U.S. government's first "commercial" satellite effort. Intelsat was founded in 1964 to provide commercial communications via satellite. It was created by 1962's Communications Satellite Act, signed by John F. Kennedy, which established the groundwork for a satellite system that would be overseen by 11 member nations. Intelsat's business in the U.S. was managed by Comsat Corporation, which handled the selling of airtime on the satellite network, much like a sales rep or agency. For decades, Intelsat was the preeminent and predominant satellite play, and it provided the world's first live global television broadcast when it transmitted back to Earth the images of Neil Armstrong stepping on the Moon in 1969. And Comsat, created originally so that AT&T wouldn't get its fingers into the satellite business, was its exclusive rep. Comsat has been public since 1963, but the government had prevented any investor from holding a majority stake.

In a competitive world, as we all know, things change. In August 2000, Lockheed Martin was allowed to buy Comsat, and in the process, relinquished Comsat's exclusivity with Intelsat. Since its inception, Intelsat has grown into a consortium with 144 member governments that owns a network of 19 communications satellites and generates more than $1.1 billion per year in revenues. After the purchase of Comsat, Intelsat's members approved a plan in November 2000 to privatize the organization in mid-2001. The company realized that it needed to be privatized to better address opportunities in the telecommunications marketplace. Intelsat made an announcement (which can also be found on its website) stating that "streamlined decision-making will make it easier to expand the business, leveraging well established, industry-leading services and global distribution channels." Looks like something NASA ought to read.

The standard bearer of commercial satellite operations, though, is PanAmSat (for Pan American Satellite). Conceived as an alternative to government-owned satellites, PanAmSat was the brainchild of Rene Anselmo, a businessman who put his own money up to launch the world's first privately-owned international satellite. Anselmo had founded the Spanish International Network (now known as Univision), which produced and transmitted Spanish-language television broadcasts from the U.S. From first-hand experience, he saw that the Latin American broadcast market was under-served and overcharged by the existing Intelsat monopoly, which provided its best and most reliable service along its transatlantic route between the U.S. and Europe. Taking matters into his own hands, Anselmo founded PanAmSat in 1984. Then he bought an RCA satellite and contracted with Arianespace to put his satellite into orbit aboard a new model launcher. When his PAS-1 was finally deployed in 1988, he had two customers, the U.S. and Peru, and faced regulatory hurdles getting anywhere else. Plus, Intelsat lobbied heavily against the use of the service, claiming it would erode its market.

Anselmo persevered and single-handedly opened up the commercial satellite market when he signed up CNN as PanAmSat's first customer for Latin American transmission. After that, the floodgates opened, and it moved to service markets around the world. PanAmSat went public in 1995 (Anselmo died two days before the IPO) and was purchased by Hughes Electronics the following year. Since then, PanAmSat has grown into a $1 billion company with a network of 20 satellites—the largest commercial geosynchronous system in the world. It is currently part of the Hughes division that General Motors did not sell to Boeing, the company believing that PanAmSat was too valuable to let go. Today, the company carries transmission that ends up in more than 125 million homes, provides Internet and satellite communications, counts every major broadcaster in the world as a client, and has $6 billion in long term contractual commitments. Anselmo's vision and business savvy created a company that defied the odds, city hall, and conventional wisdom to become one of the premiere space businesses in the world.

Loral Space & Communications has been in the satellite business longer than any other company, manufacturing satellites since 1957. In the past forty years, it has received contracts to build 210 satellites and was responsible for constructing many of the Telstar, Intelsat, and PanAmSat devices. Its manufacturing division, Space Systems/Loral has revenues of $1 billion and claims a backlog of more than 30 satellites. The company entered the satellite services business in 1997 with the acquisition of Skynet, a former AT&T company that managed the original Telstar project. Skynet owns and operates ten satellites. Another division, Loral Cyberstar (originally called Orion), provides satellite Internet services to more than 100 countries. Loral also formed Europe*Star with France's Alcatel in 1998 with the intent of creating a geosynchronous network. The entire company posted 2000 revenues of $1.4 billion with a $2.4 billion backlog. It did cut its investment in Globalstar (see above) in order to concentrate on its core businesses in the immediate future.

Orbital Sciences Corporation, founded in 1982, has carved

out a niche building satellites for low-Earth orbit and has built a total of some 90 satellites for various customers. It is the leader in small launch vehicles, both for low-Earth orbit and for suborbital missions and has launched 140 of these missions to date. Interestingly, its launch products include both ground-based and air-launch systems for lifting lightweight satellites into orbit. The company's revenues for 2000 were $725 million, with a backlog of $950 million, and a potential/pending backlog of more than $3 billion. The company claims the best launch record in the industry, with 101 consecutive successful launches. However, Orbital—like many of its corporate peers—fell prey to the pursuit of satellite operations and recently had to sell off its Orbcomm services division in order to return to the basics that have served it so well.

Société Européenne des Satellites (SES), based in Belgium, is the giant of European satellite services operators, with its ASTRA direct-to-home system serving some 87 million customers with more than 1,000 channels from a host of European and international broadcasters. Founded in 1985, SES is also a major shareholder in AsiaSat, the Nordic Satellite Company, and Star-Sat, which owns a hefty chunk of the Latin American market with its Brasilsat constellation. SES had 2000 revenue of $746 million, with profits of $461 million and a backlog of contracted orders worth more than $4 billion. The company became a global leader almost overnight with its March 2001 acquisition of General Electric's satellite unit, GE Americom, for $5 billion in cash and stock. The new company, to be called SES Global, will have a huge fleet of satellites, with 28 wholly-owned satellites—17 of which are Americom's—and partnership positions in 13 additional satellites. The Americom deal gives SES, which already services Europe, Asia, Australia, and North Africa, much-desired access to the U.S. market.

This is not an industry completely dominated by aerospace

behemoths, international megacorporations, and monstrous reserves of capital. Smaller players can be found throughout the industry, each with their own set of business paradigms and industry focus. Other U.S. players include Mobile Satellite Service (Gaithersburg, MD), founded in 1993; Mobile Telesystems (also of Gaithersburg), spun off from COMSAT in 1988; Comtech Mobile Datacom (Germantown, MD, a division of Comtech Telecomunications); and Ellipso (Washington, DC). The latter company is planning on sending 17 satellites into mid-Earth orbit at an altitude of approximately 5,000 miles in a unique elliptical configuration that it says will provide cheaper and more efficient transmission than its competitors. According to the company, this will be possible because its satellites' orbits are designed to keep them over high-population land masses a greater percentage of the time, thereby minimizing the downtime that occurs when direct satellite traffic is reduced over oceans or uninhabited regions.

The notable new big-name player is New ICO, the satellite arm of ICO-Teledesic Global. Rebuilt in May 2000 on the ashes of the bankrupt ICO Global Communications, New ICO boasts the vision and bucks of cellular pioneer Craig McCaw, coupled with investment dollars from Microsoft's Bill Gates. With $1.2 billion in new capital, New ICO plans to launch 12 satellites that will serve the usual contingent of remote-location businesses, but it will strongly emphasize its ability to deliver high-bandwidth capability for applications such as Internet access anywhere in the world—a service we believe will be a huge driver of the satcom market. In March 2001, New ICO partnered with startup Ellipso with plans to launch satellite-based Internet access in 2003. The companies plan on targeting rural and remote areas where DSL or cable modems aren't likely to be available until well after 2003. It's also likely that ICO-Teledesic will acquire Ellipso outright.

There are numerous international players, especially in areas of increasing population density but limited phone line infrastructure. These companies include Asia Cellular Satellite International (ACeS), formed in 1995 as a joint venture between Pacific Satelit Nusantara (PSN) of Indonesia, the Philippine Long Distance Telephone Company (PLDT), Lockheed Martin, and Jasmine International Overseas of Thailand. The company already serves Eastern Asia and the subcontinent, including the above nations plus China and India. It should be noted that providing service in other countries is not simply a matter of pointing a satellite in the right direction and transmitting signals to waiting users. In almost every region of the globe, a significant non-technical hurdle is doing business with the local phone companies and service providers. Many phone systems are nationalized, and successful mobile satellite phone companies must form strong partnerships and cut through high tensile strength bureaucratic red tape. No matter how good the technology, securing these relationships is a critical component to success.

One additional type of direct satellite communication well worth mentioning is VSAT (very small aperture terminal). This is a popular form of satcom that has a huge industrial presence and is known as fixed—as opposed to mobile—satellite communication. A medium that can serve both home and business users, it works with an antenna/dish and a personal computer that receive transmission directly from satellites, with each VSAT system (the name for the combination of dish and computer) acting as its own Earthbound receiving center. It allows business users to set up their own communications systems without having to rely on service such as leased lines provided by a third party telecom. An example of this is a business that needs to communicate with geographically dispersed offices or franchises, such as department stores, convenience stores, and gas stations.

In each of these cases, VSATs can be used for immediate credit card authorization, real-time inventory control and price adjustment, sending data to numerous locations in a franchise simultaneously, and continuous monitoring of store traffic and volume. Additionally, diverse data types such as stock updates, electronic signage, hotel reservations, and ATM transactions can use VSAT technology. Rite Aid, for instance, uses Gilat's Spacenet VSATs to send pharmacy prescriptions from one location to another, while the United State Post Office uses VSAT to keep in constant contact with some 27,000 locations. Hollywood's current interest in delivering digital versions of movies—instead of the bulky tape canisters that have been the staple of the movie business since the invention of the projector—is also being built on point-to-point satellite transmission. In November 2000, the Boeing Company, Miramax Films, and AMC Theatres announced Cinema Connexion. This will be a fiber and satellite-based system designed to radically alter motion picture film distribution by beaming movies directly to receivers at theaters. Connexion is also the name of Boeing's Internet service, which beams two-way Internet service to mobile users and aircraft via satellite.

The Global VSAT forum reports that there are over 500,000 VSATs in use today (not counting consumer products such as DirecTV; see below). Worldwide, nearly 200 vendors provide VSAT service.

This is as good a place as any to introduce the 500-pound gorilla of the satellite business; indeed, the entire space business. Boeing. We'll be mentioning the company quite a bit during the course of this book due to the fact that it has found ways to be part of every segment of the space business, from providing launch services to satellite manufacturing to managing the space shuttle's operations. Boeing acquired the satellite division of Hughes in 2000 and promptly set up Boeing Satellite Services, which made it the largest player in the business. The BSS subsidiary has approximately $2.5 billion in revenues and employs some 9,000 people. With Hughes' satellite division as part of its legacy, Boeing has created about 40 percent of all satellites currently in orbit and has put more than 180 satellites into space. The division claims to have a backlog of $5 billion worth of orders for satellites waiting to be manufactured and deployed—from customers in 14 different countries.

Other companies compete aggressively against Boeing in many of these areas, and some have nearly as much clout. They include France's Arianespace, the European Space Agency, China's Great Wall, Lockheed Martin, Loral, and several others. We'll look at all of them in due time, but Boeing's presence is so pervasive that it needs to be singled out here.

So, too, does TRW. Unlike higher profile companies such as Boeing and Lockheed, TRW is the stealth player in the satellite community, despite annual revenues of more than $17 billion dollars. This is due to the fact that TRW provides much of the internal electronics for the systems used in satellites, launch vehicles, ground monitoring stations, antennas, and communications equipment. Because its technology is embedded in products marketed or sold by its partners, one doesn't usually see TRW's name or logo on lots of space products (or on its automotive products; TRW makes safety systems for cars, including air bags and seatbelt systems). Yet its pervasiveness, like Boeing's, makes it an important player in the space business. You just have to look under the hood to see what it's been doing.

TRW is also one of the largest companies to make a successful transition into the commercial space market. For a significant part of its hundred-year history, it relied heavily on contracts from the U.S. Air Force and other military agencies for revenues. But during that time, TRW also gained a reputation for developing extremely high-end technology with practical applications. Today, it has customers amongst almost every company and government organization we'll site in the next several chapters. Interestingly, TRW's extraordinary success at creating advanced technology has fostered entrepreneurship within its ranks; a considerable number of the new generation and startup companies in the space business (discussed in Chapter 6) have former TRW executives in their ranks.

Satellite High Speed Internet Access (Saternet?)

A small fraction of the world's population has Internet access, and the access that is available is highly concentrated in the U.S., Europe, the Pacific Rim, and India. Any user of the Internet, regardless of the type of line or modem he or she has, will experience Internet congestion. The reason? The majority of global Internet connections are pumped through existing cable, telephone, and fiber optics networks. And demand is increasing, crowding more users into the same amount of bandwidth. Congestion is merely an inconvenience on most days, but a living, breathing nightmare when it interrupts your company email system or your corporate intranet.

What is going to happen as more people demand Internet access? Take rural areas in the U.S. As they start getting better Internet access service, they'll start using the Internet more, adding more traffic to the web. But the Internet is truly global, so we can't limit our scenario to just the untapped regions of the U.S. What happens when entire nations start demanding access? The answer is not to start laying more cable. That requires earthmoving. Yet even in cities and towns where various Internet options are viable, existing infrastructures—which might date back to the 1950s in the case of phone networks— will require adaptation or modification. The popular DSL (Direct Subscriber Lines) service requires that users live within three miles of signal-switching stations, while cable lines often have to be upgraded to handle large Internet streams.

The potent alternative is to use satellites for access and at the highest possible speeds. Satellite installations can be used even in areas where there is no phone service (or even electricity—a battery will do). Satellite connections are always on, like cable modems, but operate at speeds up to 20 times faster than telephone connections. Unlike phone systems, which have an actual bandwidth limit (which is why a 56K modem will operate at much slower speeds), and cable networks, which share Internet and TV over the same lines, satellites can deliver unencumbered high speed service that doesn't suffer the terrestrial obstacles of traditional Internet service. Satellites can leapfrog many of the bottlenecks along an Internet path (which include Point of Presence locations, network, nodes, and backbones), and provide point-to-point delivery. An added benefit is that satellites obviate the old adage that a chain is only as good as its weakest link. On the other hand, if a single ground connection along an Internet path is broken, the access fails.

New ICO is focusing directly on this market, as is the recently revamped Hughes Electronics. Hughes has begun offering DirecPC, an Internet service similar to its DirecTV offering. Using small satellite dishes, users can surf the Internet by literally surfing above the other users that are routed along ground stations. It uses VSAT technology to deliver the Internet directly to a user's home or office. With a small satellite dish—typically around 18 inches in diameter—mounted on a rooftop or window ledge by a service rep, users can get point-to-point web access almost anywhere in the world, regardless of the limitations of the local phone company.

This kind of direct access, with its attendant speed and lack of congestion, is conducive to streaming audio and video reception, two media components considered to be the linchpins of the web's future. Currently, streaming media—which resides on a server and is never downloaded onto a user's machine—takes up incredible amounts of bandwidth and is unwieldy in chunks of more than several minutes at a time. Waiting for an audio/video program to buffer and then actually run can be an exercise in high-level tedium. Conversely, limiting this type of media also limits the Internet. Such transmission obstacles have kept media companies and potential users sitting on their hands while waiting for acceptable on-demand audio and video. Again, we can turn to satellites to alleviate this, since we're already using satellites for *live* audio and video.

Live Public and Private Broadcast

It's no surprise that satellites are crucial components of the modern broadcast industry. Live TV reports from war zones, sporting events, and awards shows are transmitted using an array of equipment that link television signals directly to available bandwidth on an available satellite. In most cases, this involves having a truck with satellite equipment at the event site (say, the Academy Awards in Los Angeles) send the signal from cameras inside the hall to a designated satellite. The satellite in turn sends that signal back to national or regional broadcasters. This is an example of a public transmission.

The same technology is available to private individuals and corporations. When you attend a conference that has a keynote address beamed to remote locations or attend large corporate functions where executives are communicating directly to employees at disparate locations, a satellite is being used. This involves not only the truck and equipment for uplinking at the point of transmission but an individual truck and equipment at each of the downlinked or receiving ends. A satellite band is leased for a specific amount of time (from companies like Comsat and GE), and the satellite transmits the signal only to designated receivers. Thus, instead of a fully public broadcast, this private broadcast is beamed only to intended viewers (disregarding the occasional pirate, of course).

Satellite broadcasts are the most efficient way to "videolink" groups via video. There are numerous companies that "sell" this service (since it is really only temporary, "lease" is a more appropriate term). Neither broadcast TV signals nor cable links can provide pinpoint one-to-one communication. As companies expand their businesses into international markets and require global office locations, this type of immediate and interpersonal visual communication becomes more and more important. The same applies to business conferences and training seminars. For those that cannot attend a conference in, say, New York, a remote signal beamed to a conference hall in San Francisco ensures that the viewer on the West Coast gets the same sense of immediacy and participation, as well as interaction, that the onsite audience has.

Satellite TV

In the 1980s, huge and hugely ugly satellite dishes found their way to America's suburban and rural communities. These dishes, often more than 12 feet in diameter, brought new and varied television programs into their owners' homes. They were a visible and expensive sign of the growing consumer interest in accessing more TV channels. They also signaled the first moves away from network programming.

With the 1976 HBO satellite transmission of a remote Muhammad Ali-Joe Frazier boxing match dubbed "The Thrilla in Manila" and the satellite uplink established by Ted Turner the following year for his Atlanta UHF station, satellite TV began its steady move into the core of the TV business. Though these first transmissions were intended for cable operators who would provide cable dissemination to users, it didn't take long for both the avid viewing community and the technical community to find that there was plenty of unrestricted and unencoded programming coming right off the satellites. Thus began the era of the ugly neighborhood dish (and the solitary rural dish) where customers scanned the skies looking for free programming ranging from American sporting events to Swedish porn to Japanese newscasts. The advent of the 100 channel TV was born, although much of it was—and still is—unwatchable dreck.

These large and expensive dishes (costing around $10,000) spread like wildfire, especially in remote areas. As their price dropped in the mid-1980s, their popularity increased. Estimates are that there were 1.7 million dishes in use by the end of 1985 (Source: Orbit Communications, http://www.orbitsat.com/About Sat/History%203.htm). The satellite TV business was the Napster of its day, and users reveled in the plethora of free programs.

This practice came to a grinding halt in 1986 when content providers like HBO started scrambling their broadcasts, making them inaccessible to satellite-dish owners. Instead of 100 channels of programming, the satellite-dish owner gradually found that channels were little more than panels of video static. As pirate hardware became available to unscramble (or more accurately, decode) the encryption of these programs, satcasters came up with another idea: going straight to the consumer. Thus, a new business emerged in the early 1990s. Led by Rupert Murdoch's BskyB (formed from the merger of the British Broadcasting Company and Sky Television) in the UK, this business offered the formerly pirated satellite programming direct to the consumers, complete with a smaller dish and lower price tag. Called Direct To Home (DTH) programming, this new service was open to anyone within the coverage area and replaced the monstrosities that filled backyards with dishes that could be mounted on chimneys or even apartment windowsills. In America, Hughes Electronics launched DirecTV in 1994 and rival EchoStar unveiled DISH two years later. Both of these U.S. services now boast a combined total of nearly 15 million sub-scribers (with DirecTV making about two-thirds of that). Users have direct contact with satellite broadcasts and do not rely on their local cable operators for their programming.

In 2000, several DTH companies created a two-way satellite offering, meaning that signals could go back and forth—inter-actively. Perfect for sending a URL command to a website, for instance. It is the intent of these companies to be the interactive link in two-way communications, starting with TV and Internet access, and then merging the two together in some new form of interactive TV. New business partnerships have sprung up seemingly overnight. Hughes' DirecTV and its sister DirecPC have already partnered with AOL, while EchoStar is partnering with StarBand, a provider of satellite Internet service. The plan is to convince those individuals who already rely on satellites for their television reception to also use it for surfing the Net. With over 10 million satellite TV users, it seems that the market for Internet access is a natural follow-on, especially when it comes time to merge the two technologies into one box.

Satellite Radio

In the public perception, radio often plays second fiddle to television. The fact is that radio is still the preeminent media by which the populace is exposed to news and music. But since its creation in 1919, radio has changed little, with the exception of FM's rise to prominence over AM in the mid-1970s. It's amaz-ing that something so pervasive could change so little over so many years.

Despite its relative ubiquity, radio stations have severe limitations, namely broadcast range and sound quality. Every car driver has experienced the gradual crackling disappearance of a station as its signal fades out, only to be replaced by a new signal and new programming from a totally unrelated station. That's due to range limits. As for radio quality, it's safe to say that, while stellar in some cases, it will never be confused with CDs.

There is a change on the horizon, or over the dashboard. Enter digital radio, or to be more precise, digital satellite radio. As proposed by companies such as XM Satellite Radio (NAS-DAQ-XMSR) and Sirius Satellite Radio (NASDAQ-SIRI), radio aficionados can listen to a single station all the way across the country, with a sound quality that rivals CDs. Their concept is based on getting any kind of programming you want, anywhere you are.

XM, founded in 1992, plans to uplink 100 channels of programming to its two geostationary satellites (named "Rock" and "Roll"), both of which are currently in orbit, and then allow subscribers to download those streams to receivers anywhere in North America. And to avoid anything resembling radio fade-out, XM has also created a network of terrestrial repeaters that will still deliver signals to XM radios in case of satellite signal obstruction. (Yes, satellites can be blocked, and signals can deteriorate in severe weather conditions; the results are called "rain fade.")

XM claims that its Boeing-made satellites are the most powerful communications satellites ever built, with 3,000 watts of radio frequency power. It has also lined up powerful partners so that its 100 channels will feature programming from the BBC, USA Today, CNN, C-Span, The Weather Channel, ethnic and specialty news (BET and NASCAR), and a wide spectrum of music. XM also has various manufacturers behind it, ranging from automakers General Motors (a major investor) and Peterbilt to radio names such as Alpine, Pioneer, Clarion, Blaupunkt, Delphi-Delco, Visteon, Panasonic, and Sanyo. All of this is scheduled to happen by the end of 2001.

Sirius' business plan is similar. Founded in 1990, it too will be offering 100 channels of music and specialized content to radio listeners via three satellites already in orbit. Sirius has big partners of its own, including automakers Ford, Daimler-Chrysler, BMW, Mercedes, Mazda, Jaguar, and Volvo. Content providers include C-Span, Fox News Network, Bloomberg, CNBC, and National Public Radio. The Janus Fund took a $99 million stake in Sirius in 2001, bucking a company trend away from tech stocks.

Because the signal from these two companies is digital and can be received anywhere, they have the potential to gain back some of the ground lost by radio to auto CD players. With all the benefits of radio—diversity, news, brand, and personality loyalty—coupled with the tonal range and clarity that makes CD so desirable, satellite radio could literally usher in a new generation of radio listeners and listening habits. At a price of roughly $10 per month, with no commercials, the programming is attractive, but unproven. Both XM and Sirius will rely heavily on the installation of satellite-radios in new cars, as well as add-ons to replacement stereos. The sooner this happens, the sooner they'll start making money.

Telemedicine

At another end of the satellite services spectrum, we feel that telemedicine has tremendous potential, both socially and economically. As the age of the population increases, and medical technology becomes more available at the patient level, there will be a substantial growth in self-monitoring applications, such as testing blood sugar, measuring blood pressure and cholesterol, and monitoring heart rate and respiration. Getting this information from patients to healthcare professionals will be of paramount importance. After all, if the patient has the data but a doctor can't access it, where is its value?

Telemedicine today primarily involves telephone transmission of medical data. Conventional telephone bandwidth is a limiting factor in the ability to transfer information, especially in rural areas. For example, teleradiology, the sending of digital images such as X-rays, CT scans, MRIs, or photographs, takes up huge amounts of bandwidth on a telephone line, resulting in slow delivery. This is perhaps acceptable for non-emergency situations, but nonetheless poses a problem from the perspective of timely delivery. Medical analysis and diagnosis is based on data, and that needs to be available to physicians and surgeons on demand.

In the case of emergency situations, doctors need immediate access to patient data, and going to a location (such as an office) where they can view this information during off-hours is not only inconvenient, it may also be impractical in light of the immediacy of a particular situation. Telemedicine promises to obviate delays by providing instantaneous transmission and reception of critical data elements such as patient history, X-rays, and test results. Doctors that need instant data, which also includes Internet data, can derive benefit from having this information available to them on their home or portable computers, or via VSATs. Doctors who are not in a location near a patient—but whose expertise is called on in specific cases—can use telemedicine systems in the form of videoconferencing to remotely examine a patient or serve as a consultant to an exam.

Doctors are already able to remotely monitor patients' vital signs using modems. Using specialized devices, telemedicine systems can send data on heart rate, blood pressure, respiration, and a host of other vital signs. This usually involves the patient self-administering a certain monitor procedure and then uploading the data to a doctor's office. This system strains under the weight of data size in areas with no Internet or high-speed telephone infrastructure. In order to make such a service available to all users, satellite transmission can serve as the connection between doctor and patient. This is helpful in situations where patients are separated by long distances from their specialists (e.g., a cancer patient in Kansas and the specialist in Houston). The same process can be used by consulting physicians to take patient readings from locations where they are not able to be physically present. Combined with computer data taken from patient examination devices (including heart monitors and stethoscopes), remote doctors can review a patient's condition as if they were observing in the same room.

The benefits are obvious when considering geographic distance between individual patients and their physicians. It is less obvious, but no less beneficial, to view other areas where telemedicine is already being implemented:

- Schools. Nurses can have immediate access to physicians with the appropriate equipment on site at a school and can better administer immediate care to children who have been injured in everything from schoolyard accidents to playground fights.
- Prisons and other correctional facilities. Transporting sick prisoners out of confinement is both potentially dangerous and expensive. Many of the incarceration facilities in the U.S. are located away from urban and even suburban areas for safety reasons, making access to healthcare facilities a lengthy undertaking. By installing telemedicine equipment, prison medical personnel can access specialists and possibly eliminate the need for prisoner transport. The state of Texas was an early adopter of this process and is working with

the University of Texas Medical Branch at Galveston Center for Telehealth and Distance Education. Their system already provides for the remote treatment of more than 400 prisoners per month.

- Military. Battlefield medics are equipped with basic treatment kits and are rarely specialists. The traditional M*A*S*H* model of quickly patching up a wounded soldier and getting him or her to a medical facility could be greatly improved with immediate access to specialists and/or surgeons. Of course, battlefields aren't usually rigged with telephone or cable lines, so satellites serve as the perfect communications mechanism.

- Home care. For patients in rural areas, or for those unable to regularly or easily leave their homes, telemedicine provides a means for people to stay in touch with their doctor or specialist. This has two benefits. One is a constant monitoring of diagnosed conditions, and the second is preventive maintenance for those considered at risk (again, people in rural areas who have little contact with specialists and work in high-risk industries such as mining, agriculture, and oil drilling). A computer with the appropriate peripheral monitoring devices can provide doctors hundreds or thousands of miles away with enough data to keep these individuals under a high level of supervisory care. But, as we stated, this information is highly detailed, and thus occupies a large amount of bandwidth space.

There are certainly obstacles here, including the concern over remote vs. "hands-on" care and the ability of physicians to practice in different states. These are primarily social and legal issues that will certainly be dealt with over time. The big issue right now is bandwidth.

The next step? Satellites. There is a huge telemedicine market taking shape around the world in both industrialized and developing nations. Companies like NEC, Fujitsu, and Sony Medical Systems already manufacture telemedicine terminals and videophones, while Cisco, IBM Global Healthcare, Informix, and a host of technology companies have developed the necessary networking equipment and hardware and software tools for creating comprehensive telemedicine systems.

Global Positioning Systems

Navigation is one of the most routine of all endeavors—getting from point A to point B. At the same time, the complexity of the data analysis that goes into navigation belies its simplicity. Knowing precisely where you are, and knowing where you're going, is important to airline pilots, captains of marine craft, truck drivers, campers, and people driving in a new town—and that's barely the tip of the iceberg. Maps assist all of these individuals, but maps don't show you exactly where you are, and they certainly don't plot points in the middle of a wilderness area. Maps are a guide, but they are not a locator. They don't have, for example, a means to tell you your proximity to something such as a restroom or a police station or decent motel. For that, we now have the Global Positioning System (GPS).

GPS has become a hot buzzword in the consumer automotive and leisure industries and is now a staple of commercial transport. It refers to a system of 24 satellites launched between 1989 and 1993 that were put into MEO at an altitude of 10,600 miles by the Department of Defense. The DOD had long been concerned with maintaining troop contact and position, a problem that appeared nearly insurmountable in the uncharted

Vietnamese jungle and then again in the desert expanse of the Gulf War. Yet one of the earliest uses of the GPS system, when it was initially orbited, was to track and plan the movement of ground personnel during Operation Desert Storm. Several thousand GPS devices were deployed so that troops could operate not only in unfamiliar territory but also in a hostile environment that involved sandstorms and night movement.

After proving a valuable application in the Gulf, it was immediately clear that the GPS had uses outside of the military. Since 1996 the DOD has made the GPS constellation of satellites available to commercial users who have found that the system provides valuable tracking capabilities for drivers, hikers, campers, cross-country skiers, boaters, and anyone interested in keeping track of their location at any given point and place in time. The accuracy of the GPS is such that commercial users with ground receivers can track their position to within a hundred yards. The builders of the English Channel "Chunnel" were one of the first commercial users of the technology, employing GPS to guide crews moving in opposite directions from England and France to an exact meeting place in the middle.

The GPS system is based on data tracking, but like navigation, it employs a complex system in order to show you that wherever you go, that's where you are. It is set up in this way: there are four GPS satellites in view from horizon to horizon at any given time. Each GPS satellite monitors its own position against an atomic clock, ground stations, and against other satellites in the system so that it can define where and when it is at any given moment. A user with a ground receiver can coordinate or triangulate his or her position by obtaining readings from at least three of the available four satellites overhead. This data is received as a longitude/latitude coordinate, which— when used in conjunction with a map or display screen—will pinpoint the user's location anywhere on the globe. When all four coordinates are present, altitude can also be determined.

The rationale for such a system is obvious. Troop or ship movement in vast open spaces can be pinpointed by planners or administrators on a global map with a high level of precision. At any time, a planner can know the exact location of an object (such as a military division or a transport ship) in relation to a large expanse of territory, marked or unmarked. GPS, in practice, has applications similar to those of mobile satellite communications but is better suited to situations where movement and tracking are the primary concern and two-way data exchange is not necessary. Monitoring delivery of shipments, movement of freight, position of all the vehicles in a fleet, the location of a roving diplomat—all of these can be done using a one-way tracking device.

Tracking cargo movement (be it by truck, train, or ship) and personal movement (in remote areas) has myriad benefits to both consumers and commercial organizations. Think UPS deliveries, transatlantic container ships, mountain climbing expeditions—any situation where people and packages are leaving the security of an embarkation point and must arrive intact and safely at a destination. Now think of what happens if something should go awry. Rescue efforts are often hampered by terrain where a lost person or even a lost plane can be hidden easily from view by everything from trees to snowmass. A GPS locator can narrow down the search from miles to several hundred feet. It is not unthinkable that we will soon outfit children on camping trips or traveling away from home with these devices in order to ensure their safety and our own peace of mind.

The same applies to air traffic control. The current system relies on radar-identification of planes in order to monitor their positions. When a craft goes off radar—below tracking devices or outside of range—the radar system becomes useless. Craft equipped with GPS systems can still be tracked regardless of their position and proximity to radar. This can expedite search and rescue operations if necessary. In addition, a new set of proposals could help to ease the nation's chronic flight delay problem. Currently, air traffic controllers act like traffic cops, guiding all commercial aircraft over preconfigured routes and then lining them up over airports like cars at an intersection. Using GPS, which is already being tested by FedEx and promoted by Boeing, planes could fly more direct routes and stay out of each other's way by transmitting their locations to each other with onboard systems. That way, pilots and navigators wouldn't have to rely on ground-based control to move them in and around congested approach routes. The FAA is testing GPS as an alternative to the increasingly overburdened radar systems in place, but, like NASA, it is finding it difficult to break out of decades-old processes and procedures. Boeing has recently created an entire air traffic management division to explore and develop satellite systems that it believes will be more efficient than anything the FAA currently has in place or on the boards. And Boeing may just fund most of the work itself.

Since the GPS system has available capacity, private companies are able to create their own networks of GPS products. This market has exploded in the last five years as a wide variety of companies in various industries offer both commercial and retail GPS products for use in any and all tracking situations. Numerous software companies have integrated GPS data into their programs so that users—whether in a car, on a boat, or in the street—can locate destinations or objects relevant to their needs. A driver can find the next off-ramp on a highway, a mariner can find a port in a storm, and a pedestrian can find the nearest fast-food restaurant.

Destination-based businesses, such as the automotive, leisure, and travel industries, have been quick to capitalize on GPS technology. Rental car agencies have already taken advantage of GPS by providing in-car services that let renters know exactly where they are in a new city. Hikers in wilderness areas can also pinpoint their locations no matter where they might be—the GPS system is truly global in its reach.

The shrinking size of GPS devices, like cell phones, has brought them into the realm of convenient and inexpensive accessories. The ubiquity of GPS devices is not far off and they may soon rival cell phones as the required technogadget for anyone venturing outside of the home or office. In fact, GPS systems are already being integrated into next generation cell phones, while many handheld organizers such as the Handspring Visor and Palm Pilot already have modules and attachments that turn them into GPS devices.

On a larger scale, GPS satellites can also monitor the movement of objects previously thought too slow or too big to track, such as glaciers, tectonic plates, and coastlines. Triangulation with GPS also allows for more accurate determination of altitude or height (mountains, permafrost levels, land settling, etc.). Data derived from GPS measurements will help to identify everything from dangerous terrain conditions to animal migration.

Though the U.S. military deployed the initial GPS system and has made it available commercially, there is concern in other countries that the system is entirely under the control of the U.S. In the case of a military conflict, for instance, the U.S. could limit or even cancel service to users. As such, ESA and other agencies are planning to launch their own systems, which will greatly expand the available bandwidth for developers and users.

Remote Sensing

Remote sensing is one of those vague terms that we use or hear when referring to pictures of Earth taken from outer space—a seemingly small business endeavor in the grand scheme of things. Yet NASA claims that it and other space agencies spend more money on activities that utilize remote sensors as their primary data-gathering instruments than on any other systems operating in space (including the shuttle and communications satellites). Something must be going on.

Remote sensing can be thought of as gathering data about the Earth's surface (land and water) from a non-horizontal perspective—which is the way we usually get our terrestrial data. In the case of satellites, it means getting data from above (vertically). It might also mean getting it from "outside" (in the case of the Hubble telescope gathering data about other galaxies). Certainly, being above something such as the Earth means getting a bigger and oftentimes better view. Land-based cameras and instruments can cover areas up to tens of square miles; satellites can cover hundreds of thousands of square miles.

Remote sensing is about more than taking big or pretty pictures. The "sensing" that is done involves a variety of different technologies including radar, infrared, microwave radiometers, still and TV cameras, magnetic sensors, laser distance meters, and object plane scanners—to name a few. A quick run-through of the endeavors in which these sensors are used reads like a combined science text and a social studies review: archaeology, atmospheric dynamics, city planning, crop management, digital mapping, energy use, flood control, groundwater detection, mining, oceanography, ozone measurement, population density, precipitation measurement, rain forest monitoring, relief services, reconnaissance, soil erosion, surface temperatures, volcanology, and weather. How do all these activities benefit from remote sensing? And what benefit comes from these images, outside of scientific and governmental advancement? The following are commercial and industrial applications of remote sensing:

- Agriculture. Crop growth can be charted over time, as can rainfall and water availability, all of which are key components of crop management. Data analysis can provide an improved image of crop yields or poorly utilized farm land. New water sources can be located by identifying dense vegetation, or even areas of seasonal desert vegetation. Such data is increasingly important in areas with inconsistent or poor water management, from the Middle East to California.
- Mining and Forestry. Remote sensing can track deforestation and erosion, as well as identifying potential new sources of timber and minerals.
- Real estate development. Population patterns, as well as availability of resources such as water, power, and access, can all be revealed using remote sensing. Also, undesirable locations can be ruled out by identifying hard-to-manage areas such as those prone to flooding, weather damage, earthquakes, etc.
- Power management and utilities planning. By monitoring population patterns and growth over time, power companies can do more accurate forecasting for future power needs.
- Insurance. Remote sensing can help determine the full damage to cities and structures in the aftermath of natural disasters, such as hurricanes and tornadoes. Aerial photographs provide a complete picture of storm damage that could never be aggregated from the ground.

- Construction. Work on large-scale projects, such as highways, office complexes and campuses, and residential communities can be monitored in their entirety using remote photography.
- Oil and natural gas exploration. Finding new sources of petroleum and natural gas can be expedited using remote sensing to analyze both existing and potential oil field areas before drilling.

As soon as the first satellites were launched, governments looked for new and beneficial ways to utilize their capabilities. Certainly, communications and reconnaissance presented themselves as obvious benefits, but a fusion of these two emerged in the form of remote sensing. The concept was not new; remote sensing as a practice has long involved the use of everything from airplanes to telescopes. In 1965, NASA garnered the support of the Department of Agriculture to develop methods for studying Earth's resources from space, notably in the areas of hydrology, geology, and cartography. They created the Earth Resources Technology Satellites program, later known as Landsat. Joined over the next few years by the Departments of the Interior and Commerce, NASA finally launched Landsat 1 in 1972. Over a two-year period, the satellite generated over 100,000 images covering three-quarters of the Earth's surface. There have been six subsequent Landsats launched (Landsat 6 failed to reach orbit), with Landsat 7 having launched in 1999. Over the course of its lifespan, Landsat (as part of NASA's Earth Observing System—EOS—which includes the shuttle) has offered its services to the private sector, offering to take various types of photographs including digital and thermal starting at the price of $475 per image.

For governments at all levels, sensing provides critical and constant data for analysis. At the national level, the monitoring of population as well as terrain mapping provides the government with a better understanding of the size of its constituency and the form of the land within its boundaries. At the local level, population patterns are also important, but so are the specific conditions of the area relevant to the population. Soil analysis, crop planning, weather forecasting and reporting, environmental monitoring (smog, air, and water quality) as well as traffic movement and land use are fundamental to running efficient cities and towns. Remote sensing provides a big-picture view that can be used for regional planning, budgeting, forecasting, and zoning.

As the technology improves, it is conceivable that increased image capability will eventually lead to the replacement of illustrated maps by organizations such as police, fire, and transportation departments, as well as real estate companies, developers, architects, and delivery companies. Illustrated maps provide a general guideline to specific areas, whereas actual photographs of these areas (only available from above, especially in high-density areas) can be used for actual building location and identification.

Business has already begun taking advantage of the technology. Wal-Mart is said to have used satellite imagery to identify potential areas for new growth as well as pinpointing the locations of its primary competitors, such as Kmart. A study prepared for Wal-Mart by Space Imaging of Thornton, CO analyzed traffic patterns, counted the number of cars per parking lot in large retail lots, and determined geologically undesirable areas, such as those that had occasional flood and water drainage problems. Space Imaging is one of the leaders in the business and has come to prominence for launching its IKONOS remote sensing satellite, which can take pictures of objects as small as three feet in width. Orbiting at an altitude of 423 miles, IKONOS is the first commercial satellite to rival governmental spy satellites in the types of close-up data that it can provide.

In addition to using the satellite for customers in the industries already mentioned, Space Imaging also garnered significant publicity when it published pictures of the infamous Area 51 in 2000 and provided pictures of the damaged U.S. spy plane that was forced to land on a runway in Hainan Island, China, in April 2001. Clearly, the company knows how to attract attention. Formed in 1994, Space Imaging is privately held but is structured as a limited partnership with a long list of notable partners including Lockheed Martin, Raytheon, Mitsubishi Corporation, Singapore's Van Der Horst Ltd., Korea's Hyundai Space and Aircraft, Co. Ltd., Europe's Remote Sensing Affiliates, the Swedish Space Corporation, Thailand's Loxley Public Company Ltd., and other international investors. Space Imaging uses not only its own IKONOS satellite for acquiring images but also utilizes the services of Landsat, RADARSAT, and the Indian Remote Sensing Satellite network. It has competitors all over the world, from Russia's Sovinformsputnik to France's Spot Image. There are dozens of competitors in this field (remember, NASA claims that remote sensing is its biggest investment area), and that number will increase as more municipalities and businesses come to appreciate and understand the inherent value of "pretty pictures" from space.

The Challenges

Satellite services is the big play in the space business. But manufacturing a satellite and offering satellite services like communication are two very different businesses with widely disparate models. The satellite manufacturers like Loral, TRW, Lockheed, Boeing, and Orbital have different skill sets than the satellite operators PanAmSat, Hughes, and GE Americom. By and large, the satellite manufacturers have huge backlogs, in some cases running as high as $3 billion dollars. The length of time that it takes to construct each satellite, along with demand from the operators, virtually assures that they will have a strong market for years to come, especially at a cost ranging from $50 million to $150 million per satellite. The satellite operators, on the other hand, have to deal with the vagaries of the consumer market as well as with government regulations, which we'll talk about in a moment. Successful players, like PanAmSat, are filling their bandwidth almost as quickly as they can make it available. There appears to be no shortage of cus- tomers waiting for that bandwidth, as long as it is offered in an economically feasible fashion.

Those players that have stuck to their strengths have thrived, while too many manufacturers have ventured into an operations-based business they thought would be immediately profitable. Mainly, they didn't do enough research before jump- ing into a high margin, sexy business. Why, for example, did Motorola think that it should be in the satellite service business with its investment in Iridium? The company had a successful cell phone business, but that doesn't translate into satellite knowledge or expertise. As we've seen, the market for satellite service is there—just not the kind that Motorola was offering. Where was the market intelligence and the due diligence on that business plan? Did Orbital have a real advantage in creat- ing Orbcomm? Obviously not, or it wouldn't have had to auc- tion Orbcomm off in April 2001 to the highest bidder. Orbital just wasn't cut out to both build the satellites and manage them as well.

The key here is that demand exists, and it exists at a high level around the world. An underlying problem in addressing this seems to be the fact that engineering companies are craft- ing engineering solutions to demand. They aren't crafting busi- ness solutions to this demand. Iridium's brick-sized phone was a non-starter almost from its inception, as was its high per-call cost. The devil in this case, like so many others, is in the details. The market wants good price performance and ease-of-use, something that should be delivered from marketing departments, not engineering groups.

Since the demand exists, it's easy for space businesses like satellite manufacturers to see dollar signs in providing their own satellite services. But that ignores the fact that sticking to your knitting and partnering with proven expertise makes a better combination that starting from scratch—especially when the stakes are measured in billions of dollars. Loral found that out with Globalstar. An attractive business, yes, but not necessarily an obvious business jump. Just because U.S. Steel makes excellent beams and girders doesn't mean that it has the requisite strengths to build skyscrapers. And Boeing's proven ability to build airplanes doesn't give it a leg up on running a competitive airline. The same applies to the best satellite manufacturers, including Loral, Lockheed, and Boeing.

Many of the companies that entered the satellite services arena took their cue from Hughes, which literally created DirecTV from the ground up. But Hughes' corporate parent, General Motors, was one of the few entities on the planet that had both the pocketbook and the long-term vision to invest $2 billion. Hughes also had sister divisions that offered satellite services, so there was corporate synergy at work. DirecTV's success, and that of EchoStar's DISH program, certainly inspired companies with fewer resources and less well-thought-out business plans to jump into the market without looking very closely at the climate. More often than not, that jump was a big one, not a cautious step-by-step move into risky ventures.

Manufacturers of late have been buying their way into the service market, a much smarter and less risky proposition in that they are buying established services. Boeing's acquisition of Hughes and Lockheed's purchase of Comsat give both companies a better entrance into the market than they would have gotten by starting from the ground up. If they can maintain the revenue growth of their new acquisitions, then they should be well positioned to become successful crossover companies.

Perhaps the biggest challenge to the satellite operators right now is their terrestrial-based brethren. Bandwidth is actually a limited commodity, doled out by regulatory agencies like the FCC. Broadcasters of every type, from radio and TV stations to phone companies, have to get specific bandwidth to transmit on. They get that in the form of an FCC license, which is a precise allocation of the bandwidth spectrum. The hard truth of the matter is that these companies are competing for licenses. Cell phone operators want more bandwidth, and so do the satellite operators. Unfortunately, there is only so much to go around. Thus the terrestrial broadcasters have been pushing as a group to keep more of the spectrum for themselves and allow less of it to go to the satellite companies. They have a bigger presence than the satcasters and tend to get more notice for their efforts from the FCC. And this is all on top of getting clearance from the International Telecommunication Union (ITU), the organization that coordinates requests for orbital space from satellite services companies.

To compound this problem, the U.S. government has taken a decidedly nefarious stance against the satellite business as a whole since 1998. That year, the government accused Loral and Hughes of providing sensitive technology to the People's Republic of China during the mid-1990s. The claim, made in what has come to be known as the Cox Report (after Christopher Cox, R-Calif), was that the two aerospace companies had helped China Great Wall Industry Corporation make improvements to its Long March launcher, which had failed three times with Hughes and Loral satellites aboard. The U.S. government accused Hughes and Loral of providing the Chinese with sensitive information during a failure analysis in order to improve the Long March vehicle. Congress viewed this as a transgression that provided China with a means to improve its missile capabilities. Loral and Hughes denied wrongdoing, and there were claims that the accusations were politically motivated to show that the Clinton administration was soft on China. The end result was that satellites were classified as defense materials, and Congress transferred satellite licensing from the Department of Commerce to the State Department. Suddenly, even discussing a potential satellite deal required sign-off from the State Department, which ground the wheels of business to a crawl. During that period, European companies like Alcatel and Astrium managed to snare more than 50 percent of the satellite business from the U.S., aided in part by a soft dollar. They have now established themselves as unfettered players in the international market, a fact that will hinder American companies in the next few years as they try to reduce the government stigma of being lumped into the same category as the overall defense industry. The government created this yoke, and it will be up to the government to remove it. The alternative is to continue to restrict American satellite companies and allow their international competitors to run roughshod over them.

Overall, the satellite business stabilized in late 2000 and 2001, especially as American providers underwent significant consolidation. The struggling operators have fallen by the wayside, waiting to be picked up by second generation strategists who will have learned from the mistakes of the pioneers (a cycle that occurred in the PC industry, the biotech industry, the artificial intelligence industry, and of course, the Internet business). While this doesn't change the unenviable state of the pioneers, many of whom are burned up and burned out, it does bode well for the next generation, which can now build on the mistakes of their predecessors. The satellite companies that can capitalize on current market conditions, create viable businesses, partner with and utilize existing assets and infrastructures, and deliver cost-efficient solutions will be the ones to watch in the coming years.

4

THE BUSINESS OF GETTING THERE

Conducting business in space may ultimately be the easy part of space business. Getting into space is the hard part.

Launches

It shouldn't be so difficult, and at some point in the near future it won't be. Right now, though, there are substantial obstacles to getting into space on a regular basis, and many of them have to do with the current crop of launch vehicles and services. The core of the problem is simple: it costs too damn much to get into space. This fact of life affects every aspect of the space business going forward, from space tourism to manufacturing to more frequent satellite launches. Nothing is as important to the future of getting space business speeding forward than bringing down the cost of launches.

The conventional wisdom of the space industry is that it costs $10,000 per pound to launch viable payloads into space. This figure is cited so often that it has come to sound like a mantra: "$10,000 per pound, $10,000 per pound." With this kind of price tag, the cost for shooting a Toyota Camry into space would be $30,420,000. This is not what we like to refer to as "cost-effective delivery."

Why is it so expensive? There are myriad reasons, each with their own host of design, developmental, administrative, and personnel costs. Here is a sampling of the major issues that affect launch services:

- The use of expendable launch vehicles (ELVs) that are used once and thrown away.
- Outdated design and the type of materials and propulsion currently used in launch vehicles.
- The huge amount of administration and attendant bureaucracy that goes into coordinating each flight.
- Limited number of flights per year. When the number of customers is kept small, the ability to create economies of scale disappears. More customers bring the costs down.
- Few suppliers.
- No current incentives (tax breaks, etc.) to reduce costs.
- Failure rates approaching 10 percent. (Source: Marshall Space Center, http://stp.msfc.nasa.gov/rlv.html)
- Insurance costs.

All of these are obstacles to getting into space, and each of them adds layer upon expensive layer to a launch. The following examination of the components of the launch business will provide a better understanding as to why we're faced with such a huge financial barrier to space.

The Launch

The launch of any object involves a wide range of products, labor, and maintenance collectively referred to as "launch services." It takes all of these elements working both independently and in tandem to get a payload into orbit.

Launch services involves:

Spacecraft manufacturing. This is the creation of the launch vehicles and their various stages. It includes all aspects of production and transport up until the rocket is delivered to the launch site. Estimated cost for today's crop of ELVs ranges from the low end of $30-50 million dollars for Russian rockets on up to $300 million for high-end vehicles like Lockheed's Titan, capable of carrying the heaviest or multiple unit payloads.

Ground Operations. Launch sites have to be able to ignite a rocket, get it off the ground, put its payload into orbit, and monitor its progress. This involves a wide variety of resources, such as personnel and computer hardware, that are on hand at each launch. Each site has a receiving area (usually situated at the end of a rail line or a seaport), a launch port (some have landing ports for aircraft), antennas, specialized computer hardware, and electronics. They perform functions ranging from signal monitoring and telemetry control to communications and technical support.

Investment. Before a rocket is launched, it has to be paid for. Orders for launch vehicles and the subsequent launch services come primarily from governments, followed by consortiums, corporate customers, and investment organizations.

Insurance. Before a rocket is launched *and* paid for, it has to be insured. The premium can range from eight to 15 percent—although in some cases it may be as high as 20 percent—of the cost of the actual launch vehicle, payload, and services (Source: Cox Report).

Those are the essentials. Now, here's a quick tally of the cost of entry to space. (These are all based on estimates and then averaged, since the relatively small number of players in the business keep these numbers secret and don't break them out in their annual reports or corporate filings.)

Launch vehicle	$150 million
Payload (satellite)	$100 million
Ground services	$10 million
Insurance	$39 million ($260 x 15%)
TOTAL COST:	$299 million

And that's the cost before a single dollar of revenue is ever brought in from selling satellite services such as communications, GPS, remote sensing, et al.

The biggest number here belongs to the launch vehicle itself. We're all familiar with these rockets. They have evolved from those Atlas, Delta, and Titan launchers that powered satellites and astronauts into space during the 1960s and 1970s. Launch vehicles typically consist of various stages that drop off once their fuel has been expended, with each stage taking the payload closer to its final destination. The technology underlying these launch vehicles hasn't changed much in the past few decades. The use of these traditional vehicles results in huge costs due to the fact that 1) every launcher has to carry all its own—and very heavy—propellant with it, and 2) once the propellant is gone, the launch vehicle is useless and therefore discarded, like an empty beer can.

Many of the launch vehicles in use today were born of designs from the Cold War. By and large, they still carry the same names as their forebears. But the advent of cheaper Russian rockets (made possible with propulsion and materials advances), ESA's Ariane launcher, and the next generation of vehicles in development by startups (see next chapter) has introduced some new players to those that have been around since the 1960s.

The primary launch vehicle manufacturers and their respective rockets are, according to Obireport.com, as follows:

International
    Cosmos International GmbH: Kosmos 3M
    Eurockot Launch Services GmbH: Rokot
    International Launch Services (ILS): Atlas, Proton, Angara
    MKK Kosmotras: Dnepr
    LeoLink: Zenit 3SL
    Starsem: Molniya, Soyuz
    United Start: Kosmos 3M, Start
Australia
    SpaceLift Australia: Start
China
    China Great Wall Industry Corp. (CGWIC): CZ Long March
Europe
    Arianespace: Ariane
    EADS: Ariane, Starsem, Eurockot
India
    Antrix Corp.: PSLV, GSLV
Israel
    Israel Aircraft Industries Ltd.: Shavit
Japan
    Rocket System Corp.: H-2
Russia
    RSC Energia: Kvant
    GKNPTs Khrunichev: Proton, Angara
    IKP KompoMash: Riksha
    ZAO Puskoviye Uslugi: Kosmos 3M, Start
Ukraine
    NPO Yuzhnoe: Tsyklon, Zenit

United States
  Boeing: Delta series
  Lockheed Martin: Atlas, Titan
  Orbital Sciences Corp. (OSC): Pegasus, Taurus
  United Space Alliance (USA): Space Shuttle

Some of these companies have partnered with each other to offer a wider range of vehicles. Different launchers can carry different weights or are better suited for delivery to different orbits, such as geosynchronous, low-Earth, etc. Boeing offers the Zenit and Energia rockets via its Sea Launch partnership, while Lockheed offers the Proton as part of its involvement with ILS. EADS makes use of rockets from its holdings in Arianespace, Starsem, and Eurockot, while Eurockot markets the Khrunichev Rockot.

Alternative Engines

The sheer weight of these conventional rockets, due in large part to the amount of fuel they must carry, keeps their prices high. There could be considerable cost saving using 1) improved engines or 2) alternate launcher and/or fuel types. In the former category, a great deal of investment has been put into scramjet engines. A scramjet is radically different in all respects from conventional engines. Whereas traditional engines, such as turbojets, use rotating compressors, the scramjet has no moving parts. Instead, it relies on the movement or "breathing" of air into its structure. Air is compressed into the engine as it rushes forward, and hydrogen from the air is injected into the engine. Combustion within the engine creates gas expansion that accelerates its exhaust, which in turn creates thrust. The engine is called hypersonic because it can propel aircraft to speeds of more than seven times the speed of sound, or Mach 7. By comparison, the SR-71 traveled at three times the speed of sound.

The benefit here is for atmospheric flights (at least for the time being) since air is required for the combustion process. That still allows a scramjet-equipped vehicle to operate at an altitude of 100,000 feet, or three times the altitude of jet airliners. In summer 2001, NASA began physical testing of its hypersonic combustion engine, a scramjet, in its X-43 Hyper-X experimental unmanned aircraft.

The investigation of alternative rocket types is taking two tracks. The first one is the use of evolved expendable launch vehicles (EELVs). The second is the nascent development of reusable launch vehicles (RLVs). EELVs are part of an Air Force mandate drawn up in 1995 that seeks to radically overhaul the existing U.S. launch vehicles, specifically the Delta, Atlas, and Titan boosters. RLVs are part and parcel of the new generation of space companies seeking to create a better and more efficient way to use launch technology. Since EELVs are currently in testing and slated for use by the government beginning in 2003, we'll cover them here. RLVs will be covered in more detail in the next chapter.

EELVs came about as a response to the lack of evolution in launchers during the 1970s and 1980s, when launch technology was focused on getting the shuttle regularly into orbit. Not coincidentally, rocket design and large-scale improvement suffered. Realizing the deficiency, the U.S. Air Force funded a program to revamp the current lineup of Boeing and Lockheed Martin rockets to the tune of $3 billion. The objective is to reduce launch costs by anywhere from 25 to 50 percent, with the net result being a savings of some $5 to $10 billion during the period between 2002 and 2020. It will attempt to do this by standardizing systems, components, and support functions across the board for launches and launch vehicles. This means a complete redesign and rebuilding of some of the existing infrastructure, such as launching pads and ground stations.

EELVs, though, are still expendable, and only used once. It is a good evolutionary step, and a necessary one in driving costs down. This is the kind of development the government should be funding, since improving the rockets it uses will translate into better rockets for commercial customers. Such investment takes the onus for all new development off of private industry. Use of taxpayer money in this way has a direct effect on reducing costs-of-entry to space and should make space more accessible to customers in the near future. Companies like Ariane have urged the U.S. to allow them to participate, and it's a certainty that EELVs will be the launch vehicle of choice by the end of the decade.

The same cannot be said for RLVs, although they ultimately will drive launch costs down even further than EELVs. RLVs aren't discarded after one launch, as all launch vehicles to date have been. They are used for a series of launches, one after another, with the length of service determined by the manufacturer—many of whom are space business startups.

Everyone in the industry, including NASA, understands the cost benefit that RLVs will bring. NASA's Advanced Space Transportation Program (ASTP), begun in 1994 with the development of the National Space Transportation Policy, cites the need to create RLV technologies that will help to bring the cost of launches down to one-tenth the cost of today's systems. Two years later, the National Space Policy reaffirmed these goals and stated its commitment to regaining and maintaining U.S. leadership in space. It also specifically stated that NASA should make investments that would "reduce the payload cost to low-Earth orbit by an order of magnitude from $10,000 to $1,000 per pound, within 10 years, and by an additional order of magnitude, from thousands to hundreds of dollars per pound within 25 years, to $100 per pound within 25 years, and to tens of dollars per pound within

40 years." (Source: http://procurement.nasa.gov/EPS/LaRC/
Synopses/1-063-DIG.1299/synopsis.html) Again, this is a NASA
goal.

Five years after this was laid out, NASA is no closer to
achieving that 10-year goal than it was on the day the policy
was adopted. In fact, NASA has shut down the very programs
that would help it achieve these goals, such as the X-33 and
X-34 reusable spacecraft.

With reduction of launch costs serving as the Holy Grail of
space business, there are quite a few companies eager to get
into the business. Various organizations are claiming that they
can bring the price down below $8,000 per pound and as low as
$1,000 per pound with RLVs. While this has yet to be proven, it
is unfortunate that the development for RLVs is now a private
industry initiative, and not one that the government has stood
behind.

ELVs, then, are the vehicles of choice—indeed the only vehicles available—at the moment. And launch vehicle manufacturers and launch services companies are putting them into space
at an increasing rate.

The Suppliers

Relatively speaking, there are only a handful of launch suppliers in the world. There are certainly hundreds of companies
involved in every launch, from software design to signal monitoring to insurance, but when it comes to physically getting a
payload into space, the number of players can be counted on
your fingers. Interestingly, there is an almost inextricable link
of partnerships within the international space community,
whereby almost everyone is partnered somewhere with someone else. For example, Boeing is a partner with Russia's Energia
in Sea Launch, while Energia is Lockheed Martin's partner in
International Launch Services (ILS).

Domestically, the biggest player is Boeing. As we stated earlier, Boeing is involved in almost every single aspect of the space industry. It builds satellites, it builds launch vehicles, it manages launch sites (such as Sea Launch), and it oversees satellite and flight operations. All of this makes Boeing a significant player not only in the U.S. but internationally, where it does face substantial competition. In many cases, international entities such as Arianespace and China's Great Wall have built on their governmental history. Realizing, with much more foresight—and much less history—that commercialization would be crucial to not only their long term survival but also to providing services in a growing market, other countries quickly made provisions for spinning off and then partnering with the commercial entities.

American space companies have no such governmental leeway nor incentive. NASA is still the single largest organization awarding contracts, and it does little to promote the commercial growth of its partners (outside of giving them contracts for NASA work, which is in effect a transfer of taxpayer dollars—it's not really NASA's money). This creates a situation where a huge benefactor funds new projects but is not interested in seeing its partners do any development outside of those it funds.

This strange catch-22 of the American space industry may be catching up to it. The current situation has launch companies and the majority of their customers appreciating the need for better and more efficient launchers and technology; but NASA, as the largest contractor, continues to invest specifically in technologies and launchers that have been proven. As an example, look at the X-33. Lockheed Martin was willing to work on the development of this vehicle as long as it had NASA as a partner to help offset the costs. But when NASA sought to trim its budget in 2001, it slashed the X-33, claiming that the technology had not moved far enough along. So, LM was stuck with the prospect of working on and funding the X-33 on its own. But its most immediate customer for the X-33, NASA, had just decided to pull out. What to do? The corporate answer is not to invest in technology that your customer won't buy. This is an insidious situation, one we'll explore more in the next chapter on investments.

Internationally, promoting space science and promoting commercialization are supported in tandem—and at the same high levels of industry and government. Such support has aided both the Chinese and the Europeans in creating ferocious space competitors to the U.S. and Russia in less than two decades. This despite the fact that both the U.S. and Russia have what amounts to a twenty-year headstart over the rest of the world's space programs.

Europe

The Europeans have become a dominant force in the space business—primarily in launch services—through the auspices of the European Space Agency (ESA). This agency in many ways is to the European nations what NASA is to the U.S. Founded in 1973 by ministers from ten European countries, its initial charter was to unify two separate space programs, the European Launcher Development Organisation and the European Space Research Organisation. These organizations had been formed in the 1960s in the early days of the Cold War but had not attained any degree of success or visibility. They were dwarfed by the Russian and American space programs in every way, so much so that European satellites were carried into orbit by the Russians and Americans.

ESA formally got under way in 1975 with a mission to play catch up. Its initial members—France, Germany, Italy, Spain, UK, Belgium, Denmark, Netherlands, Sweden, and Switzerland—provided researchers, technology, and ground facilities. Joined later by Ireland, Austria, Norway, Finland, and Portugal, as well as Canada (identified as a cooperating state), ESA put its efforts into building a launch vehicle. In December 1979, it unveiled Ariane, a launcher designed to put telecommunications satellites into orbit two at a time. The Ariane proved that Europe could be self-sufficient when it came to launches.

Since then, ESA has become a recognized player in both the research community and the commercial space business. It was a major partner in the development of the Hubble Space Telescope and sent its Giotto spacecraft closer to Halley's Comet than any other probe. ESA is a full partner in the International Space Station and is planning on sending a lander to the comet Wirtanen in 2003. ESA claims that across Europe there are now more than 40,000 people employed directly by the space business, with another 250,000 employed indirectly via suppliers and materials manufacturers. Interestingly, ESA has a policy of seeking bids and awarding contracts to member nations relative to those countries' contributions to ESA's budget. Thus, every country gets a crack at providing products and services to ESA's space missions, and everything from ground stations to astronaut training centers are located throughout Europe. Oddly democratic, as opposed to the rather dictatorial nature of America's space agency.

Ariane was the European equivalent of the Atlas and Delta rockets used in America, and it proved to be a reliable launcher. In 1980, the ESA created Arianespace, a commercial venture to handle bookings for its Ariane rockets (in the same way that Comsat represented Intelsat). Technically, Arianespace qualified as the world's first commercial space transportation company in that it was not government regulated and could accept business from just about every nation on the planet. Headquartered in France (also ESA's headquarters), Arianespace courted partners in America and Asia and then made one of the most astute moves of any space company to date: it built its spaceport right next to the equator. Instead of trying to find space over the crowded countryside of Europe for launching its rockets, it set up a launch facility in Kourou, French Guiana that gave it an ideal location for launching geosynchronous satellites (remember that GEOs are usually situated over the equator in order to have optimum ground coverage, and that vehicles launched from the equator can use the rotation of the Earth to help achieve orbit—which saves money and time). Kourou has been the site for nearly 100 liftoffs. It supports both a launch zone and an assembly zone, which allows two missions to be prepared simultaneously.

Arianespace claims to hold more that 50 percent of the market for payloads that have been delivered to geosynchronous orbit. It has performed more than 130 commercial launches, comprising nearly 200 satellite payloads. During one particularly productive stint in the three years from 1995 to 1997, Arianespace launched 44 satellites, or more than half the world's geosynchronous satellites. That averages out to launching a new satellite every three and a half weeks—an impressive feat for any launch company. Currently, the company has a staff of 350 employees and had 1999 sales of 6.4 billion French francs.

The biggest name in the European space business is now European Aeronautic Defence and Space Company, called EADS. An aerospace giant on the order of Boeing and Lockheed—it ranks third in the world in terms of revenues—EADS is a major defense contractor and the majority shareholder in Airbus. It was founded on July 10, 2000 (the same day it went public) as a space consortium comprised of three aerospace partners: Aerospatiale Matra S.A. (France), Construcciones Aeronáuticas S.A. (Spain), and DaimlerChrysler Aerospace AG (Germany). EADS' space division, which includes manufacturing and launch services, accounts for just under 15 percent of the company's total revenues, which were $21.5 billion in 2000. The company employs some 100,000 people at more than 90 sites in Germany, Great Britain, France, and Spain. The company is also a satellite manufacturer, having produced satellites for numerous scientific missions as well as for Intelsat and INMARSAT, among others, via its Astrium division (itself a multinational consortium). EADS owns a quarter of Arianespace and uses the Ariane rocket for heavy-lift launches, Starsem for medium-lift launches, and Eurockot for small-lift launches.

Interestingly, the ESA admits that it has not been able to compete effectively in the market for actual satellite manufacture. While it does build satellites for its own use, it notes that non-European countries still prefer to go to American manufacturers like Hughes and Loral. ESA believes that the military interest in developing state-of-the-art satellite technology has helped the U.S. in this regard. By contrast, the Europeans do not share a single military and thus have no dedicated military budget for technology development on par with the U.S.

China

China, despite the fact that it has never conducted a manned mission, is an aggressive player in the launch industry. Since 1980 the country has run a business called the China Great Wall Industry Corporation (CGWIC), which is essentially China's answer to both Boeing and NASA. It is a "state-owned enterprise" yet in recent years has been reorganized to attract revenue from outside the country by providing launch services and satellite development and maintenance to any and all comers.

Great Wall is uniquely positioned in this market, relying on a military infrastructure built up during the Cold War. Its Long March launch vehicle is a workhorse that has been in operation for nearly 20 years, having successfully put 17 Chinese satellites into orbit before the company went commercial. It has three launch centers (spaceports) across the Chinese mainland (Xichang, Taiyuan, Jiuquan—all serviced by major Chinese transport routes), each with a different service mission and unique expertise, such as geosynchronous satellite launches or LEO satellite launches. In 1985, China decided to put these assets to work bringing business into the country as a provider of satellite launch services.

CGWIC had it first commercial launch in 1987, a science satellite for France's Marta Group. It followed these quickly with launches for a number of countries, including Germany, Pakistan, Australia, and the U.S. In 1994, the government established the China Aerospace Great Wall Enterprises Group as a mechanism for making CGWIC a full-service international space industry competitor. In addition to CGWIC, the enterprise consists of 50 interrelated companies including, with China Great Industry Corporation as its core, the China National Precision Machinery Import & Export Corp., China Astronautics Science and Technology Consultant Corp., Great Wall Industry Import and Export Corp., Great Wall International Transportation Service Center, Great Wall International Exhibition Corporation, and the China Aerospace International Travel Service. Admittedly, this is a diverse group with a core business that focuses mainly on importing and exporting space, scientific, technological products, and electromechanical products. It also undertakes contracted international engineering projects, scientific and technical consultation, transportation, exhibition, traveling services, and even real estate management. But give them time. Altogether, there are 12,000 employees in the Great Wall company, with CGWIC its star property. In 1998, the company was already 36th on the list of China's largest foreign trade enterprises, and its annual revenue was $725 million, with about two-thirds if that coming from CGWIC.

In the past 15 years, Great Wall has racked up a successful

track record of launches. It put up several of the early Iridium satellites in 1997, as well as AsiaSat, Globalstar, and Echostar satellites. All told, the Long March series has been launched 65 times and has put 27 international satellites into orbit. A string of three bad launches in 1995 and 1996 created a crisis for the organization, but it has since regained its footing with nearly 20 consecutive successful launches.

Like all international space industry competitors, CGWIC has joined forces and created partnerships with every entity that it can. For instance, the satellite it launched for AsiaSat was manufactured by Lockheed Martin, a relationship that many felt was too close for national security comfort. Allegations arose that Lockheed helped CGWIC with some technical fixes for the Long March to ensure that the satellite it made for AsiaSat got where it was supposed to be going. In fact, the U.S. State Department has scrutinized every deal that the U.S. space industry has with the Chinese, deals that included Loral and Boeing. Part of this is due to the U.S. government's understandable concern that the Chinese space program is progressing at a pretty good clip, which could certainly raise military concerns. At the same time, China is getting more and more business, and one would think that the political establishment would realize that U.S. companies are losing business to China, which until 1987 had no viable space program. To add fuel to that fire, the Chinese also have had two successful tests of a planned manned spacecraft, the Shenzou. The country hopes to launch a two-man crew into orbit sometime in 2003.

Russia/Ukraine—Former Soviet Union

By any measure, Russia was the country that first saw the potential of space. Regardless of the impetus—national pride, the Cold War, military defense, offense—and the grander accomplishments of NASA, Russia was there first.

Given the turbulence of its recent political history, it's surprising that Russia is still alive, let alone still in the space business. But alive it is, and it remains an energetic and aggressive, if cash-strapped, player in the industry.

Russia's space heyday came during those days when the Soviet Space Agency actively competed with NASA—and by extension, the entire U.S. Its scientists pushed the notion of satellites into a realm where none had ventured before, and it sent men into space and landed them safely on solid ground. Aggressive and quirky, the Russian space program prodded NASA at every turn.

When Neil Armstrong landed on the Moon, the Russian space program seemed to have suffered a withering setback. It had theoretically "lost" the race it had begun. Once an American had set foot on the Moon, the Soviet Space Agency could never claim anything but runner-up status.

During the 1970s and 1980s, Russia changed course, concentrating on putting people into space and keeping them there (Russia also put a woman cosmonaut in space two decades before American Sally Ride ventured into space). It began with the launch of Salyut 1, the first manned space station, in 1971. America followed the next year with its short-lived Skylab project. Once again, the Russians had pioneered another space endeavor: maintaining a manned space station. This success led to the Apollo-Soyuz test project, which was more of a docking test than it was a long-term plan for a permanent station. In 1986, the Soviet Space Agency appeared to have found its ultimate mission in Mir, the longest-running and most successful space station to date. Assembled in stages 235 miles above the Earth using modules based on the original Salyut stations, Mir (which is the Russian word for "peace") was initially designed as a five-year project. The collapse of the Soviet Union left Mir without a place to call home; the cosmonaut on board at the time, Sergei Krikalev, wasn't even sure that there was a country left to come and get him back. Like the Soviet Space Agency, Mir was literally cast adrift. Since no decision as to launching its replacement could be made, it was simply decided to let Mir continue orbiting. Its control fell to Energia, one of two primary Russian agencies responsible for launching and monitoring Russian spacecraft. Energia is also the commercial arm of the revamped Russian Aeronautics and Space Agency.

Like many of the man-made objects in space, Mir continued to perform its duties long past its expected lifespan. Before it was deorbited in March 2001, Mir was in the running to become the first space station to welcome visitors. Mark Burnett, producer of the popular *Survivor* reality television show, had approached Energia about the possibility of sending the winning contestant from a show to be called "Destination Mir" on an all expense paid trip to Mir. The deal was a go until increasing concerns about Mir's safety scuttled those plans. That didn't stop the Russians from courting other space travelers. Approached by Dennis Tito in 2000 with a $20 million proposal to hitch a ride on a Russian trip to the ISS, the Russian Aeronautics and Space Agency plotted a new and unique strategy for its space program. They would be the first to take a tourist into space. Rebuffed at almost every turn by NASA, the Russians saw both the economic and public relations value of taking a paying customer along for the ride. In that regard, the Russians are still light years ahead of the American thinking about who should or should not be allowed to travel into space.

The exploitation of Mir aside, Energia and its Russian space rival Khrunichev Space Center are both actively involved in bringing the former USSR's space legacy to the international market. Energia has traditionally been viewed as an organization of the state that performs much of the launch and maintenance of spacecraft, especially those involving manned flight, including Yuri Gagarin's first solo flight. Khrunichev has been a bit more commercially oriented, building systems for corporate customers and relying on actual business revenues rather than state budgets.

Energia and Khrunichev utilize communist-era spaceports, the Baikonur Cosmodrome in Kazakhstan and the Plesetsk Cosmodrome in Russia. While they do have satellite building capabilities, it is their launch services that have attracted international business. The two are partners with Lockheed Martin in International Launch Services (ILS), a company that provides launches from both Cape Canaveral in Florida and the Baikonur Cosmodrome in Kazakhstan. Energia is also a 25 percent partner with Boeing in Sea Launch.

A third player in the former Soviet Union's space industry is the Yuzhnoe Design Bureau, based in the Ukraine. Originally created as the Experimental Design Bureau in 1954, it was charged with creating ICBMs during the Cold War. In the 1970s it provided both France and India with launch services for satellites from those two countries. Since the breakup of the Soviet Union, Yuzhnoe has concentrated on launch service business for both Russia and international partners. It is a 15 percent partner in Sea Launch.

One of the biggest customers of the launch services provided by these organizations is Intersputnik, the Russian-led satellite company. Formed in 1971, Intersputnik was founded by members of the former communist bloc (Bulgaria, Hungary, East Germany, Cuba, Mongolia, Poland, Romania, USSR, and Czechoslovakia) to coordinate the satellite communications needs of these countries. It began operations of its satellite system in 1979 and started offering commercial services in 1992. In 1997 it teamed with Lockheed Martin to form LMI to offer full range satellite services, from manufacture and launch to maintenance and operation.

Japan

Japan's space program has been one of fits and starts with some stellar successes and spectacular failures. Operating in near isolation, it developed its own space program in the late 1960s with the formation of the Institute of Space and Astronautical Science (ISAS), based at the University of Tokyo (many of Japan's new technology initiatives are associated directly with research labs and universities). In 1970 ISAS launched Japan's first satellite, the Ohsumi. At the same time, though, the Japanese government created the National Space Development Agency of Japan (known as NASDA). NASDA's charter was to make Japan an international space power, but it was positioned directly against ISAS, which was overseen by a different agency and had a separate budget. The two organizations began competing for dollars and resources, including talent and technology.

By 1975, NASDA had developed its own launch vehicles and was sending satellites into orbit. Up until 1994, NASDA had a perfect record of 30 launches and employed a thousand people. That year it introduced its H-2 rocket, which was to give it leverage to compete on an international scale. But in the next six years, a combined total of six rockets and satellites failed, a series of major setbacks that have seriously thrown its future as a launch services organization into doubt. The head of NASDA resigned, and the government put a hold on any budget increases for NASDA. Hughes (now Boeing) cancelled a contract for ten H-2s, valued at $836 million, citing its lack of confidence that the launch vehicles would actually work. These failures overshadowed the fact that rival ISAS had launched the first non-U.S., non-Russian interplanetary probe in 1998 or that NASDA looked to be on schedule to deliver its planned module for the International Space Station, something that neither the U.S. nor Russia could claim.

The Japanese government is investigating the possibility of merging the two agencies that oversee NASDA and ISAS. There is also speculation that NASDA could be broken up into parts and end up reporting to different agencies. All of this has thrown Japan's commercial space program into disarray, and the heads of its core research programs—like the Selene Moon lander and its plans to have a Moon base by 2020—are wondering if the other shoe will ever drop.

Sea Launch

Sea Launch may be the most innovative launch development of the past decade, and in many ways its portends the future of the international space business. Established in 1995 for the purpose of launching vehicles from an equatorial launch platform in the Pacific Ocean (154 degrees west longitude, to be exact), partners in the venture each brought specific space business skills to the program.

Boeing (U.S., the majority holder with a 40 percent stake) provides payload fairing (the connection of payload to launch vehicle and release mechanism), analytical and physical spacecraft integration, mission operations, and home port management. The home port, and Sea Launch's headquarters, is in Long Beach, California.

RSC Energia (Russia, 25 percent stake) provides upper-stage rockets, launch vehicle integration, ground systems, and mission operations.

Anglo-Norwegian Kvaerner Group (Norway, 20 percent stake) designed and built the launch platform and the assembly-and-command ship, called the Sea Launch Commander.

Yuzhnoe/Yuzhmash (Ukraine, 15 percent stake) manufactures the first two stages of the launch vehicles while providing launch vehicle integration support and mission operations.

Sea Launch's first commercial launch was in October 1999,

when it lifted a DirecTV satellite into orbit. Since then it has delivered payloads for PanAmSat, Thuraya (a Middle East telecom operator), and the XM Satellite Radio company. It has contracts for additional launches, including a second XM satellite. Of course, the company benefits from its Boeing pedigree in that Boeing can send its own satellites into space via Sea Launch.

International Launch Services

International Launch Services (ILS) was founded in 1995 after a series of mergers involving the interests of Lockheed Corporation, Martin Marietta, Khrunichev, and Energia. Lockheed had been marketing Khrunichev's launch vehicles, while Martin Marietta had its Atlas rockets. After the acquisition of Martin, Lockheed proposed putting its various rocket programs together under ILS.

In 2000, ILS had 14 successful launches and signed contracts for 17 future launches worth more than $1 billion. The company claims to have a total backlog of $3 billion in orders for 40 future launches. Its customer roster is impressive in that it contains a huge international clientele (some of whom are competitors), including Alcatel, AsiaSat, Boeing Satellite Systems, EchoStar, Eutelsat, GE Americom, Intelsat, Loral Space and Communications, NASA, PanAmSat, and the U.S. Air Force and Navy. The company's launch sites are Cape Canaveral in Florida and the Baikonur Cosmodrome in Kazakhstan.

Ground Stations

Getting a satellite or space station launched is only the first step in a long process. A successful launch, for instance, is not the same as a successful mission. Once the launch vehicle has reached the appropriate altitude it must deploy its payload. Then that payload has to perform the operations that it was designed to do. A satellite in space not doing its job is nothing more than $100 million worth of space junk.

Responsibility for the launch, and then the ongoing monitoring of a satellite, falls into the purview of ground control, also known as ground segment operations. Technically, these ground operations are separate for launch vehicles and orbiting payloads. We'll start with launch vehicles.

A huge amount of the capital and personnel employed in the space industry is related to the pre-launch development of launch vehicles. This includes the design, development, manufacturing, testing, and delivery of the launcher. Since each rocket must be fitted to its prospective payload (to take into account weight, shape, release mechanisms, etc.), every launch vehicle is treated as a unique unit. Thus, early stage ground operations involve everything from materials, propulsion systems, and computer-aided design on to component testing, propellant testing, and aerodynamic testing.

That's all before the vehicle gets to the launch site. Once there—it is usually delivered by rail or ship—final assembly, payload mating, propellant tank mating, and systems analysis is performed. When the vehicle is launched, the ground operations switch over to computerized control, monitoring, and analysis. When a rocket is off the pad, it can be watched, adjusted or aborted, but it can't start over. Thus, the critical first step is getting into space (which is what launch insurance is all about; we'll talk about that in a moment).

The ground component of the launch phase monitors the vehicle until the payload is delivered to the appropriate orbit. During this phase, a ground crew continually monitors the launcher's progress and makes minute corrections as necessary based on data sent back from the launcher itself. All ground stations use antennas (usually dishes), signal generators and amplifiers, and communications equipment such as modems and phones. A huge amount of the operation of this equipment is handled by computer.

When the payload is delivered, the launch vehicle is no longer of value. It then falls uselessly back to Earth—a multi-million-dollar empty vessel that can never be reused. And this happens *every* time a satellite is launched (unless it's deployed by the shuttle).

At this stage, the owner of the satellite, such as a telecom, takes over the control of its product. The ground station at that point has two functions. The first is to monitor the satellite itself and make sure that it is performing according to plans. The ground station receives continuous data about the satellite's position and operation and sends corrective signals back to the satellite when necessary. The second function is to transmit and receive the data that the satellite is designed to relay. This can be telephone calls, Internet messages, TV programming, weather information, or live point-to-point communication. It is the ground station's responsibility to route this data to the appropriate ground locations. In some cases, such as remote sensing or photographs, the data that is received from the satellite is stored as digital data and reviewed at a later time.

The Administrative Business of Space

As in any business, the business of launching a rocket and then making sure its payload is working properly demands a requisite amount of organizational or corporate infrastructure. This includes technical support, sales and marketing, public relations, and staffing. In addition, insurance and investment are huge components of each and every space launch and come with a unique set of parameters not found in many other industries.

Technical Support

Like computer companies or phone companies, a staff is maintained that troubleshoots any problems with the launch vehicle. The difference is that the troubleshooting has to be done from as far away as 22,300 miles—onsite inspections are not an option. The industry relies exclusively on signal data and computer control to fix bugs and make programming changes. Perhaps the most public example of this was when JPL lost control of the Mars Pathfinder and then had to reboot the system computer from an entire planet away to correct the problem.

Marketing and Media

Launch services companies and satellite operators generate business like any other company. They employ sales reps, they print glossy brochures, they write up proposals. The small number of vendors and the small numbers of launches per year ensure that competition and bidding are particularly aggressive and often fierce. This activity is the reason there are so many partnerships in the business; various partner companies can bring different economies of scale to a specific project. It's also why an Intelsat payload may be designed by Loral but launched by Boeing, or a PanAmSat satellite may be built by Boeing and launched by Great Wall. Because the entire cost for spacecraft manufacture and launch routinely rises into the hundreds of millions of dollars, customers look to providers to keep costs down. That means contracting out various parts of the cycle to different vendors.

The media plays a large role in the outcome of bids. Satellite launches are monitored closely by the industry, with more than a dozen magazines and websites reporting on successful bids, signed contracts, launch failure or success, and mission failure or success. Chief among these are Space.com, Satellitetoday.com, spacedaily.com, and spaceref.com. A company like Sea Launch can show its raft of successful press clippings to prospective buyers while Japan's NASDA would rather that not so many potential buyers knew the full details of its six year cycle of failure.

All media companies have their own agendas, which is to publish news and information, sell enough units to justify the ad rates that will allow them to stay in business, and hopefully to turn a profit. As with the entertainment industry, the sports business, or the financial services business, there are a host of information providers that have selected niches they address, ranging from consumer interest to business-to-business trade news.

Insurance

By some estimates, insurance is the biggest expense in the space industry after manufacturing. The nature of space launches—putting delicate equipment on top of extraordinarily explosive cylinders of fuel and then propelling them into space—means that there is a high degree of risk and thus financial exposure involved. An aborted launch, a rocket that explodes, or a satellite that doesn't switch on each add up to a failed mission. That in turn means that many millions of dollars have been ultimately spent for nothing. Since there aren't any ways to get investment back from an exploding fireball or a satellite that drifts silently into the Van Allen Belt, insurance is a very big deal in this business.

The first insurance policy for the space business was drawn up for Comsat and its launch of the Early Bird satellite. Ten years later, launch coverage became available and was extended to cover production and operation. It was a slow growth business, with most of the participants utilizing a modified form of aviation insurance. The situation was not helped by the fact that in 1982 insurers paid out more than they made from premiums (Source: Military Insurance Company). In fact, the 1980s were rife with lawsuits over blame, coverage, and payouts. As launch technology improved the rate of success in the 1990s, insurers actually made money, and more underwriters entered the market. The industry hit the wall briefly in 1998, when payouts were double the $850 million received in premiums. Since its inception, the industry has taken in nearly $5 billion in premiums and paid out nearly $4 billion. Market capacity hovers right around $1 billion per launch, with $300 million being about average (Source: Report to select committee of the U.S. House of Representatives, 1999).

Premiums are usually based on a percentage cost of actual equipment and expected revenues with per launch premiums running as high as $50 million. This provides a nice return to insurers when all systems perform smoothly. The current leader in the business is Marsh Space and Aviation, a French company that claims to issue as much as 60 percent of any year's space insurance premiums.

Interestingly, the U.S. government has a long-standing policy of not insuring its launches or any of the attendant operations or facilities. If something does go wrong, the repairs and payouts come from taxpayer dollars. If a rocket or payload goes up in flames, so do your dollars.

Here are the areas where insurance enters into the space picture:

- Pre-launch. Essentially, this covers any damage to the launch vehicle or satellite prior to launch or revenue loss from delays. Insurance can be obtained for the spacecraft after manufacturing is complete. Testing, integration of components, storage, transit, and launch site preparation all fall under this heading.

- Launch. Easily the most sensitive area for insurers. This insurance begins when the launch vehicle (hopefully) is ignited. Various aspects of the launch are covered, such as liftoff and deployment of payload. Typically, the industry has a 180-day period of coverage, more than enough to get a payload into orbit.
- In-orbit. Once a satellite is deployed, it can be insured for continued operation. Usually, policies that cover satellite operations are drawn up annually and subject to review of the satellite's performance.
- Liability. Just like car insurance, this form of insurance covers damage to third parties—such as persons or objects—resulting from launch or in-orbit disaster. This includes injury or damage from falling debris, in-orbit collisions, explosions, and a host of other potential forms of destruction.
- Service interruption. Exactly what it sounds like. If a launch vehicle is unable to lift off on time, or malfunctions, or if a satellite goes dark for a period of time, this insurance covers delays, transfers, and lost revenue.

There are other forms of insurance that cover a range of potential losses, such as a government revoking a satellite broadcaster's license or the inability to broadcast a live event due to severe weather interruption, etc.

- Brokers

  International: Aon Space; International Space Brokers Inc. (ISB)

  France: CECAR & Jutheau, a subsidiary of Marsh & McLennan; European Space Brokers (ESB)—ISB affiliate; Inspace, a subsidiary of Gras Savoye

Great-Britain: Blanch Crawley Warren, Aerospace Division—ISB affiliate; Sedgwick Aviation Ltd.— Marsh & McLennan affiliate; Willis Corroon Inspace

United States: Frank Crystal & Co. Inc.—ISB affiliate; J&H Marsh & McLennan LLC; Space Machine Advisors Inc.

- Underwriters

  Australia: Australian Space Insurance Group (ASIG)

  Belgium: Aviabel SA; Kemper Europe Réassurances

  Bermuda: ACE Ltd.

  France: AGF; La Réunion Spatiale; SCOR Réassurance

  Germany: DaimlerChrysler Services AG (Debis); Münchener Rück (Munich Re Group)

  Great Britain: Brockbank Insurance Services Inc. (BIS); Marham Space Consortium; Venton Underwriting Agencies Ltd. (VUA)—Lloyd's affiliate; Wren plc—a Lloyd's syndicate.

  Italy: Assicurazioni Generali S.p.A.

  Japan: Dowa Fire & Marine Space Industry Department; The Sumitomo Marine & Fire Insurance Company, Ltd.

  Russia: OAO Avicos; Ingosstrakh. In Russian; Megus Insurance Co. Ltd.

  Sweden: OdysseyRE Stockholm—Fairfax Financial Holdings affiliate; Skandia Insurance Company Ltd.

Switzerland: Swiss Re

United States: AXA Space Inc. (formerly INTEC); Great Lakes Insurance Associates (GLIA); Reliance Insurance Group; U.S. Aviation Insurance Group (USAIG)

Investment

All of what we've discussed thus far is part of the status quo of the space business. Two new factors in this equation will dramatically change how this business operates and how it will grow in the future. The first is investment. The second is the emergence of successful startups. Their importance cannot be overstated, and they are the focus of our next two chapters.

5

INVESTMENT

As we've outlined it here, the space industry encompasses everything from satellite operations to launch services to global positioning satellite applications. This cuts a wide swath across vast numbers of "established" businesses, including telecommunications, aerospace, defense contracting, television broadcast, Internet services, and home entertainment.

NASA vs. Industry

Because the various components of the space industry are so deeply entrenched in many of these businesses, the space industry is considered horizontal in its scope and its business offerings. The upside of this is that space does not rely solely on any particular business or industry for its overall revenues and growth (although for years it relied almost exclusively on the government). The downside is that it makes it difficult to categorize space by any single business practice or definition. Is space business launch services? Yes. Is it GPS? Yes. Is it satellite communications? Yes. Is it remote sensing? Yes. Is it high-speed Internet access? Yes. It is all these things, but it is not limited to any of them.

Therein lies the conundrum of what constitutes the space business. Because it is not easily classified, the capital markets view space as a subset of other industries, primarily telecommunications and aerospace, but also defense contracting. In those instances when space is considered a stand-alone industry, it is usually filtered through the lens of NASA projects and experimental science.

This view belies the fact that the space industry now gets more of its revenues from private industry than it does from government. This has been the case since 1996, when business with the private sector actually surpassed government contracts by a 53 to 47 percent margin. That disparity has steadily increased in the ensuing years as the space business has transitioned out of its limited role as a provider of satellites, launch vehicles, and ground systems to governments around the world.

That stigma of being associated with government business—and by extension military and space agency business—has limited the perception of what space businesses have accomplished and how they are poised for the near-term and long-term future. NASA-sponsored space initiatives, and indeed all government sponsored missions, are contributing a smaller percentage of overall revenues. And, from an investment perspective, government-sponsored space business is actually an impediment to the creation and sustaining of long-term commercial space success.

Why is this? John Higginbotham, chairman of venture firm SpaceVest, explains: "Government has never been designed as a business. Neither has NASA. They are both fundamentally incapable of running or creating businesses because they are designed—by their nature—to be procurement-oriented."

This is the seminal point in understanding why space ultimately needs to be free of government oversight or control. Government agencies do not make and sell products; they acquire them. In sum, they are buyers. Thus, their interest is in low-cost, easily developed solutions, which is a basic consumer mentality. Businesses, on the other hand, have to develop products and services that are in line with the specific needs of customers. In many cases, the best products and services are not those that are priced lowest or those that are easy fixes. In fact, when businesses contract out for goods and services to other businesses, they are oftentimes looking for solutions that require complex development, investment, and innovation.

Higginbotham has a basic set of comparisons that show how government differs from the private sector when it comes to nurturing new businesses or fostering growth in existing ones. As simple as they are, these conservative generalizations illustrate just how difficult it is to succeed when government is driving the bus. The cultural divide, as they say, runs deep. Bear in mind that we're talking about large deals running into the millions of dollars and not just off-the-shelf products.

Government = Buyers.
Industry = Sellers.

Government = Cost-driven. Lowest cost.
Industry = Price-driven. Market and profit determine costs.

Government = Winner takes all. Individual contractors usually get an entire project and then the government owns the outcome.
Industry = Win/Win. The buyer and the seller benefit equally.

Government = A single source buy at the lowest possible cost. Innovation is not a factor.
Industry = Can involve multiple sources for best outcome. Client has a problem, works with seller(s) to develop best solution. Innovation is primary factor.

Government = Fosters enemies. If you're selling to another government, or even another government agency, then you're at odds with the given government organization.

Industry = Fosters alliances. Clients and providers work together to benefit each party, creating enhanced revenue streams for both.

Government = Personnel ranked by "time in grade." Many government employees are interested in keeping their jobs to gain tenure and reach pension status.

Industry = Personnel ranked by "making the grade." Performance determines an employee's status and elevation in the company.

Government = Public value (poorly measured).

Industry = Shareholder value (accurately measured).

Some of these are generalizations, but they are inherent and fundamental differences between the two entities. So what's the point? The point is that the space industry is in a transition mode away from working solely with and relying solely on government. Any expectations that government will lead the way towards the future of the space business are sorely misplaced. Even though NASA makes public overtures to supporting commercialization of space, the fact is that it is inherently incapable of doing this successfully. It's not because NASA and its people are bad or misguided; it's because they aren't set up to make business work. They have, however, rationalized their involvement in business by touting the fact that they're experienced procurers. To them, procurement as an endeavor is equivalent to a fundamental understanding of conducting successful business. In fact, procurement is only one aspect of business, and as for its contribution to running a successful company, it probably falls far down the list in terms of the highest-rated skills. Contrast the importance placed on procurement employees with the premium placed on stellar salespeople and product developers and the picture becomes crystal clear.

Dr. George Mueller, CEO of launch-vehicle startup Kistler Aerospace, points out that there are other factors at work. Government programs have a raft of "regulations that are more social than commercial in nature. The government has to enforce a lot of policies among its contractors, like EEOC (Equal Employment Opportunity Commission) and affirmative action. Implementing and monitoring that adds somewhere between 100 and 500 percent to the cost of any program." He also feels that lack of specific vision will always keep government from being the driver of business. "A lot of agencies are in the business of self-perpetuation—keeping themselves alive. No one takes the position of setting a goal and saying 'we'll do whatever it takes to get it accomplished.' That also creates a lack of morale and the creation of competing projects that take away from a single objective."

The awarding of contracts for EELV development [see previous chapter] to competitors Boeing and Lockheed dilute the available funds rather than creating a process to develop a fully funded project with a stated goal. Mueller knows from whence he speaks; he was the head of the Apollo Manned Space Flight Program for NASA from 1963 to 1969, responsible for the Gemini, Apollo, and Saturn programs as well as the Kennedy, Johnson, and Marshall Space Flight Centers. He also worked on the original plan for Skylab and has been referred to as the "Father of the Space Shuttle."

Thus, we can't expect government to create new businesses by simply creating contracts. What about government-funded commercial initiatives, such as those that come from the Small Business Administration? The above set of strictures apply to funding business ventures through government investment pools or small business initiatives. It is too limiting because it begins with a procurement model. As Higginbotham states, "The government has a commercial strategy unblemished by success." For instance, how many of today's leading technology companies have been funded by government? Microsoft? Yahoo? Oracle? Apple? AOL Time-Warner? Not a government-funded name in the bunch. On the other hand, try to name successful leading-edge companies that have been birthed by government funding. Try; we'll wait.

The reality is that government investment fuels only those kinds of companies that fit the government model, which again is procurement driven, and thus low-cost oriented. These aren't the kinds of companies that become leaders in their respective industries. And entrepreneurs can run afoul of their government benefactors by taking matters into their own hands. All government agencies have a built-in "not invented here (NIH)" mentality. If the agency hasn't had a particular product or service constructed and designed to its rigid specifications, it is reluctant to use it.

Many in the space community use the Northrop F-20A as the prime example of technology losing out to the government's NIH mindset. In 1980, Northrop—in a rare display of defense contractor entrepreneurship—received government clearance to develop a jet fighter for the export market, as there was a ban on selling the existing F-15s and F-16s overseas. When Northrop demonstrated the jet, then designated as the F-5G Tigershark, it was considered superior in many ways to the F-16. However, the government decided to allow a version of the F-16 to be exported, and as a proven commodity, it was purchased by countries hungry to have the same fighter that the USAF used. In 1985, though, there was a delay in developing the next generation F-16s on order from the USAF, so

Northrop offered the Tigershark as an alternative—and a cheaper one at that. Despite the delays and cost overruns, and some tangible benefits of the Tigershark, the USAF stuck with the F-16. Northrop then tried to get clearance to sell the Tigershark to Taiwan but was denied by the State Department. With the government turning its back on the plane, and no way to sell it outside the U.S., Northrop was forced to pull the plug in 1986 on what by all accounts was a stellar aircraft. A billion dollars of its own money went down the drain, and the F-20 is literally a museum piece.

Could the same thing happen to launch vehicles developed by independents outside of NASA's sphere of influence? Certainly, and it is a big risk. If NASA decides not to use an independent RLV and the State Department forbids its use by other countries (remember, satellites fall under the category of defense armaments), there could be some serious blood spilled on the way to commercializing space.

That said, the government did fuel the creation of most of today's aerospace industry and the early days of the satellite business, primarily during the Cold War. Those companies performed admirably and achieved the objective set forth by the government: win the Cold War. That's done—we won, and these companies did an admirable job. But transition time is here. These companies all have to identify new missions for themselves, and many have started. This is why forward-thinking traditional aerospace companies are entering the commercial space business. They are buying existing satellite operators, creating new infrastructure, and examining ways to reinvent themselves in a less defense-oriented climate. Boeing, TRW, SAIC, and Lockheed are Cold War veterans that are adapting to the new model and finding ways to transition to a different market focus. Their partnerships with international players, many of whom were former enemies, show commitment to building new businesses. Note, however, that they are not about to give up their existing businesses and rush to create new technology and products. That would cannibalize a still very strong bottom line, and no smart company kills off its old products in the name of technology. For that, we'll have to look to the startups covered in the next chapter.

The only time that government helps drive commercial innovation is when it creates an environment or infrastructure and then gets out of the way. Take GPS. Funded by the U.S. military to the tune of $12 billion, GPS satellites did exactly what the government wanted them to do: track troop movements and monitor international fleets. There was no mandate to make GPS a commercial success. When it was determined that there was excess capacity on the satellites, the military offered that capacity to the private sector to do with as it wished. No push, no stated goal—just opening up the market. Then the entrepreneurs rushed in. Auto makers, transport companies, sporting goods manufacturers, digital device developers, and others created their own products using the GPS infrastructure. They now have a booming set of businesses on their hands. It'll get even bigger in the years to come as 95 percent of the cell phones produced in the next two years are estimated to have some GPS capability.

However you choose to view it, government funding is a dead end. Government has a role—to serve the public good—and business has a role, which is to engage in commerce. This separation has worked well, as capitalism proves itself daily outside the purview of government. Thus, it will fall to the capital markets to fund space development. These markets are the only entities with the resources, tools, and capital to create the kind of space businesses that will change industry in the way that Intel, Microsoft, and Hewlett-Packard have.

The trouble right now is that the market analysts and the

fund managers don't understand what constitutes a space business. As was stated at the outset, these financial professionals
view space as a subset of other, more well-established industries. And since they don't understand it thoroughly, they won't
make a huge commitment to invest in it. This is only natural;
fund and pension managers are risk averse. They use hundreds
if not thousands of matrices to analyze the investments they
make in order to narrow the risk and minimize their exposure.
Quite frankly, these matrices don't yet exist for the space industry.

SpaceVest

Education is of paramount importance if investors are to
understand the dynamics of commercial space endeavors.
SpaceVest's Higginbotham says that companies like his are
generating the educational tools and matrices that will allow
Wall Street to accurately determine the potential of space. Once
Wall Street understands the market, it will begin to feel comfortable with making investments. After all, pension fund managers won't invest in anything they don't understand. That
would be imprudent, and it would be based on speculation. And
any savvy investor will tell you that speculation is related more
to Las Vegas gambling than it is to making sound financial
decisions.

The failure of Iridium in its first go-round has certainly
caused unease in the market, as that had been the most high-
profile commercial space venture during the late 1990s. Its
demise scared off a large pool of potential investors, investors
who were looking for strong and fast returns. Kistler's Mueller
notes that even without Iridium contributing to confusion in
the capital markets, ". . . it takes a certain kind of investor to get
involved in space commercialization. They have to be willing to
invest large amounts of money in a space business infrastruc-

ture, and they have to wait for at least three to four years to see rewards. They have to have a view towards the long term."

Creating sophisticated investors is the overarching requirement for getting more money to flow directly into the space business. It also takes vision, the kind of vision that the auto companies had in the 1920s looking out from their Detroit offices towards the future, and the same kind of vision that electrical engineers had sitting in their garages on the West Coast in the 1960s and 1970s imagining what their hand-built computers could do for business. The space industry will have to nurture this by developing business plans that demonstrate how their companies will enhance reward and reduce risk.

Analysts will have to acquire and develop their own knowledge, conduct due diligence and research, and create financial models that are insightful and can be reproduced with statistical confidence. As they've done for years, they will have to take careful measure and apply a sound portfolio theory to space businesses, one that is as germane and viable as those that are applied to the chemical, transportation, agriculture, and computer industries.

SpaceVest currently has a portfolio of more than 20 companies in which it has invested, ranging from remote sensing to satellite services to Space.com.

Other Venture Firms

In addition to SpaceVest, other venture firms have begun to put money into the space industry. Kleiner Perkins Caufield & Byer, one of the preeminent venture capital firms in the technology business, has invested in WildBlue, a startup that plans to offer high speed internet access via satellite service with its own satellites in 2002. Kleiner Perkins' entry into the space business adds a new level of support and credibility to space investment based on its three decades of success with companies such as Lotus, Sun Microsystems, Genentech, AOL, and Amazon.com. Kleiner Perkins has invested in more than 100 publicly traded companies, which now have a market capitalization of some $80 billion. For its part, WildBlue has strengthened its appeal for the investment community by partnering with some of the biggest names in the space industry and large media companies, including EchoStar, Liberty Media, Space Systems/Loral (SSL), TV Guide, Arianespace, and TRW.

Investments are also coming from corporate ventures. Liberty Media, the company founded by John Malone, has been increasingly aggressive in pursuing the space market, which it views as essential to its telecom and entertainment businesses. The company recently revamped its own satellite business as Liberty Satellite and Technology (LSAT), and it holds 32 percent of satellite services startup Astrolink and 19 percent of Wild-Blue. In addition, it has two percent of XM Satellite Radio and small positions in several other space companies.

Perhaps most striking is Liberty Media's offer to contribute $500 million to 2001's "Deal of the Year"—Rupert Murdoch's plan to buy DirecTV. Murdoch's News Corporation has long lusted after a sizable entry into the U.S. market, and DirecTV (a part of General Motor's Hughes Electronics) would certainly provide that. DirecTV has nearly 10 million subscribers and is the third largest provider of subscription TV in the U.S. after AT&T (15 million) and Time Warner Cable (13 million). Adding this number to News Corp's Sky Global systems would create a subscriber base of roughly 23 million satellite service customers worldwide. Who else is planning on putting money into this satellite takeover? Microsoft, to the tune of $3 billion. The total cost of the deal is expected to be between $7 and $8 billion. Obviously, some smart people are putting money into this space venture.

While competitors like EchoStar are also interested in

DirecTV, the importance of this deal resonates far beyond the confines of TV broadcasting. If Murdoch acquires DirecTV, it ups the ante in the war between satellite service providers and cable operators. The cable companies have been upgrading their land-based systems furiously, trying to stem a growing tide of residential business that is turning to satellite TV and Internet access. A global satellite system the size of what Murdoch has in mind would dwarf comparable cable systems, in part because cable companies are land-locked.

And Murdoch is an especially aggressive competitor. He has said he will slash prices and use his other holdings (Fox TV network, 20th Century Fox Films, Gemstar-TV Guide, etc.) to bolster the content that he can offer directly to subscribers. He can also lower his cost for subscriber acquisition by combining his buying assets for transmission and receiving equipment, passing on those savings to boost his subscriber base. Interestingly, it is likely Murdoch will sell off Hughes' stake in PanAmSat to both pay off debt and to avoid the responsibility of managing PamAmSat's business of offering satellite service to other companies. With only a few missteps, Murdoch has built a monstrously successful company with satellite service as one of its key components. That as much as anything should point the way to the future of commercial space endeavors; Murdoch sees a value and is willing to pay a price for it. DirecTV at its core is a space business, a salient fact that separates it from its cable competitors.

With all of this activity, it is no coincidence that the investment climate is warming up at the same time that traditional space businesses are moving into the commercial service market. Those that participate in the investment opportunities early on will reap the rewards when the market cracks wide open. As Higginbotham points out: "As soon as the investment community realizes that they've been left out, everyone will jump in."

6

STARTUPS AND THE NEW GENERATION
OF SPACE COMPANIES

There is an upside and a downside to being a startup company in a market in transition. The upside is that as the market changes course, opportunities are ripe. The downside is that because there is a market history, there are usually large competitors firmly in place.

In new or emerging industries, there are no ground rules and startups can forge their own paths. The Internet business is a premier example of this. New companies were created with little more than an idea, and in many cases, no plan for how to turn that idea into a revenue generator. The financial marketplace initially embraced this "new economy" and eventually found it to be severely lacking. But because it was new and had no model upon which to build, skepticism was put aside, at least temporarily.

The space industry doesn't have the luxury of inventing the rules as it goes along. Nurtured for decades on government contracts, the space industry has a very visible history that includes monumental successes (the Moon landing, Mars Pathfinder, Hubble Telescope, PanAmSat) and spectacular failures (the Challenger explosion, the Mars Polar Lander, Iridium).

This history is also the legacy of the aerospace and telecom businesses, which are now established commercial industries. Breaking into this club with a new or revolutionary idea is not an easy task for any nascent business, regardless of pedigree.

But the fact that the entire space industry has to adapt itself to changing market needs and conditions does kick open the door for solid business plans and ideas that can improve the efficiencies of the industry. Nowhere is this truer than in the launch vehicle business. Dominated, as we have seen, by a few select international players with roots in the Cold War, it has relied on the same technology and inflated costs that have sustained it for nearly half a century. The "$10,000 a pound" mantra is accepted as gospel throughout the business. Even as the space community has demanded lower prices, it won't be the long-timers like Boeing, Lockheed, and Ariane that change this equation. But they are capable of changing it. In fact, the conventional wisdom holds that per pound costs could easily be brought down to under $5,000 per pound right now.

Why is this true? The launch vehicle/services companies developed their products for the government, and they are government-approved products in the strictest sense of the term. The government historically buys products designed to its specifications until it calls for another product to be developed. As such, there is still a big market for Boeing's Titan and Delta rockets, and Lockheed's Atlas expendable launch vehicles. These ELVs are expensive pieces of equipment, but they are government sanctioned and they sell well to the private sector. They are also, along with their international counterparts, about the only game in town.

Development of the next generation of ELVs, the evolved expendable launch vehicle, is only just beginning. The EELV is a small step up from the ELV, and it doesn't approach the ideal of being reusable, but the EELV is what the government is funding. Therefore, it doesn't behoove Boeing or Lockheed to go off on their own and create reusable launch vehicles (RLVs) when one of their biggest customers is still willing to pay for ELVs and is funding the production of EELVs. That customer hasn't asked for RLVs—in fact, that customer killed the funding for RLVs.

Look at the position this puts the launch companies in. They understand that they must transition to a more commercial model, which demands that costs come down. Yet, they have a huge customer in the government, and that customer is perfectly happy to use older technology and proven hardware without consideration for what new innovation could bring. What is a launch company to do? It can't discard its old product line simply in order to speed up the commercialization process. This would upset the relationship it has with government, which is comfortable with the fact that the products it buys were designed to government specs (that's why the government bought the $500 toilet seats all those years ago). And introducing new, lower cost reusable vehicles would undoubtedly cannibalize sales of those existing products.

Thus, we find the proverbial rock and a hard spot in the marketplace. The launch companies walk a fine line between keeping the government side of their business intact and lucrative and spending money to cultivate commercial business with the development of new products. If they stick to the former, they might ignore the latter. If they develop the latter, they risk the ire of the former. It's like asking these companies to develop independent left brain/right brain personalities. Given the current market, it is unreasonable to make such a request because as public companies they are still required by their bottom lines and shareholders to extract profits from their core businesses.

The launch companies will evolve; the technology impetus

for better efficiency and higher capability will ensure that. They just won't be the first ones to make inroads. For that we will have to rely on startups.

Startup companies always find themselves in unique and awkward positions. They require lots of upfront capital to get started, and they find themselves competing for resources, business, and mindshare. They are also lighter on their feet, more flexible, and less encumbered by the constraints that shackle established companies. Companies like PanAmSat have embodied all these aspects of being a startup and have succeeded. Others, like Iridium, have fared poorly. The difference between success and failure has boiled down to several key components: identifying a viable market need, creating a good product or service to meet that need, and then executing the whole plan with solid business administration and sense. Again, PanAmSat hit this on every cylinder; Iridium had a series of backfires.

In many way, startup companies, and those enterprises that have been around for a number of years and moved past "startup" status, are the outliers of the space industry. Flying under the radar of their behemoth-sized counterparts, they can take risks and use advanced technology in ways that their more closely scrutinized brethren cannot. Like their predecessors in the computer industry, they are worth watching for the technical innovation they will bring to the space business. Not to mention the agitation factor they supply, prodding and prompting the industry's less-adventurous companies to respond more quickly to market demands.

The real market for startups began in the mid-1990s, when the space industry began getting more of its revenue from the private sector than from government. Opportunities for partnerships that didn't involve agencies like NASA or ESA appeared in every sector, and those individuals who saw opportunity dived in. Of course, there had been startups formed prior to that time, but they saw their market potential increase with the introduction of commercial business into the mix. An example of this is SPACEHAB, a company founded in 1984 that is now poised to take advantage of opportunities available on the ISS. Not technically a startup, but indicative of the new breed of non-traditional space businesses, SPACEHAB is one of those space-based companies that will help coalesce the definition of space industry for the capital markets. It helps that SPACEHAB is a public company, although chances are that you've never heard of it.

Startups are, and will be, increasingly important to all areas of space business, from launch vehicles to satellite services to remote-sensing application development. Because the length of time it takes to get to market is longer than, say, a software company—due to the physical and manufacturing requirements of space business products—there is a correspondent length of time involved in getting these companies to profitability. It may be a year or more in the making, but the growth of these companies will profoundly alter the space industry as it has never been changed before.

There are many companies talked about in this book, and quite a few more will be examined. They range from new divisions of existing businesses (like Boeing Satellite Services) to companies that are offering new products based on space commercialization (Digital radio providers XM and Sirius). For the purpose of showing just how diverse this group is, we've chosen to examine a few companies in isolation in the section below. The following companies represent a strong cross-section of the activity occurring in the space industry on behalf of what we consider to be startup or next-generation companies. Some of them have been successful; others have already failed. Some are well funded; others are cash-strapped. Some have obvious paths to space; others are taking what can best be described as "radical" routes. Nonetheless, they provide an accurate snapshot of what the market looks like as commercialization opportunities begin to manifest themselves.

Kistler

As a pure-play space business, Kistler Aerospace is at the vanguard of how the space business is sure to evolve. The company is building a reusable two stage rocket launcher called the K-1. The plan is to use the two stages to put payloads into LEO and then have the used-up stages fall back to Earth using airbags and parachutes. This is not a radically new idea: the Mars Pathfinder and Russian manned missions used airbags and parachutes.

In 1993, Kistler was established by Walter Kistler, who has started several electronics firms and was an initial investor in SPACEHAB. The company's timing was based on the fact that there was a shortage of vehicles available for launch in the early 1990s. Plus, Kistler believed that an RLV was the most direct way to bring down launch costs for the commercial market.

Dr. George Mueller was hired as CEO. Mueller's background as the overseer of the Apollo programs gave him unique insight into the pitfalls that occur when managing launch programs. Along with Chairman Robert Wang and an experienced technical team, Kistler began work on its two-stage rockets in 1994. Kistler's RLV resembles a traditional rocket in everything except its reuse. Unlike other efforts to create an RLV using a single stage to orbit (SSTO) vehicle, Kistler is convinced that two stages are more appropriate and effective for low-Earth orbits. The second stage of the K-1 lifts payloads from 135,000 feet up into low-Earth orbit, where payloads are deployed from a module positioned at the top of the stage. It then fires onboard engines that aim it back towards the launch site, where it lands with the aid of chutes and bags.

All of Kistler's competitors are using "the airplane approach" with a single vehicle that launches and returns without separating at any point in the mission. According to Mueller, "Most current efforts don't consider staging in their designs, like the X-33 [the abandoned NASA RLV prototype]. The reason is that they're being designed by people with an aircraft background, and so they think in terms of a single vehicle. Physically, it's unclear whether this approach will work to get the necessary altitudes for higher orbits."

Kistler's unmanned vehicles are being designed for use up to a hundred times each. The company wants to have a fleet of five vehicles, which it claims will allow it to offer weekly flights. This is part of its plan to offer "launch on demand" to any customers who want to get into space without the traditional wait of months or years. And, says Mueller, it can bring the costs down under $1,500 per pound right away, and ultimately believes it can get down to the $500 per pound level within a few years. In this way, Kistler would serve as freight delivery service for the industry. Citing a Teal Report that states that an estimated 2,100 payloads will be delivered between 2000 and 2009, Kistler sees a huge opportunity in helping satellite operators get full constellations into orbit quickly (because the time between most launches is measured in months, constellations are "assembled" piecemeal as each new satellite is placed into the appropriate orbit relative to the other satellites in the constellation). As these constellations grow in number, Kistler sees an important market emerging in replacement satellites as old or dead ones are taken out of service in favor of newer models.

Focusing on LEO markets at present, Kistler does have long range plans for developing a MEO and GEO market, but satellites that operate at these altitudes are typically heavier than those used in LEO. Because individual satellites deployed at

GEO tend to handle huge amounts of traffic (which would be dispersed among a greater number of smaller satellites in lower altitude constellations), they also require more onboard equipment, bulking their weight up to several tons or more. The first generation K-1 will not be designed for such heavy payloads, although the company believes it can modify the K-1 to individual customer specifications so that it can eventually meet this demand.

Who are these potential customers? As far as Kistler is concerned, it is any entity within the three traditional sectors that needs cheap launches: commercial, military, or civil space. Commercial companies who use LEO orbits include those satellite operators involved in telephony and broadband Internet access, as well as remote sensing and scientific research. The military has LEO needs for observation, messaging, and tracking. In civil space, Kistler has already identified the ISS as a potential customer. Resupply of the space station is going to be an ongoing endeavor and high launch costs are already plaguing all of the ISS participants. If NASA is serious about following government directives to use commercial launch services when possible, then Kistler is uniquely positioned to take advantage of the frequent cargo flights that the ISS will require.

Kistler has contracted with the Nevada Test Site (NTS) corporation to use former government grounds for testing its rockets. But due to a long standing FAA regulation that rockets be launched from the coast so as not to fall back over inhabited land areas, Kistler can't launch its RLVs from the U.S. Thus, there is no place for its RLV to land on U.S. soil. It will perform its launches from the Woomera range in Australia, where there is plenty of open space for landing and recovery without threat to urban areas. The company is building its own launch facilities in Woomera.

The NTS and Woomera are not the only contractors involved

in assisting Kistler. Like government launches, it takes a host of companies and organizations to make any launch successful, and Kistler has signed on with a host of them, making its partnerships read like a who's who of the space business. GenCorp Aerojet is supplying the propulsion system, Draper Laboratories is providing guidance and navigational software, Honeywell has created the vehicle management system, Irvin Aerospace designed the landing system that incorporates parachutes and airbags, Lockheed Martin created the fuel tanks, Northrop Grumman built the composite structures including the structural components, Oceaneering developed the thermal protection systems, and organizations ranging from NASA Langley to the Huntsville Sciences Corporation and ATA Engineering have provided testing and analysis services.

Like all startups and independent space companies, Kistlers's big concern going forward is funding. Having raised a half-billion dollars to date, the company needs to raise several hundred million more to make its K-1 RLV a reality. In May 2001, the company found an unexpected source of capital: NASA. As part of its new Space Launch Initiative (SLI) to explore various RLV technologies, NASA awarded Kistler $135,400,000 to perform flight demonstrations of its proposed RLV. It's not a bulk award, however; Kistler gets $10 million up front for development and proof-of-concept, then receives the remainder based on successful flight operations. Interestingly, the only one of the 22 SLI contractors to receive more money than Kistler was Boeing, which received $138 million for its planned RLV program.

Rotary

Rotary Rocket is one of those space companies that was ahead of its time and ahead of the funding curve. Founded in 1996 by Gary Hudson, the company developed the Roton Atmospheric Test Vehicle (ATV), a manned RLV which stood only 63 feet high. The Roton's innovative traffic cone design—it included a helicopter like cap that would cushion its descent back to Earth—attracted a great deal of attention, especially after the company conducted three successful short flights of the craft (unmanned) over the Mojave Desert in California.

Funded by Gold & Appel, SA and Tom Clancy (who invested $1 million of his own money), Rotary got off to a quick start with $30 million in cash. The plan was to staff the SSTO rocket with two crew members who would pilot the single stage vehicle in to LEO, deliver a payload weighing up to 7,000 pounds, and then descend gradually back to precise Earth sites using its rotor blades. It claimed that the rotors would be more practical than parachutes or airbags in achieving successful landings.

The company was focusing on quick delivery and repair of satellites, as well as controlled and safe flights. Rotary engineers claimed that a manned RLV would be more manageable (comparisons were made to the Atlas rocket that propelled NASA's Mercury missions), and that the rotors could be used to ensure crew safety in case of aborted liftoffs. A fully loaded Roton with payload and crew could be launched for $7 million, or about $1,000 per pound.

That was the plan. Rotary had the misfortune of timing its flights during the Iridium fiasco and just prior to NASA's shutdown of the X-33 program. Suddenly it found that its sources of further funding had dried up as potential investors recoiled from the idea of putting money into space business. Hudson said that he needed another $150 million additional dollars to make the Roton a go but that the money dried up. As he told Space.com: "We had one outstanding failure . . . the failure being the financing." He left the company in 2000 and its assets were seized in early 2001 for failure to pay taxes. Since then, there has been no further development on the Roton.

Kelly Space & Technology, Inc. (KST)

Kelly Space is currently the only other serious startup in the race to create RLVs. There are others, notably Space Access and Pioneer Rocketplane, but neither have attracted the funding to get their businesses properly launched. Kelly is determined to avoid the pitfalls of the rest of the space business by eliminating the launch vehicle—as we know it—altogether. Its plan is to tow payloads into space.

Former TRW engineers Michael Kelly and Michael Gallo founded the company in 1993 with a plan to create a unique RLV for use in LEO missions. They created the Astroliner, which looks like a small jet. The Astroliner is towed down a runway behind a modified Boeing 747, called the Eclipse tow launcher. During the takeoff and initial phase of the flight, the Astroliner will essentially act as an unpowered glider riding behind the Eclipse on a tow line. At an altitude of 20,000 feet, the tow line will disengage, and the Astroliner will "launch" into orbits of up to 400,000 feet using its own power—an interesting combination of liquid oxygen engines and air-breathing propulsion. At the proper altitude, the Astroliner forward loading bay will open and deploy its payload with a small second stage booster. The Astroliner will then fall back to Earth where it will land on a runway like a conventional airplane.

While tow-lining a vehicle into space may seem far-fetched, tow-lines are used frequently in the aviation industry and the idea barely raises an eyebrow among those familiar with the concept. Kelly believes that using the two-launch technique to eliminate the initial launch phase will save millions of dollars in launch cost. The initial boost will be handled by the 747, and the use of conventional runways means that the Astroliner does not need to be launched from dedicated launch facilities. The company also points out that most mission failures occur in the first phase of launch operation, a condition that can be obviated by using conventional takeoff techniques. And Kelly claims that keeping the delivery vehicle separate from the actual boost vehicle also adds efficiency and safety. The horizontal processing of payload, from loading to deployment, also reduces errors and increases the rate of success.

In 1996, Kelly received an $89 million contract from Motorola to handle the deployment of 20 Iridium satellites. This was a big boost to the company and its profile in the space community, right up until the time that the Iridium project imploded. The company did have a successful demonstration of its technology in 1998 and has since gone on to win several contracts from NASA to investigate next generation RLV technology based on its tow-launch process. Like Kistler, Kelly is actively searching for funding to take the company's Astroliner and Eclipse aloft.

Spacehab

SPACEHAB is an anomaly in the space business. It derives the bulk of its revenue from space agencies, but its unique business positions it to capitalize on the future of space commercialization. This is because SPACEHAB is currently the only company in the world developing and producing inhabitable space facilities.

Founded in 1984, SPACEHAB has a long history of developing pressurized modules for use in space research aboard the Space Shuttle. SPACEHAB builds and owns three of these modules, which it then leases out to NASA for onboard use as self-contained research labs or cargo-holding areas. It configures these modules depending on the specific needs of each flight, whether for experiments, living space, or equipment storage. For instance, science and educational projects that go into orbit on the shuttle are pre-packaged into these modules. By and large, the working areas in the payload bay of the Space Shuttle are comprised of SPACEHAB modules.

SPACEHAB's biggest venture to date will be its work on the ISS. Teaming up with Russia's Energia, SPACEHAB is responsible for designing and producing the space station's Enterprise module. This module is to be the centerpiece of the ISS as it will provide an area for doing commercial work in space. Scheduled for launch in 2003, Enterprise will be 27 feet long and 9.5 feet in diameter with 1,800 cubic feet of work volume. It will be partitioned into three areas, specified as research, ISS services, and multimedia. The research partition is designed to host commercial microgravity activities over extended periods (current experiments only last as long as a shuttle is in orbit). The ISS services partition will be used for crew support and cargo stowage. The third partition is the most unusual: it will house a studio for broadcasting information from the ISS back to Earth. A SPACEHAB subsidiary called Space Media Inc. is planning on using this capability to broadcast video and web data from the ISS to Earth viewers. It is also proposing live interactive discussions with crew members during their stay on the ISS, an endeavor clearly targeted to the consumer and educational market.

When NASA cancelled its plans to build the ISS's habitation module, SPACEHAB and Energia offered to convert part of the Enterprise into replacement living quarters, for a fee. Having spent almost $20 million on development so far, the estimated cost to finish the module is at least $40 million more. If NASA opts to use the Enterprise, it would have to pay a fee to SPACE-HAB and Energia. No decision has been made yet, but SPACE-HAB undoubtedly likes the idea of getting more money from NASA to house its astronauts. In the meantime, it is looking for additional investment to assist with the funding.

SPACEHAB is unusually diversified for a non-mainstream

space company. As an ongoing business, publicly traded SPACEHAB (NASDAQ–SPAB) generates more than $100 million a year in revenues. Not all of its revenue comes from its modules, though. Through its Astrotech subsidiary, the company offers its payload planning and packing skills to commercial businesses. Positioning itself as an alternative to government-owned payload processing facilities that are used for prepping satellites and research projects, Astrotech charges a fixed fee for processing and support of payloads, ranging from final mechanical assembly and electrical testing to transport to the launch pad and propellant loading. To date, it has provided this support for more than 150 missions. It also owns Johnson Engineering, a company that oversees astronaut training operations—formerly run by ex-astronaut Eugene Cernan. Johnson manages the Neutral Buoyancy Pool, a well-known facility that trains astronauts for the idiosyncrasies of space by submerging them in water. It also builds trainer mockups of the space shuttle and the ISS at its Space Vehicle Mockup Facility, which is used to ensure astronaut flight readiness by familiarizing them with the space vehicles before they ever leave the ground.

With all of these operations and expertise at hand, SPACE-HAB could very well become a company that prepares future space tourists and houses them as well. It's a nice turnkey operation, and one in which there is negligible competition.

Bigelow

Bigelow Aerospace is a company whose primary business right now is manufacturing components for the aerospace industry: molds, prototypes, machined parts, and the like. But the founder and head of Bigelow Aerospace, Robert Bigelow, has bigger plans for his little company. He wants it to be the first space lodging company. And unlike most of the other startups in the space business, Bigelow already has $500 million dollars committed to reaching that goal. He didn't have to go far to get it; it's his own money.

Bigelow is the founder and owner of Budget Suites of America, a chain of corporate lodging facilities scattered across Arizona, Nevada, and Texas. These hotels, which accommodate the long-term visitor with apartment-complex-style amenities, have made Bigelow a wealthy man. And he wants to use that wealth to open up a space hotel that will house 100 vacationers at a time, plus 50 crew members.

Even in a business accustomed to unusual and even revolutionary ideas, Bigelow's vision is considered extreme. His commitment, however, is backed up by the kind of money that other startups have yet to see. A longtime space devotee with a keen interest in UFOs (he helps fund the National Institute for Discovery Science, an organization that investigates UFOs), Bigelow created Bigelow Aerospace in 1999 to realize his dream of hosting space travelers. His idea centers on building a circular space station half a mile wide that spins on its axis, generating artificial gravity and removing the queasiness of the space experience. It will have all the amenities of an ocean liner, with a restaurant and observation deck. More impressively, it will be a lunar cruise ship, orbiting the Moon and giving passengers a view of the fabled dark side. Passengers will be taken back and forth to the station via space shuttle.

Such a station will cost more money than Bigelow has in his bank account, so he may ultimately look to partner with others to form a consortium, which he thinks is the only way that space businesses can really break the chains of NASA's dominance. Bigelow's big concern is that NASA will get too comfortable with the eventual profits its realizes from commercializing the ISS, and that it will want to exert control over all future commercial endeavors, and perhaps even run them itself. (Some information from *The Washington Post*, Sunday, July 25, 1999).

Bigelow has lots of supporters in the space community and even inside NASA (articles about the reclusive millionaire often refer to the fact that $500 million buys a lot of respect). Despite the grandiose size of his dream, he is seen as an agent for change who is willing to put his money where his mouth is and take on the space agency monopoly. He has already begun petitioning the FAA for the right to build his space hotel, a request that forces the agency to start considering the potential realities of space tourism (obviously, the agency doesn't have standard forms for processing such requests). Bigelow has said that even if he doesn't achieve his space hotel goal in his lifetime—he's in his mid-50s and says he's committed to spending the next 15 years on it—at least he will be using his money to push for a change in the way that space is commercialized. And since that money is his to use as he pleases, no one can tell him not to do it.

Beal Aerospace

Another entrepreneur with a lot of cash, Andrew Beal founded Beal Aerospace in 1997. Beal was, and is, president of Beal Bank, the largest private bank in Dallas, Texas. Like many of his space business peers, he believed that NASA and the federal government were standing in the way of getting business into space. His idea was direct and straightforward: form a private launch services company using proven technology and sell to the private sector—all without becoming a contractor beholden to the government. Instead of setting his sights on creating new forms of space vehicles, Beal decided to one-up NASA. He planned to build the biggest, most efficient launch vehicle ever devised. Using composite technology and private funds, Beal set about creating a high-capacity launch vehicle that would propel even the heaviest payloads into GEO.

He succeeded—in part. In early 2000, Beal Aerospace fired the second largest liquid-fueled engine ever built in the U.S., the BA-2. Only the engines used on the Saturn V rockets, which carried the Apollo spacecraft, were larger. Viewed from a different perspective, the Beal engine was the largest engine ever built without the use of public funds. Beal put somewhere in the neighborhood of $200 million of his money into developing that engine.

But later that same year, Andrew Beal pulled the plug on his company. He had battled the government over everything from export licenses to subsidies, even going so far as testifying before Congress on May 29, 1999 to argue against government funding of experimental programs that he believed would lead nowhere. Finally, in a written statement released on October 24, 2000, he said that there was just no way that his company could go forward and compete with NASA's various and sundry initiatives—initiatives that threw curves at every company interested in stepping up to the launch plate. His statement minced no words:

"The BA-2C program was the largest privately funded program ever in existence to build a large capacity space launch system. Unfortunately, development of a reliable low cost system is simply not enough to ensure commercial viability. Several uncertainties remain that are totally beyond our control and put our entire business at risk. The most insurmountable risk is the desire of the U.S. government and NASA to subsidize competing launch systems. NASA has embarked on a plan to develop a 'second generation' launch system that will be subsidized by U.S. taxpayers and that will compete directly with the private sector . . .

" . . . There will never be a private launch industry as long as NASA and the U.S. government choose and subsidize launch systems. While Boeing and Lockheed are private entities, their launch systems and components are derivatives of various military initiatives. Very little new effort takes place without significant government subsidy, control, and involvement. While we believed we could compete successfully against the government subsidized EELV launch vehicles, the characteristics and depth of subsidy for NASA's new initiative as well as its ultimate performance are impossible to determine or evaluate.

"Once it became clear that NASA and Congress intended to proceed with their new competing launch systems, our only remaining choice was whether to cease operations entirely, or to evolve into a government contractor role like Boeing and Lockheed and seek government contracts to assist the development of the NASA system. We have elected to cease operations."

Some may consider the failure of Beal Aerospace to be a shocking indictment of NASA's leverage over space commerce. Others view it in the Kafka-esque context of business as usual. Unfortunately, it's both. As a footnote, many of Beal Aerospace's assets were sold off in early 2001. One of the buyers was NASA.

SpaceDev

SpaceDev bills itself as "the world's first publicly traded commercial space exploration and development company." It uses two slogans in promoting its business: "If we want to go to space to stay, space has to pay" and "space is a place, not a government program." Formed in late 1996, SpaceDev's mission is to provide low-cost entry to space. To that end, it will focus on projects that involve small payloads and small launch vehicles. In the latter case, it is developing hybrid rocket/motor-based spacecraft, ranging from a micro-launch vehicle to a small maneuverable craft that can perform orbital operations such as satellite inspection, repair, and parts replacement.

Ultimately, though, SpaceDev wants to do commercial deep

space missions. It notes—correctly—that deep space missions to date have been predominantly government defined and government managed. SpaceDev wants to change that by taking over the portion of the equation that is "government managed." It realizes that the government is still ultimately the sponsor of most research labs or university projects, and that is where the bulk of its business has come from to date. SpaceDev has set itself up to run counter to the traditional government contractors by offering fixed-fee proposals and using off-the-shelf components (many contractors develop custom products and then charge for "cost plus," including time and additional resources). The company went public soon after its formation, and is traded over-the-counter (NASDAQ—SPDV). In 2000, its revenues were $3.9 million.

SpaceDev's early work was primarily in doing studies for government organizations. In conjunction with the Jet Propulsion Laboratory, it investigated launch alternatives for sending small payloads to Mars. It also did a study for the National Reconnaissance Office to examine the feasibility of small satellite "hitchhikers" or "ejectables," meaning payloads that are dropped off en route to, but not actually at, their desired destination. Such ejectables could use the company's micro-motor technology to reach their ultimate destination. These two studies now serve as the basis of SpaceDev's commercial offerings. The company also formed a strategic partnership with Boeing to conduct a study of the commercial potential of beyond Earth-orbit commercial missions. In April 2001, SpaceDev received a $1 million contract from JPL to study options for a potential Mars sample return mission in 2011.

In addition to ongoing studies, the company has received a contract for an actual mission, the CHIPSat explorer. Managed by the University of California at Berkeley, The CHIPSat (Cosmic Hot Interstellar Plasma Spectrometer satellite) project is worth $4.9 million to SpaceDev, which will serve as developer, builder, and operator of the satellite. It is scheduled for a 2002 launch aboard a Boeing Delta rocket. Another SpaceDev mission, the Near-Earth Asteroid Prospector (NEAP), is being organized by the company itself. The destination is the Nereus asteroid, which SpaceDev estimates will take four months to reach. The mission involves sending a single vehicle to Nereus with multiple ejectable and attached payloads. The attached payloads would be part of the project for its duration, while ejectables would be detached at specified orbits. The company is expecting to carry payloads ranging from science, entertainment, and engineering equipment on to undefined "novelty" objects. Prices for each payload will range from $2.5 million to $12 million according to SpaceDev's fixed-price list. It hopes to receive enough funding for each of these payloads to be able to launch the NEAP aboard an Ariane launch vehicle before 2006.

X Prize

The X Prize is an endeavor that hopes to foster homegrown space innovation in a manner resembling the garage companies that fueled the personal computer revolution. Started by Peter Diamandis, the X Prize is a competition that plans to award $10 million to the first developer of a working RLV. But there are a few stipulations:

- The RLV has to be manned by at least one person, with the capability of actually carrying three people. The passengers have to return in good health.
- The RLV has to reach an altitude of 62 miles.
- The RLV has to be privately funded.
- The RLV has to make two manned flights within a space of 14 days.

This is no small task, regardless of the size of the teams involved. Any effort that could come close to succeeding will most likely spend more than the $10 million just to get their ideas into working order. Yet 19 groups from around the world have already signed on in hopes of winning the purse.

A former aeronautical engineer-turned-entrepreneur, Diamandis started the X Prize competition with money donated from the city of St. Louis (the organization's headquarters and primary sponsor) and other investors—plus revenue from an X Prize-branded credit card. The organization is halfway to raising the entire $10 million, but many feel that the contest isn't really about the money. Like the aviation prizes awarded during the 1930s for innovation, it has more to do with the spirit of achievement and proof of concept than it does winning a small fortune. The organization compares it to the America's Cup yacht race: teams have spent up to $40 million to win a race that has no monetary reward. But the $10 million does get people's attention.

The prize has attracted a wide variety of participants, from commercial entities such as Kelly Space & Technology and Pioneer Rocketplane to private groups planning to launch from hot air balloons and using "blastwave-pulsejet propulsion." The contest is open to anyone up until the prize is won.

Celestis

Perhaps the most unusual space business formed to date is Celestis. The company began offering post-cremation memorial services in 1997 which involve launching a "symbolic portion" of the cremated remains (cremains) of people into space. For roughly the cost of terrestrial Earth funerals (from $5,300 to $12,500), about seven grams of ashes are encapsulated into a satellite along with the departed's name and a message, and then launched by an Orbital Sciences launch vehicle. Destinations include near-Earth orbit (the memorial satellites remain in orbit for up to ten years), the Moon, and deep space. To date, the company has launched three satellites, which have included the remains of *Star Trek* creator Gene Roddenberry and counterculture icon Timothy Leary.

Celestis is not the only organization to send cremains into space. In 1998, NASA included a small portion of noted astronomer Dr. Eugene Shoemaker (the NEAR Shoemaker satellite was named for him) in its Lunar Prospector, which landed on the Moon in 1999. As a testimony to Celestis' unique position in the industry, NASA used a Celestis space capsule to house Shoemaker's remains.

Starcraft Boosters

No discussion of space startups would be complete without a mention of Edwin "Buzz" Aldrin. The second man to walk on the Moon, Aldrin is an avid proponent of opening space to commercial ventures. He speaks frequently on the topic and is easily the most recognizable and outspoken former NASA astronaut to espouse the values of space commercialization.

He is working with a small company in Los Angeles called StarCraft Boosters, which is designing the Starbooster system. Part expendable launch vehicle and part reusable launch vehicle, the Starbooster concept involves fitting a conventional ELV to an RLV. The RLV first stage reaches a specified altitude before releasing its second stage (the ELV component) to lift payloads into orbit. (Interestingly, this is the converse of the way that the space shuttle system works; the shuttle's first stage is expendable, but its second stage—the shuttle vehicle itself—is reusable.) The Starboost then returns to Earth for future use.

In addition, Aldrin has developed a concept that he calls "the Cycler," which is a vehicle system that could sustain perpetual orbits between Earth and Mars. It includes orbiting inter-planetary stations that would cycle between Earth and Mars using the gravity of each to keep it moving. Aldrin has plenty of experience in the area; his doctoral thesis before becoming an astronaut was on orbital mechanics. His relationship with NASA coupled with his aggressive insistence on developing space for business have made him one of the primary spokes-men for space commercialization in the last decade.

7

THE NEXT INVESTMENT FRONTIER

L et's take a baseline position and state that low-cost entry to orbit will be available in the next few years. If that is the case, then now is the time to look forward, to start investigating those avenues of space commercialization that can become reality in the near future. When travel into space is routine and economically feasible, our use of space will change forever. Space stations, space labs, space manufacturing facilities, and space hotels are destined to follow. A decade ago, it would have been preposterous to speak of this in concrete terms. But that was before the ISS, before Dennis Tito. The entire landscape is evolving with impressive speed.

The Commercial Possibilities

We know the argument over how to get launch costs down will continue over the next few years; it has to. But our scope is not limited to exposing the issues and pointing out the potential paths to commercial development. We'll also explore what will happen when space commercialization becomes a reality. Thus, the business possibilities in this chapter will be predicated on our assumption that easy access to space will soon be a reality.

There already exists a commercial portal to space—the International Space Station. The ISS will have a dedicated commercial module, built by Russia's Energia and SPACEHAB—not by NASA. So the potential of doing commercial space work is already there. It's not the kind of access that will be cheap, nor will it allow for completely unfettered business endeavors. It is, however, a start, and deserves examination here as the first step toward a full-fledged industrial move into orbit.

International Space Station

The ISS is the first step in establishing a permanent address for business in space. Unlike Mir, which suffered from the view that it was merely a pet project of the USSR and its communist regime, the ISS is supported directly by sixteen nations and indirectly by many more. Its mission statement includes plans for commercial use, the first such offering ever made to private industry. (The space shuttle's occasional experiments on behalf of various private organizations cannot be considered dedicated commercial endeavors.)

The ISS benefits from points of view that aren't limited to those held within NASA. The sixteen countries involved in the station all have vested interests, and many of those interests are related to promoting commerce. Of course, the station itself is a product of international industry and government cooperation occurring on a scale never seen before. Each participating country or space agency has to build and provide one or more specific components to the ISS, and training of the station crew is incumbent upon the participating countries (hence, Tito's training for the Russian flight in Russia and not the U.S.).

Following are the commitments that have been made by the ISS participants. Some of them are in flux, especially in light of budget concerns and the resultant amount of agency politics:

United States—NASA

The U.S. is building the primary laboratory module (Destiny), a habitation module that will provide living quarters for seven crew (currently on hold), a centrifuge module for creating various levels of gravity during experiments, a crew return vehicle (CRV) for emergencies (also on hold), a propulsion module, four solar arrays, truss segments, and others. It is responsible for thermal control, life support, guidance, navigation and control, data management, power systems, communications and tracking, ground operations, and launch-site processing facilities.

Canada—CSA

The Canadian Space Agency built the 55-foot-long robotic arm ("Canadarm") that is used for in-space assembly of the sections of the ISS. Theoretically, the arm is capable of hoisting the entire weight of the ISS. It was this component that was delivered by Endeavor in April 2001.

European Space Agency—ESA (including Belgium, Denmark, France, Germany, Italy, Netherlands, Norway, Spain, Sweden, Switzerland, and the United Kingdom)

The European Space Agency is building a pressurized laboratory (Columbus) as well as logistics transport vehicles (LTVs, essentially cargo and supply craft). Its Ariane rockets will be used for some launches.

Japan—NASDA

Japan's contribution to the ISS is a laboratory module with an attached exterior platform (meaning outside the ISS' internal modules) that will be used for experiments. Like ESA, it will also be building logistics transport vehicles.

Russia—Rosaviakosmos

Russia is responsible for two research modules, a self-contained residence module called the Zvezda Service Module, a docking and stowage module, a science power platform of solar arrays, logistics vehicles, and Soyuz vehicles for crew return and transfer (ultimately to be replaced by the U.S. CRV).

Brazil—INPE

Brazil is building the "Express Pallett," a specialized work station designed to hold equipment and experiments.

The ISS will be massive when it is finished, spanning 356 feet in width and weighing more than a million pounds, orbiting some 220 miles above Earth. Its living and working space will be more than 46,000 cubic feet, or roughly the equivalent of the passenger cabins of two 747s. Fourteen space flights have been required to construct the ISS to its current stage, and it is expected that at least 70 more will be needed to finish it (the original estimate was a total of 44 needed flights).

All of this comes with a hefty price tag. The most recent U.S. General Accounting Office projection is that the station will cost about $60 billion by the time it is completed in 2006. This number includes launch costs and doesn't take into account maintenance and operation, which is estimated to add another $96 billion over the ISS' ten-year lifetime.

Cost overruns and delays have unfortunately been part and parcel of the ISS to date and are likely to be an ongoing feature of its evolution. Every participant has been plagued with this problem; it's one of the primary reasons that Russia accepted Dennis Tito's money for his trip. In 2001, Congress slapped around NASA and prime contractor Boeing for major cost increases that have nearly quadrupled the early estimates of

$17 billion for the station when it was proposed in the mid-1990s. These costs were certainly not in keeping with NASA's pledge of "faster, better, cheaper" space development and management, known officially as FBC. NASA's response to budget concerns? To kill development of the habitation module and the CRV.

Here again we have NASA stepping on the prospect of commerce occurring on the ISS. Think about this. The habitation module was specifically designed to provide the ISS with long-term living quarters for seven crew. Currently, the station can handle only three people for extended stays. It takes 2.5 people to manage the station, leaving one half of a single crew member's time available for conducting experiments or doing research. This means that any work not directly connected to keeping the station running is done "part time." Without a habitation module to house another four people, the current situation is equivalent to just keeping the lights on. This cut literally guts the core from the ISS mission.

Next, NASA dispensed with the CRV. This was intended to provide the crew—seven of them—with an escape vehicle in case of emergency. No CRV, no emergency vehicle. Would you work in a building without a fire escape or a set of back stairs? The ISS crew shouldn't, either.

Nearly everyone in the space community agrees that without these two modules, the ISS is not going to be able to serve as the portal to space it was intended to be. To add insult to injury, these were part of the same cuts that resulted in NASA pulling the plug on its RLV research. What happened to pushing the envelope? What happened to the big picture? Why isn't somebody managing the direction of the agency with an eye to the future? By way of defense, Daniel Goldin blamed much of the poor cost management on NASA's lack of expertise in predicting what it would take to build the station. However, not noticing potential overruns in the billions of dollars also shows a lack of expertise in running a business.

Amid the flurry of cost-cutting and face-saving, the Italian participants in the ISS have expressed interest in building the habitation module, which would take the onus off of NASA. The French contingent, for their part, has offered to take a look at handling the CRV.

It's interesting that while the Russians have decided to take money where they can find it (e.g. Dennis Tito), NASA tends to view the prospect of getting outside funds from tourists or advertising to be small potatoes. A million here, a million there doesn't seem to add up quickly enough. But no organization should know better than NASA that that equation does add up rapidly, which accounts for its own overruns. Cognitive dissonance seems to be at work within the agency.

NASA isn't the only organization to change its mind about contributing specific components to the ISS. Russia decided in 2000 to replace the docking and stowage module with the Enterprise commercial module. The reason for the switch was to put a business-oriented lab on the ISS from which Russia (and its partner SPACEHAB) could derive revenue. As was pointed out in the last chapter, this module will be divided into three segments: one for microgravity research, one for multimedia broadcast, and the third for stowage (as part of the original module's responsibility). Russia and SPACEHAB are also considering the prospect of using this module for crew quarters.

In spite of its problems—which one would expect in a multinational, big budget undertaking of this sort—the ISS will continue to grow. And bit by bit it will begin to offer commercial services to businesses around the globe. It has already received its first bit of revenue in the form of Dennis Tito's trip, which made the ISS the world's first space hotel, if only for a few days. But it was the first instance ever of actual space tourism, and it will be hard to ignore this factor of space business from here on out.

Space Tourism

It only takes one event to alter the reality of a situation. Dennis Tito's trip to the ISS in April 2001 brought unparalleled attention to the space station almost overnight. From being yet another space project to which people might have paid scant attention, the ISS is now on everyone's radar. Part of that has to do with Tito's iconoclastic dismantling of the notion of space as belonging only to the space agency elite. Now, real people can go to space. It might be the wealthy at first, but they were also the first passengers on ocean liners and airlines.

Was the hype over ISS' first paying passenger simply a media creation? Not at all. There was not much coverage of the ISS prior to 2001, even though assembly began in 1998. Yet the week prior to Tito's arrival, the space shuttle *Endeavor* went through some trials and tribulations trying to attach a robotic arm to the ISS and later suffered computer failure. During this time period, visits to NASA's website spiked by 75 percent, and the site attracted 567,000 individual visitors. By contrast, the number of unique visitors to the web home of TV's top-rated program, *Survivor*, was 320,000 that same week (Source: Nielsen-NetRatings). The space station's web traffic was almost twice that of the popular reality show. Obviously, space is still a hot property when people can get involved, either by watching streaming audio, getting updates from inside the station, or imagining that space may finally be within their grasp.

Elitism and space travel have always been synonymous. The best and the brightest forged the path into space, and it was tacitly acknowledged for decades that that was the way it should be. As space travel became more routine, and flight safety improved, the barrier of elitism has worn down. The pioneers made their mark, and the way has been paved. Space agencies still hold strongly to the tenet of elitism, but it misses the point. If explorers and pioneers were the only ones allowed to go into uncharted territory, then settlements would never occur in the wake of people like Columbus, Vasco da Gama, and Lewis and Clark. The world would be limited to those designated as explorers. It was only when businesses and people seeking new lives followed in the footsteps of the explorers that the potential of the "new lands" was fully realized. As a report prepared by Bigelow Aerospace points out: "The last great American space project, the moonshot, occurred over thirty years ago. The reason for this lack of progress is that the astronauts made it to space, but the entrepreneurs never did." (Source: http://www.bigelowaerospace.com/pb_589900_v1.pdf)

Tito's trip put a nice dent in that elitism, and there are a number of companies waiting to push a big hole through that dent and make space tourism a reality. After all, tourism is a multi-billion dollar business, approaching $500 billion in the U.S. alone. In many U.S. states and quite a few countries, tourism dollars account for a large percentage of revenue and income. By some measures, employment related to tourist activities makes the tourism business the nation's second largest employer.

Thus, tourism is a valid industry by any standards, though many are content to write it off as pseudo-industry, primarily because it does not traditionally produce products. Like entertainment, another long-scoffed-at business, tourism has been denigrated because of its status as something that contributed to the leisure of individuals, not their labor.

Yet what are companies like Disney and AOL-Time Warner without their substantial tourism assets? They are thought of as media-industry titans, but even a cursory examination of their properties reveals huge contributions from theme parks, children's TV programming, and revenues from the licensing of cartoon characters. Investors may snicker at the actual sale of one pair of Mickey Mouse ears or a Bugs Bunny tee-shirt, but these items form the foundation of corporate behemoths.

In the same vein, space tourism has been the one aspect of space business that routinely raises eyebrows and rolls eyeballs. Taking a back row seat to "serious" space endeavors such as science, exploration, and even manufacturing, tourism is last on the list of businesses that NASA and the space community plan to consider. So decried is the term that space agencies refer to the carrying of non-commissioned passengers as "public space travel" or "passenger space travel." For some reason, they just don't like the idea of tourism.

Maybe they should go back and look at their own studies in considering space tourism. In 1998, NASA presented a study done in conjunction with the Space Transportation Association called "General Public Space Travel and Tourism." This study found that space tourism could be a viable industry rivaling that of the satellite business within two decades. Once certain biological and technical concerns have been addressed—including everything from obviating motion sickness and reducing cost per launch to finding ways of dealing with noise abatement and debris collision—the report has nothing but high hopes for space tourism. To quote from the report:

"As these technical-operational goals are achieved, the price per ticket could drop below $50,000 per passenger and might eventually reach the range of $10,000-$20,000 . . . However, with ticket prices well below $50,000, it is believed that there could be the order of 500,000 space trip passengers/year. (Transporting these many (sic) people/year would require the carrying to/from space of hundreds of millions of pounds of payload per year—roughly 1,000 times more than today's U.S. civil, commercial and industry (sic) annual space trip payload, but still many factors of ten less than is carried by commercial airlines.)

"Overall the assessment to date suggests that if EO transportation system-services can be developed that demonstrate acceptable safety, reliability, comfort and affordability, and are sized to serve large enough markets, financially viable general public space travel and tourism businesses can be created by the private sector."

The study concluded with a recommendation that "Our national space policy should be examined with an eye towards actively encouraging the creation of a large public space travel and tourism business."

NASA isn't alone in having explored the value of space tourism. Back in 1993, Japan's National Aerospace Laboratory (NAL) conducted a survey in which more than 3,000 Japanese citizens revealed that 70 percent of people under age 60 and more than 80 percent of those under 40 stated they would like to visit space at least once in their lifetime. Nearly three-quarters of respondents said they would pay up to three months salary for this "trip of a lifetime."

What is the appeal of going into space, beyond the standard line that "no one else I know has ever been there"? There are actually quite a few factors:

- The view of our home planet from hundreds of miles up may be the most awe-inspiring view a human can ever have.
- The flight itself is the ultimate thrill ride, putting any theme park ride or roller coaster to shame.
- The opportunities for near-weightlessness, not currently available on terra firma.
- Opportunities to view space from a different perspec-

tive, or to watch land-based activities such as other launches, hurricanes, volcanoes, etc.

Part of the allure of the Concorde, in addition to the obvious time saving, is the view that it offers and the experience of flying at supersonic speeds. Those who've ridden the Concorde are rarely asked about the cost/benefit ratio—they are asked about the experience.

Interestingly, space tourism as a terrestrial pursuit already attracts more than ten million visitors a year. This includes visitors to various space centers, such as Cape Canaveral, Johnson Space Center, et al. as well as the Air and Space Museum in Washington, D.C. and a host of other space-themed attractions around the country. Each of these could certainly serve as a marketing and promotions unit for the day when we really go into space. Turning that ground-based wonder into actual desire for a space trip is almost like preaching to the converted: there are millions of people interested in space. If only a fraction of them decide they want to go, an entire business is waiting to be built to serve them.

What kinds of tourism will space generate? Those that make the most sense (and in some cases, cited by the NASA/STA study) include:

- The quick up and down. In many ways, this is not dissimilar from the tethered hot air balloon flights that are offered at county and state fairs. A non-orbital launch into space gives passengers an incredible view and experience over the course of an hour, far surpassing those amusement park rides with names like "space shot" or "orbital thrill." The passengers remain in the transport vehicle for the duration of the flight and may get to experience a period of the artificial "weightlessness" of microgravity.

- Orbitals. Passengers could orbit the Earth several times within a set span of time (say three orbits in five hours), giving them a bird's eye view of every area of the globe, perhaps coupled with a period of microgravity. Again, passengers would stay inside the transport vehicle during the course of the trip.

- Short stays. Transport vehicles would dock with orbiting stations (or more appropriately, hospitality suites), where passengers could disembark for an overnight— or several nights'—stay. Activities would include experiencing microgravity and an "astronaut experience." Requirements and resources for such a stay would be minimal; it would be akin to an overnight camping trip.

- Extended or resort stays. Space tourists would dock with orbiting stations and stay anywhere from several days to several weeks. Activities would involve not only extended weightlessness but also the possibility of a space walk.

People want to go to space, and why shouldn't they? Cost, safety, and availability are the primary factors against. NASA has shown that it can be done safely, so while safety is always a consideration, it is one that has been addressed by every single flight to date. Availability is also in NASA's control; after all, it monitors and authorizes launches. That's two out of three. The only remaining one is cost, which is an industry-wide concern. Certainly long-term revenue-generating endeavors such as satellite deployment are more important economically than giving a citizen the ride of his or her lifetime. But what if tourists are willing to pay their own way? That changes the equation to one where customers pay not only the entire cost of their trip but also enough to add some profit to the deal. Again, we can look to the travel and tourist industry for some guidelines about how to proceed:

- Vehicles will have to have an amortization schedule that resembles that of commercial jets. A certain number of passengers must be flown over X number of flights to not only pay for the vehicle, its maintenance, and its operation but also to return a profit to its operators.
- No one is looking for luxury accommodations. Anyone who has ever flown coach from the U.S. to Asia understands that prolonged flights can be endured with minimal creature comforts.
- An entire fleet does not need to be deployed in order to begin service. One of the world's best airlines, Richard Branson's Virgin Atlantic Airways, began service in 1984 with just one 747 that made continuous round trips between London and New York. Today, the airline services nearly two dozen destinations and is valued at more than $1 billion. Ever the forward-thinker, Branson has made allusions to going further into the sky—with his own space shuttles. He even established a company called Virgin Galactic Airways in April 1999.

But are we really talking about a component of the space transportation business, or are we looking at an extension of the hospitality industry? Perhaps Stanley Kubrick was prescient when he showed a Hilton Hotel and a Howard Johnson restaurant in the early scenes of *2001: A Space Odyssey*. Providing people with comfortable and comforting accommodations, as well as offering them amenities, has long been the purview of the hospitality business, from low-end chains like Motel 6 and Days Inn on up to high-end resorts and hotels as operated by Starwood and Ian Schrager. Robert Bigelow thinks that he can combine his expertise in running Budget Suites of America with the space plans of his Bigelow Aerospace company to provide the best of both worlds. Once there is a permanent location established as a space destination, it makes a great deal of sense to staff it fully with people who understand the nature of the hotel business. NASA bureaucrats or corporate scientists hardly make the most gracious of hosts, so that role will fall to the professionals: Marriott, Holiday Inn, Starwood, and others who are already successful at running that business on the ground (remember our earlier admonition that for a business to succeed in space its terrestrial analog must also be successful).

The locales built for getting people into space will also have to be part of the equation. Spaceports, a rather sci-fi term, will be similar to airports, but without the congestion and the continuous air traffic. These spaceports would have to be located in relatively out-of-the-way locations so as not to disturb their neighbors with noise and traffic. Such out of the way locations may at first seem to be a detriment to getting the customers in. But then, forty years ago, no one would ever have expected Anaheim, California or Orlando, Florida to be the country's leading vacation destinations.

In anticipation of the paying visitors to come, several companies have set themselves up as the forerunners of space tourism. Space Adventures, formed in 1997 as a partnership between several high profile travel and expedition companies, already offers several quasi-space trips. For the low, low price of $12,595, it will fly passengers to 82,000 feet (almost three times the flight altitude of commercial jets) in a Russian MIG 25. It's not quite suborbital, but it gets you higher than any of your friends or business associates have ever gotten. And that price includes two nights in a Moscow hotel. The Arlington, Virginia-based Space Adventures also offers zero-gravity flights aboard its own version of the famed Vomit Comet, the U.S. aircraft used by NASA to simulate weightlessness by going into freefall (and named by astronaut trainees). For a mere $5,400, passengers travel to the Yuri Gagarin Cosmonaut Training Center in Star City, Russia and board a specially outfitted Ilyushin-76. From there, they get to experience a parabolic flight that will send them floating around the interior of the plane's cabin as the craft descends from the top of its arc—the same technique used by the Vomit Comet. To date, Space Adventures claims that it has sent more than 2,000 people on these near-space trips.

The big offering from the company is its planned suborbital space flights, scheduled for travel sometime between 2003 and 2005. For $98,000, Space Adventures will send tourists to an altitude of 62 miles for a time period of 30 minutes to 2-1/2 hours (the company is hedging its bets here until it determines what type of RLV it will actually use). The company is already accepting reservations.

A similar set of offerings is available from Incredible Adventures of Sarasota, Florida, including a parabolic flight, flying in a Mig 25, and prebooking of planned suborbital flights in the next few years. Between the two travel companies, an estimated 200 people have signed up for—and put deposits on—the yet-to-be scheduled space flights. (Source: St. Petersburg Times, 6/11/00: "With Stars in Their Eyes, Travelers Look to Space.")

Then there are those companies like Bigelow Aerospace and Space Island Group that are taking the big-picture view. Hoping to establish space-based hotels, the two companies are proceeding slowly into the market, although their marketing has already begun. While Bigelow's dream will grow out of its established aerospace manufacturing business, Space Island is hoping to build on NASA's discards—literally. The company, founded in 1997 by ex-TRW engineer Gene Myers, plans to use 12 discarded space shuttle external fuel tanks in the construction of a wheel-shaped space station based in LEO. This "space island" would rotate in order to provide artificial gravity for guests and hopes to open for business in 2007. Myers estimates it will cost a billion dollars or so per year to get his project going, and he's targeting sponsors and pension funds for the money. He also plans to devote a section of the island to manufacturing to augment the tourist trade.

There are some wild cards here, the most interesting of whom is Richard Branson of Virgin Air. In an interview conducted after he had established Virgin Galactic Airways, Branson said, "We're looking at various things that could enable people to go to space for a reasonable price. I hope in five years a reusable rocket will have been developed, which can take up to ten people at a time maybe to stay at the Virgin Hotel for two weeks! I'd love to do it, and I hope the dream will become a reality. Also, I would be on the inaugural flight, of course." (Source: VIRGIN.net interview, http://www.virgin.net/chat/ archive/archive_40.htm). Branson is an avid adventurer and entrepreneur, as his balloon trips, airline, record company, and retail stores attest. He is the prototypical "adventure capitalist" and has been known for overcoming staggering odds and opposition in his efforts to build successful businesses. His participation in, and the promotion of, space tourism would significantly ratchet up the current level of activity.

All of which takes us back to the Russians, who took the first paying passenger into space. After the success of Tito's trip, Energia announced in May 2001 that it would offer seats on Soyuz flights in the future, perhaps as many as two of the three seats available per craft. The agency will most likely use a

Soyuz craft that is not in rotation for an upcoming ISS flight, meaning that it will serve as a designated tourist craft. Although the missions won't dock with the ISS, they will orbit the Earth, allowing customers to experience space up close and personal. The training for these flights is expected to be three months per passenger, and the cost may be about half of what Tito paid. As we said at the outset, it only takes one event to open the door. If Russia goes through with this particular plan, the door may be wide open for space tourism sooner than anyone ever expected.

Microgravity: Research and Manufacturing

Every process, event, occurrence, and situation on Earth is affected by gravity. Gases rise, solids fall, liquids flow, and even though we don't formally acknowledge it, all of our research and manufacturing is conducted with the effects of gravity in mind. Liquids are mixed and alloys manufactured with consideration for where the heaviest components will end up as well as their effects on mixing with lighter components. This is true of everything from batteries and baked goods to steel cable and semiconductors.

If we were to minimize or mask the effects of gravity, we would have a greater understanding of the inherent properties of the matter that we deal with every day. Because gravity tugs at molecules in every element, even the relationships between elements could be more thoroughly examined if we could study them—or work with them—outside the encumbrance of gravity.

Space provides this opportunity. Microgravity—a state where the pull of gravity is one-millionth of what it is on Earth—exists at a point about 4 million miles from Earth. (Source: http://mgnews.msfc.nasa.gov/db/understanding_ug/understanding_ug.html#under2). However, microgravity effects can be achieved in near-Earth orbit aboard the shuttle and ISS due to their continual state of freefall—hence, the seeming weight-lessness of astronauts (remember that Earth orbits aren't com-pletely free of gravity; the weightlessness is generated by the speed of the craft and its position relative to Earth). In essence, this microgravity is artificially generated, but for the purposes of research and manufacturing it will serve commercial and industrial purposes quite well in the near future.

Microgravity research and manufacturing in space will pro-vide benefits impossible to attain on Earth. It will allow for the creation of purer chemicals and materials than we've ever cre-ated before and will allow us to analyze their properties in more detail and better understand how to use them back on terra firma. This isn't speculation: successful microgravity experi-ments have already been conducted on the shuttle, and the ISS will have a module dedicated to commercial microgravity research and manufacturing. NASA's Marshall Space Flight Center in Huntsville, Alabama oversees the agency's Micro-gravity Research Program (MRP) and has been conducting ongoing microgravity experiments in five areas: biotechnology, combustion science, fluid physics, fundamental physics, and materials science.

Microgravity manufacturing will initially be done by researchers and then by small teams of space workers aboard space stations or platforms. Some have speculated that early operational space manufacturing facilities will be staffed by robots (and potentially nanobots, see below). By taking humans out of the equation, we eliminate a huge number of factors that contribute to space costs (primarily life-support, maintenance, and safety systems). Remotely controlled and fully-pro-grammed robots could perform manufacturing duties without the direct aid of humans. These activities are already common in manufacturing, from spot-welders on automotive assembly lines to terrain-monitoring wheeled vehicles, which have been used in volcanoes and on Mars. Creating space platforms that are outfitted with robots performing manufacturing functions would be the equivalent of automated assembly lines used in facilities all over the world.

As stations are set up initially near Earth and eventually further out in the solar system, facilities will resemble terrestrial ones, with people living near where they work and utilizing robots for specific tasks to supplement the human workforce. Many of the space business endeavors outlined in the remainder of this chapter, notably manufacturing and mining, will likely involve both robotic control and human participation.

Microgravity: Proteins/Pharmaceuticals

The most promising near-term processing in space involves protein crystal growth, and ultimately all crystal growth. Why? There are more than 100,000 different proteins in the human body that affect everything from fighting disease to oxygen transport in the blood. Understanding these proteins and how they interact with the body and each other is critical to developing medicines and treatments for a variety of health issues.

Analysis of proteins centers on their physical structure, as a protein's crystal structure determines its function. Three-dimensional models are needed to properly evaluate the components of the crystal and identify which of its components specifically affect its ultimate function. Once they have been properly studied, drugs can be created that target a particular component by locking into the structure.

That's in an ideal world. In actuality, their size and lack of uniformity make protein crystals difficult to study in terrestrial labs. The analytic process typically involves the utilization of X-ray diffraction to analyze the structure of the crystals, but this technique requires the presence of fairly sizable molecules in order to view them. Proteins that are more uniform in size, have larger molecules, and fewer impurities are easier to analyze, making it easier to determine and ultimately understand the protein's structure and create the appropriate drug.

On Earth, protein crystal growth suffers from the sedimentation and buoyancy that occurs in solution, leading to interference between the crystals as they move about as well as the effects of differing densities within the solution. Fortunately, space removes these effects from the process. Microgravity experiments on the shuttle, where these effects are minimized, have already produced larger and more uniform proteins for analysis, due to the fact that protein growth can be controlled with more precision than is possible on Earth.

Once they've achieved a higher level of purity, proteins can then be synthesized and even altered. This is critical for the development of structure-based drug design, also known as rational drug design. The end result is that mass quantities of the protein can be manufactured more efficiently and with greater potency. This would have a huge impact on the production of crystalline-based rational drug design, ranging from insulin for diabetes patients to new drugs to combat the AIDS-related HIV protease/inhibitor complex.

The benefits in microgravity manufacturing of pharmaceuticals have already been proven. In October 1998, Bristol Myers Squibb Pharmaceutical Research Institute (Wallingford, Connecticut) and BioServe Space Technologies (University of Colorado, Boulder) sponsored a shuttle experiment to study the orbital manufacture of the chemotherapy drug actinomycin D. The results of the experiment were such that Squibb believes production of the drug in space would lead to a 75 percent increase in output over the same process used on Earth. Additional studies showed that increases of up to 200 percent in output could be achieved for other drugs such as antibiotics. (Source: http://www.spaceandtech.com/digest/sd2001-01/sd2001-

01-001.shtml). Other companies including DuPont Merck, Eli Lilly, GlaxoSmithKline, and Schering-Plough have all begun utilizing microgravity research data to aid them in future drug development.

So protein growth in orbit has already begun and has obviously been one of the more important results of shuttle experiments. As for the ISS, a report prepared by consulting firm KPMG for NASA ("NASA: Commerce and the International Space Station") contains the following statement: "The National Institute of Health has said that that crystal protein growth is the number one research tool that we'll be using in the next century." When the ISS commercial module is up and running, this research will take a huge step forward as development can begin right away. The resultant products and materials will be shuttled back and forth to Earth much as is done now in replenishing the ISS. From there, larger manufacturing facilities will be the next step, developed by commercial organizations.

Microgravity: Fluid Dynamics

The way that liquids flow is due in great part to gravity (other components such as viscosity, vibration, and friction are also a factor). Thus, our understanding of liquid properties is based on gravity-induced conditions, which limits the way we can use liquids in any processes (although centrifuges have provided some indication of how liquids will behave in reduced gravity). Whether freezing, boiling, or mixing, liquid processing has to take gravity into account. For example, air rises through liquid, sediment falls in it, and gas bubbles can be suspended in it. Air and particulate matter are routinely trapped in liquid, and the position of these objects affects the way that liquids solidify, break up, or become gases. Even the movement of fluids through our bodies is subject to these factors, and understanding the fluid dynamics of our circulatory and endocrine systems could result in better delivery systems for medicine.

Interestingly, granular systems such as clay, sand, and soil behave similarly to liquids when enough force is exerted on them (think of the rippling ground that occurs during earthquakes). Experimentation with normally solid matter in liquid-like states could lead to better design of structures affected by this behavior, including bridges and buildings.

Microgravity offers the ability to use liquids in such a way as to change the gravitational dynamic. Sedimentation and air can be evenly flowed through the liquid, resulting in a less stratified end-product. Plastics, fuels, dyes, adhesives, and other products would be more uniform in their construction if the affects of gravity, heat (convection), and temperature could be more precisely controlled. We can take this a step further and consider food processing applications that result in contaminant-free ingredients or packaging.

If fluid behavior could be managed at different stages of the manufacturing process, greater control could be exerted over product quality. Removing or mitigating the effects of impurities during, say, the molten state of steel, could improve its strength and resistance to corrosion. Even getting a better handle on the transportation of volatile fluids and vapor-liquid mixtures, such as in power plants and refineries, could lead to better efficiencies and more stable (i.e. safe) environments.

French oil giant Elf Aquitaine has been using results of microgravity research (done in conjunction with ESA) to help it better understand the thermodynamics of deep oil reservoirs, as well as the behavior of fluids injected into the fractures of those reservoirs from which residual oil is to be extracted. Such phenomena and processes can only be modeled on Earth but can actually be observed in space. (Source: http://esapub.esrin. esa.it/pff/pffv6n3/hiev6n3.htm). Another company that has funded fluid-based microgravity research is Coca-Cola. The beverage giant participated in space shuttle experiments to help it develop new carbonation systems for its products and explore effects that space might have on taste perception (which could be applied to similar changes experienced by target populations, such as the elderly).

These are perfect examples of the way in which microgravity experimentation and manufacture may ultimately affect products and consumption in a way we never could have imagined.

Microgravity: Materials

In addition to creating better products or improving the efficiency of manufacturing, microgravity may provide the foundation for the creation of new alloys and classes of products that can't be manufactured on Earth because the disparate components won't form or mold under normal conditions. The following are specific areas where microgravity can contribute to better products and processes:

- Composites and alloys. Composite materials such as alloys are used in a wide variety of products from airplanes and automobiles to power plants. They are created by mixing two or more different materials together to produce a desired product that is typically lightweight or has greater strength and corrosion resistance. The process usually involves a liquid or molten stage when the materials are mixed together. As solidification occurs, the new material crystallizes, providing the alloy with its primary properties (tensile strength, heat resistance, etc.). The uniformity of these crystals determines how successful the alloy will be in its final application. During the cooling process,

though, the molten material continues to flow, creating unavoidable irregularities in the crystal structure
that result in less-than-perfect alloys. As a result,
Earth-built alloys have some built-in weaknesses
(although at an acceptable level) because their internal
structure is impossible to control in light of convection
and other gravity-related phenomena.

Such alloy construction would be improved in microgravity
where convection is eliminated as a factor. Crystals formed during cooling would be uniform from top to bottom, increasing
the purity of properties throughout the entire product. Mixtures
could also be modified due to the relative absence of gravity,
resulting in materials we have not yet been able to build on
Earth due to issues of density and sedimentation.

Even traditional metals such as steel would benefit from in-
orbit production. Making steel is fraught with contamination
along every step of the process, from the raw materials to the
furnaces to the molds. This contamination, as well as the unset-
tling effects of convection during the molten phase, make steel
an incredibly impure product. By creating steel that has a more
uniform internal structure, steel could actually be made
stronger and lighter. For instance, Dr. Dale Webb of Texas A&M
University estimates that a steel bolt with strength of 100,000
pounds per square inch could be improved to handle
20,000,000 pounds per square inch if it were made out of "perfect steel" produced in space. It would also be smaller and
weigh less than one manufactured on Earth.

- Glass and optics. Optical fibers, lenses, filters, and
  electrical components made from glass will all benefit
  from space manufacturing. Delicate and high-quality
  glass products are extremely difficult to manufacture

terrestrially because they have low viscosity, are susceptible to very low levels of contamination, and tend to develop crystal imperfections during processing. Microgravity will help in the manufacture of these products by lessening the viscosity issues and minimizing airborne contamination.

- Ceramics. We think of objects made of ceramic as being brittle. In fact ceramic has a higher strength than many metals and is used in high-stress and high-temperature environments where metals are inappropriate. Its brittleness is a function of our mixing, molding, and firing processes. Control over each of these steps of ceramic manufacturing in space could create nearly indestructible objects for use in electronics, the refining industries, household items, and even high-quality bone replacement.

- Containerless processing. Many materials, especially chemicals, react with their containers during processing. This may include leeching elements from the container itself, simple reaction with the container material, exposure to container contaminants, or the affect of a container's temperature. Microgravity allows materials to be suspended and manipulated without touching their containers.

- "Unmixables." There are some materials on Earth that simply won't mix properly no matter how intricate the process. This is the proverbial "oil and water" problem, in that gravity will ultimately pull these materials apart and long-term combinations are not possible. Space will provide the antidote to such conditions, allowing us to experiment with mixing that is not possible on Earth. Solar cells are a good example of this in that some of their components, like aluminum and glass, do not easily mix with other compounds due to problems associated with viscosity, contaminants, and weight. The production of solar cells in space would obviate some of these processing constraints and lead to a host of new mixing procedures that can't be implemented on Earth.

Preliminary data on these materials has already proven helpful in terrestrial manufacturing. Numerous industrial firms, including Ford Motor, General Electric, Pratt & Whitney, and Alcoa, have used data from NASA to improve the casting and molding of precise and low-cost components for their products.

Microgravity: Medicine

Organic tissue and cells, such as skin, are grown in labs on Earth but suffer from a significant detriment: they must be grown in flat trays, which promote two-dimensional, but not three-dimensional, growth. Given that the human body exists in three dimensions, the possibility of growing tissue that more closely simulates the natural growth process is highly preferable. Seeing how cancer cells spread and invade tissue in a 3-D environment would also mirror the actual process and provide better examples of how and why such growth occurs.

This 3-D capability is considered the one remaining task of optimizing the spectrum of medical research into living tissue. Cell optimization has occurred, as has culture optimization, yet process optimization is still limited by the environment, which relies on flat growth panes and centrifuge experiments. Liquid flow in culture also affects how cells aggregate and work together since it often results in unnatural separation and dilutes the result.

Microgravity will point the way to more accurate delivery of medications in the human body. Even though bodily fluids flow upward and downward, propelled by various organs and muscles, they are still at the mercy of gravity. Compounds traveling through the blood stream, for instance, are subjected to fluid dynamics that affect them on their way to their intended destinations. A more thorough understanding of exactly what occurs to medications circulating through the body will allow developers to create more efficient delivery vehicles, especially those that are time dependent.

Biotech firm Amgen (Thousand Oaks, California) is using the unique properties of microgravity on human bones to test a naturally occurring compound called osteoprotegerin. Microgravity has been found to cause bone loss and Amgen scientists want to use this environment to investigate osteoprotegerin as a possible treatment for osteoporosis. Chiron Corporation, another medical firm, has applied microgravity research to a new treatment for bladder cancer and metastatic melanoma.

Microgravity: Combustion

Fully 85 percent of the energy used on Earth involves combustion, essentially the burning of material. Be it in the form of solid, liquid, or gaseous fuels—from coal to gasoline to propane—combustion is ubiquitous in power generation. At the same time, it is greatly affected by the Earth's natural forces and environment, including air pressure and flow, oxygen availability, gravity, and contaminants. Beyond that, there are the physical properties of combustion itself, such as heat transfer and fuel mass, that are influenced by their immediate surroundings. In addition, a huge amount of combustion results in significant waste as a by-product, notably air pollutants and toxins.

Combustion in space is an entirely different story. Flames, for instance, do not behave in orbit as they do on Earth—they can be freestanding and formed in the shape of balls. Investigation of the processes of flame ignition and flame in space will not only give us a better understanding of what takes place during combustion but also help to create combustion systems ideally suited for use in space. They may also provide insights to creating more efficient and cleaner-burning fuels as well as improved combustion processes.

A huge amount of experimentation involving combustion has taken place on the space shuttles, performed in sealed containers called "gloveboxes." This research will be ongoing on the ISS, sponsored largely by universities and research labs.

Space-Based Solar Power

Energy consumption. Two relatively innocuous words that meant almost nothing five years ago. But once the millennium rolled around, energy consumption hit the top of the charts as an issue of national importance in the U.S. With rolling blackouts in California disrupting everything from traffic and radio stations to web servers and alarm clocks—and soaring demand in the rest of the country—energy concerns replaced the fascination over plummeting Internet stocks almost overnight.

In the U.S., we're complacent about our energy policy. People have forgotten about the long lines at the gas stations in the 1970s and seemed oblivious to the price creep of fuel in the late 1990s. That's because when there's enough energy to go around, it really doesn't matter that it becomes more expensive. At least it's there.

The California problem—indeed, our national problem—has people scared because now the energy or the fuel isn't always there, regardless of the price. Even if you're willing to pay a premium on your energy bill for your house in Marin County, it's not going to help avoid blackouts. When the energy grid goes down in your area, no amount of money is going to get it turned back on (unless you have your own generator; but that's a different issue).

The reason the current situation is important is that it's indicative of the "fear, relax, forget" nature of how we view energy. For as long as anyone reading this can remember, there have been periods of time where politicians, private industry, and the general public have joined in an outcry against our reliance on oil as a primary energy source. This happens during times when people fear that we're running out of the black gold. They demand investment in and experimentation with alternate energy sources. Then the oil tap inevitably opens up, and everyone relaxes because there is—once again—enough oil, and thus enough energy. Over time, everyone forgets about the initial crisis. Until the next time.

This isn't a screed about national energy policy. You can get that in the daily op-ed section of your local newspaper. But the situation does lend itself, for our purposes, to an examination of how space commercialization might ameliorate the situation in the future.

We're already using solar power in space—lots of it. There are no extension cords running up to the ISS powering its computers, and there are no gas-burning engines keeping satellites whizzing around the Earth at 17,500 miles an hour. Where does the power for satellites and the space station come from? The Sun. Solar power. More precisely, space solar power, known as SSP. All those silvery panels that emanate like wings from orbiting objects are collectors designed to capture sunlight and convert it into efficient, nearly waste-free energy.

On Earth we've used this same solar power for small, almost inconsequential appliances like calculators and wristwatches. Using tiny cells, sunlight is converted into just enough energy to power these devices. On a larger and more productive scale, there are solar panels that heat houses and water, but to date their adoption has been limited to sunny desert and remote areas. This is primarily due to the upfront costs of installing these solar panels and their relatively large size, not to mention the need for constant sunlight to keep them operational.

We haven't developed a good solar power collection system on Earth for a number of reasons. First, the entire Earth only receives one part in two billion of the Sun's radiant energy. (Source: Space Solar Power Newsletter: Climate Change and Energy Options Vol. 1 - March 1997 - http://www.netdepot.com/~preble/). And due to the atmosphere, rain, clouds, time of day (solar angle), and air pollution, the strength of the Sun on any specific point of the globe is much less than it is thousands of miles above the Earth in the emptiness of space. There, the Sun's rays are unimpeded and there is no atmospheric loss. It has been estimated that the intensity of the Sun at geosynchronous altitude is twice that of what strikes the Earth at equatorial regions during days of perfect clarity. By the same token, a solar collector in space would receive up to ten times the amount of sunlight that a similar area would receive on the ground (ibid).

Since we know that there is plenty of unobstructed sunlight in space, and we currently use solar collection panels to capture that light and turn it into power, the next step is sending it back to Earth. This sounds like a smoke and mirrors operation—pun only slightly intended—that might involve reflecting sunlight and heat back to Earth. But that's not how it will be done, at least not in our scenario. The smart money is on converting space solar power to a form of energy that can be transmitted harmlessly back through the atmosphere and not via a shaft of searing heat from outer space.

We already retrieve transmissions from our satellites every minute of every day in the form of communications and broadcast signals. If we could convert solar power into transmittable energy, then it follows that we could receive that transmission at our ground stations as well. Not coincidentally, we already have a transmittable form of energy that we use in our kitchens and in our cell phones: microwaves. In space, solar power can be converted into microwaves and transmitted to Earth antennas in much the same way that broadcast signals are.

A blueprint for creating a space-based solar power system was outlined in 1968 by Dr. Peter Glaser of Arthur D. Little (although the idea of transmitting energy wirelessly was posited by Nikola Tesla back in 1881). Glaser's plan was to place large solar collector panels—measuring miles across—into geosynchronous orbit. At that altitude, the large collector panel, called a solar power satellite (SPS) would be free of atmospheric interference and would be minimally visible in the night sky. Current satellites are configured to turn sunlight into power; however, that power is consumed solely by the satellite. The SPS would generate much higher levels of energy, perhaps as much as several Earth-based nuclear power plants. It would be constructed in space (much like the ISS) and could be maintained by small robots, as there would be few moving parts that would require service or replacement.

Once it had captured the solar energy in photovoltaic cells, the SPS would convert that energy onboard to microwaves, similar to those used in microwave ovens, but at a much lower density. These microwaves would then be sent back to Earth where they would be captured by a large receiving antenna (called a rectenna). Microwaves do not lose their energy as they pass through the atmosphere or through clouds and storms, so there would be no waste during transmission. The rectenna would be attached to a transformer station that would modify and attune the energy for use as AC current and then distribute it to the local electric grid for distribution to customers. Without getting into the specifics of AC/DC, phasing, rectifiers, capacitors, magnetrons, and other aspects of electrical minutiae, suffice it to say that this conversion has been demonstrated with high degrees of efficiency and minimal waste.

There is strong argument for the use of SPS in that they are in direct sunlight 24 hours a day (with the exception of the weeks just prior to and following an equinox, when the SPS would be in Earth eclipse for about an hour a day). Their orbital altitude allows them to be positioned above a fixed spot on the Earth, and the ability of microwaves to penetrate cloud layers and precipitation make the SPS a continual and pollution-free source of energy for any location on Earth capable of setting up a rectenna.

Discussion of transmitting microwaves from space is going to create a huge amount of fear in the minds of many people. Microwave ovens have always been the source of various urban legends about radiation leakage, and cell phones have been at the center of a brain cancer scare for several years. The fact is that microwaves are not the same type of radiation as, say, ultraviolet or X-rays. The latter are classified as ionizing radiation, which is generally considered dangerous, while microwaves are non-ionizing and fall into a wide range of electromagnetic frequency (EMF) radiation, which at low levels is not considered harmful. The debate has raged on for years, despite various studies stating that there is no evidence that microwaves cause cancer or other health problems. According to a study by the U.S. National Research Council, "No clear, convincing evidence exists to show that residential exposures to electric and magnetic fields (EMF) are a threat to human health . . . There is no conclusive evidence that electromagnetic fields play a role in the development of cancer, reproductive and developmental abnormalities, or learning and behavioral problems." (Source: NRC release, October 31, 1996, National Academies, http://www4.nationalacademies.org/news.nsf/(ByDocID)/ B495ECAC8C6EA4B085256774006354B1?OpenDocument). These findings have been supported by reports from the American Medical Association, The American Physical Society, and several other organizations during the 1990s. This has calmed the fears of many people, but not all, over the use of this kind of radiation. One way to alleviate fears is to place the rectennas and receiving stations in remote areas, and even offshore.

An additional concern over the use of SPS is the potential impact they might have on communications satellites orbiting below them in middle and low-Earth orbit. There is the possibility that satellites passing through the microwave beams might experience disruption or corruption of their processes. Proponents claim that the microwave power isn't strong enough to do any damage, while opponents want more studies done.

In fact, numerous studies have been done regarding the prospects and potential, as well as the downside, of space solar power. NASA did a "Fresh Look" study on space solar power in 1995, and then followed it up with the Space Solar Power Exploratory Research and Technology (SERT) Program in 1999-2000. The preliminary results were presented at a House Subcommittee hearing in September 2000, stating that more work needed to be done over the next few decades. The hearing also featured "The Technical Feasibility of Space Solar Power" as voiced by the director of Aerospace and Science Policy of the American Institute of Aeronautics and Astronautics (AIAA). The director, Jerry Grey, stated that international work on space solar power was already proceeding ahead in Germany, France, Japan, Russia, and Canada, where significant advancements have been made in wireless transmission, solar array technology development, multiple use applications, and actual demonstrations. The AIAA also found that significant strides had been made in using lasers to transmit the converted solar power from the SPS to the ground, but that social stigma attached a "weapon perspective" to use of any space-based laser. The biggest obstacle of all? Lowering the cost of access to space, namely in the area of launch services. By this point in the discussion, that shouldn't come as a surprise to anyone.

Our ability to use solar power is a given, as is our ability to receive transmissions from satellites. Getting solar energy to help us with our on again/off again energy crises seems like a no-brainer. All it will take to change the equation is one functioning space solar power generator. Just one.

Space Mining

Space mining has been the subject of countless science-fiction books and movies, although we're not always told exactly what they are supposed to be mining for. In actuality, there are two reasons that space mining will eventually become a large component of the space industry. The first reason is the recovery of valuable materials (i.e. minerals, gases) that are scarce here on Earth. The second reason is that space mining will allow us to use space-based resources for orbital construction, rather than trying to cart everything up from the Earth. As we'll see, this will be essential to permanently moving beyond Earth orbit in the future.

Mining in space will either be done on planets (like Mars) and large satellites (like the Moon) or on asteroids and comets. The first type of mining will probably be done on near-Earth asteroids, those that stray from asteroid belts and provide the inspiration for science-fiction movies where collisions threaten life as we know it. Asteroids are believed to be rich in minerals that are scarce—and therefore precious—on Earth, especially gold, platinum group metals, and nonmetals like gallium and arsenic. These resources have high material value for Earth-based industries, such as platinum for use in jewelry and high-durability alloys and nonmetals for use in computer components. Even less valuable material like iron ore may have a purer form on these heavenly bodies. Astronomers believe that the structure of asteroids may be such that these elements could be concentrated individually in rich cores, making mining a more direct process than it is on Earth. Bringing large quantities of this material back to Earth may justify the expenditures of sending robot mining "crews" and probes to asteroids to retrieve the elements, or—as has been suggested—steering the asteroid back to Earth where it can be mined after crashing into a desert area. Somehow, this latter strategy doesn't seem to be something that the FAA or State Department would approve of.

As we establish outposts on other planets and moons, asteroids could provide the raw materials for space-based manufacturing. Iron ore and nickel mined from asteroids and even meteorites would be used as the raw materials for building structures such as habitats and facilities as well as heavy equipment—negating the need to haul those minerals from Earth to other destinations.

More important, water and methane could be extracted from comets and asteroids to provide hydrogen, oxygen, and natural gas for use by space travelers and in developing propellants. According to John S. Lewis, co-director of the NASA/University of Arizona Space Engineering Research Center, "The most economical sources of space materials are those bodies that have the greatest richness of valued commodities and that are most accessible from the earth: these are the near-earth asteroids. All they lack is economically attractive amounts of helium 3." (Many researchers believe helium 3 is a perfect fuel source for the future; it is potent, nonpolluting, and has almost no radioactive by-product.) (Source: http://www.space.com/science astronomy/helium3_000630.html and Scientific American, http://www.sciam.com/askexpert/astronomy/astronomy3.html).

Landing on asteroids has already been done. NASA's NEAR Shoemaker spacecraft descended onto the surface of the Eros asteroid on February 12, 2001. From there it transmitted radio signals back to Earth. Before its touchdown, NEAR flew by the Mathilde asteroid, which was measured to be 40 miles long by 30 miles wide—roughly the size of metropolitan Phoenix, Arizona, or about 25 times the size of the island of Manhattan.

We're talking about just the asteroids that come near Earth, of which there are more than 1,200 (Source: http://neo.jpl.nasa.gov/neo.html#number). One planet over, the belt between Mars and Jupiter is thick with asteroids of varying sizes. The Jet Propulsion Lab cites an estimate that the wealth of minerals in this belt is equivalent to $100 billion for every person currently living on Earth (Source: http://ssd.jpl.nasa.gov/why_asteroids.html), or enough to make every man, woman, and child worth about two Bill Gates.

Other celestial bodies, such as planets, will be mined in the same way, with extraction of their essential resources used in the service of colonies on those planets.

The next step in obtaining this mineral wealth is putting robot miners on an asteroid. The equipment will have to be launched in a way similar to the Mars Pathfinder and NEAR Shoemaker and will have to be manipulated via preprogramming and ground-based communications. While the robot miners themselves would have to be durable and sturdy, the relative lack of gravity on asteroids might make the actual removal and transport of heavy metals a relatively easy process. And, since they won't initially require manned launches, the cost and safety considerations of these projects are far lower than they are for manned space flights.

Second-generation robots and human miners will be able to concoct their own fuel from asteroids and comets, further reducing the cost for asteroid landings. Comets in particular are believed to have significant quantities of organic and volatile materials, making them ripe for the production of propellants.

Better yet, solar power could serve as the energy source. Ultimately, as happens on Earth, mining equipment will be moved to a new location when veins or cores are tapped out.

The impetus for making space mining happen will be one of two events: 1) the need for more resources due to lack of supply on Earth, or 2) establishing of extraterrestrial colonies. No one is suggesting that we replace Earth mining with space mining, just as we're not suggesting that we replace all our fossil fuels here with space solar power. But we've successfully landed spacecraft on an asteroid, and we know that asteroids are rich in valuable elements and resources. The value of these elements should be enough to make industry give space mining a serious look in the near future.

Technology Applications in Space: MEMS

One of the most impressive aspects of the computer industry is its ability to continually shrink the size of its silicon chips while increasing their functionality. Components that once filled an entire circuit board have been condensed into systems the size of an M&M, residing on microscopic layers of silicon. As they have become smaller, their performance and capability has improved.

While many of these chips have a specific function, such as accelerating the rendering and display of graphics on your computer screen, a new form of microprocessor chip is already taking the functionality of these chips to a higher—actually lower—level. Called MEMS (MicroElectroMechanical Systems), these chips have numerous functions built into a single microprocessor. Linking these individual processors in groups creates powerful devices and machines whose sizes are measured in millimeters. These systems are a fraction of the size of their traditional counterparts, such as satellites. Everything about MEMS is scaled down; their internal components, their power supplies, and their containers. They will be to modern devices what the Palm Pilot is relative to the original room-sized ENIAC computer: smaller, more powerful, and portable. Think of MEMS as groups of miniaturized versions of computers, cameras, or sensors fitted together to perform multiple functions in one tiny package. In effect, complete systems on a single chip.

These microscopic systems can perform functions normally associated with individual and disparate components, such as communications, sensing, and activation. With research spearheaded by organizations like Sandia National Laboratories and companies like MicroChips (Boston, MA), MEMS hold great promise in confined environments (like the human body) and in replacing big, bulky, and costly equipment. Work is already underway on tiny monitors that can be tracked or activated just below the surface of the skin. MEMS implants might contain insulin or other chemicals that need to be regularly injected into the bodies of patients, and they would be activated either by wireless remote or by sensors embedded in the skin. In this way, they would be similar in concept to implanted devices such as pacemakers but with a wider variety of potential applications. Experimentation with a host of other implanted devices, including miniature cameras for patients losing their sight, is going on at research centers including Johns Hopkins and the Massachusetts Institute of Technology.

The use of MEMS in confined areas such as power plants or processing facilities also has great potential. Placing clusters of tiny sensors together with a microprocessor for analysis could increase the use of monitoring devices that are currently large and expensive to install. More sensors spread over an area means more analysis of an environment and ultimately more control. Several hundred MEMS in the core of a nuclear power plant or a semiconductor clean room would certainly be preferable to use of a few. MEMS could theoretically even crawl into small areas to perform reconnaissance and provide video feeds, be it during military action or in the aftermath of an earthquake. They will also be used to enhance the capability of current devices, such as cell phones and digital assistants. MEMS could convert these devices into scanners, or even tiny printers and video players.

The Aerospace Corporation, a California consortium of space companies, has created MEMS-based picosatellites. These satellites each weigh less than half a pound and are roughly the size of a paperback book. The Aerospace Corporation has tethered two of these satellites together to create a single orbital satellite. While still in the testing stage, these picosatellites have the potential to replace much larger satellites for the purposes of local or dedicated communications. Putting a constellation of these picosatellites into orbit would still cost less than the cost of launching individual satellites weighing a ton or more that require huge launch vehicles to put them in orbit. Picosatellites also use tiny batteries and will cost less to produce and maintain on a per unit basis that large satellites. Remember that satellites can cost tens of millions of dollars to design and manufacture; the goal of picosatellite research is to bring that cost down substantially, perhaps into ranges measured in the thousands of dollars. This will create an additional benefit in that the cost of replacement will be relatively small as well. Bringing down the manufacturing costs will bring down the attendant insurance costs, which will bring down launch costs.

If that isn't enough to change the dynamics of the satellite business in the future, Sandia Labs is developing similar satellites about the size of a fist that would be launched into space using what might be considered modified cannons, thereby eliminating the cost of the launch vehicle altogether.

In space, the entire concept of the equipment used in each mission will change. Travelers will be continually monitored with skin-implanted MEMS, as will the quality of their air. MEMS will also replace large banks of electronic equipment that currently require significant amounts of storage space on space flights. In preparation for the day when that will happen, the Defense Department and NASA are currently exploring the use of MEMS for use in onboard guidance and self-maintenance systems.

In the immediate future, MEMS will provide a multitude of functions on a piece of silicon that fits under your fingernail. While this will make digital equipment smaller than anything that has come before, MEMS are ultimately limited by the construction techniques used in our current manufacturing processes as well as by the properties of Newtonian physics. But the most radical change in our computing machines, as well as in the development of new materials, will come from a technology that uses the principles of quantum mechanics: nanotechnology.

Nanotechnology

Dropping to a level of existence smaller than that of MEMS, nanotechnology may change the way we view the entire world. Nanotechnology has created a great deal of interest over the past several years as humans get better at understanding the realm of physics known as quantum mechanics. Here, the normal rules of Newtonian physics as it applies to light and gravity are completely turned upside down. In quantum mechanics, light is both a particle and a wave and separate objects can appear to be linked across time and space. Exploration occurs at the atomic level, where individual molecules, atoms, and their sub-components, called quarks, have their own behavior and are not always what they appear to be. It flies in the face of our visible world and often defies logic, yet we build lasers and microprocessors based on the properties of quantum mechanics.

It may not be comprehensible to most people, but that doesn't stop quantum mechanics from being applied to our daily lives.

Part of the reason for the recent spate of interest is that scientists have gotten better at manipulating molecular structures. Another reason is the National Nanotechnology Initiative, which is a government pledge to spend $500 million on research and development. The technical reason, however, is that for the first time in our history, we are able to build things up from the atomic and molecular level. Man has always created objects, from skyscrapers to sculptures, by cutting, whittling, trimming, molding, shaping, melting, and generally hacking away at existing substances, be it iron ore, trees, clay, or stone. Conversely, nanotechnology allows us to go down to the level where we can construct objects by piecing them together molecule by molecule. From there we can scale up, creating smooth-as-silk steel or unbreakable plastic just millimeters thick.

The possibilities of nanotechnology were first discussed by physicist Richard Feynman in 1959. Feynman was a Nobel Prize winner who may be remembered most for his role in the *Challenger* disaster investigation (he showed how O-rings could lose their flexibility at low temperatures by dunking them in ice water during a hearing). More than 40 years ago, Feynman delivered a paper called "There's Room at the Bottom" that outlined how science could benefit from taking a molecular view of the world—and looking up from there.

But how do we look up from a realm that is invisible to the naked eye? After all, we're talking about doing work that is measured in nanometers—one billionth of a meter, or roughly the size of two atoms. To put it in perspective, a pinhead is approximately one million nanometers wide. A more practical way to consider how much a billionth of a meter is may be to think of it in relative terms: the distance between New York and

Los Angeles is almost 3,000 miles, and a billionth of that is approximately one inch.

Using scanning electron microscopes, researchers have begun to build nanomachines. Simple gears and levers built from a few atoms have been developed at companies like IBM and Hewlett-Packard and at universities such as Yale and Rice. Taking the nanomachine concept a step further, IBM announced in April 2001 that it had created transistors that were several nanometers wide (current chip-level transistors are about 500 nanometers wide) using carbon nanotubes. These nanotubes, which are in reality infinitesimally small fibers of carbon, are likely to become the basis for the first generation of nanomachines. When linked or threaded together, these nanotubes can form incredibly durable materials that are 100 times stronger than steel and capable of withstanding temperatures over 5,000 degrees Fahrenheit, yet are of incredibly light weight.

Assembling these nanotubes, which resemble rolled chicken wire, into practical materials may ultimately be the work of nano assemblers. These tiny programmed machines will literally grab molecules and link them together to create various materials out of a molecular stew, spinning and weaving to produce a near-perfect product. Some nano theorists envision a day when these assemblers not only construct the materials but also assemble them into a finished object or structure, such as a syringe or a skyscraper. Or, as both Feynman and the movie *Fantastic Voyage* suggested, nanotechnology can create small medical devices that will be inserted into bloodstreams to carve plaque from arteries or destroy individual cancer cells. Critics, however, picture a world where nanomachines float in the air, potentially poisoning us or disintegrating matter by tearing it apart at the atomic level. The debate over nanotechnology's potential use and abuse has already filled numerous books and articles, and we won't delve into it here.

Our interest in nanotechnology is its use in space, especially for strong and lightweight material applications. An obvious initial use will be for vehicle construction, which currently suffers from its own weight. Breaking free of the Earth's gravity is a difficult proposition for almost any object—when was the last time you tried to jump straight up?—but propelling hundreds and thousands of tons of equipment into the air requires a commensurate amount of fuel. Lots of vehicle weight and lots of fuel add up to lots of cost. Reducing the weight, while potentially making a more stable vehicle, immediately drops the cost. In addition, due to the harsh conditions of space flight, from extreme temperatures at either end of the thermometer to the extreme effects of gravity, friction, and velocity, nanotubes offer a promising alternative to our mill-manufactured steel.

Nanomachines in the form of small computers and sensors will also help to reduce weight concerns and provide more direct monitoring of system functions as well as the personal health of space travelers. It is possible that nanomachines will ultimately be used to extract microscopic pollutants from the air aboard space flights as well as to repair stress damage to components. Tiny "nanobots" will traverse the exterior of a craft repairing fractures, holes, and other minor damage caused by impact from space debris such as meteor particles and space junk.

Futurists see large-scale manufacturing facilities operated by nanobots that use solar power to keep them operative. These factories could assemble products in Earth orbit or in deep space. Applications range from the construction of massive solar panels with dimensions measured in miles to orbiting storage platforms and even habitats awaiting human arrival. Once a nano-facility was constructed on, say, Mars, the nanobots could use mineral resources to replicate themselves and build terrestrial stations that undertake everything from mining and mapping to observation and communication. Since these nanobots would operate at the molecular level, they could also create artificial environments that produce local air and water, given the presence of hydrogen and oxygen in either the atmosphere or the rocky surface of the planet itself.

Getting There: Propulsion

Earlier we discussed the recent testing of scramjets, air-breathing engines that use oxygen and hydrogen as their propulsion mechanisms. Although a vehicle that can essentially use air as a form of propellant would seem to be the ultimate spacecraft, it does have its limitations, most notably in space where there is no air. For that we have to look at other forms of propulsion.

Propulsion and propellants have remained essentially unchanged for decades. They still involve combustion of chemicals ranging from gasoline to liquid oxygen in order to create lift and thrust. Once the propellant is gone, so is the thrust. In deep space, vehicles won't be able to carry unlimited amounts of propellant to carry them from planet to planet, or galaxy to galaxy. To achieve that, we will eventually have to look elsewhere.

But where? The mythical "warp drive" of *Star Trek*'s starships has inspired numerous theories and possibilities of how we might propel craft without relying on current propulsion techniques. The resultant scientific literature has produced some ideas that have potential, while others will require monumental leaps in our understanding of space, time, and quantum mechanics. Here are some of the most intriguing concepts.

- Ion propulsion. The Deep Space 1 spacecraft launched in 1998 utilizes an ion propulsion system instead of a traditional chemical propellant engine. This technology has been around in various forms since 1960 but was never used as a primary propulsion method for any spacecraft due to the fact that its success had never been proven (quite the Catch-22). NASA finally took a chance on the technology with Deep Space 1, the mission of which—not coincidentally—was to test new technologies.

The propulsion technique involves using the gas xenon to serve as a propellant. The xenon is given an electrical charge, or ionized, and is then electrically accelerated. The xenon ions are then channeled and emitted as exhaust from the craft at a high rate of speed, which literally forces the craft in the opposite direction.

The benefit of the ion system is that is incredibly efficient and much lighter than chemical propellants. For example, Deep Space 1 carries nearly 82 kilograms of xenon propellant and will take about 20 months to use it all. A similar chemical propulsion system would have only one-tenth the efficiency. The downside is that ion propulsion cannot be used for high acceleration missions (such as from the Earth to the Moon) because the engine provides only a relatively gradual thrust. For long-distance travel, however, this will be perfectly acceptable as the fuel efficiencies will be more important than high acceleration in getting to destinations like Mars.

The initial success of Deep Space 1 will likely lead to greater consideration of ion propulsion for similar long duration missions in the future, as well as consideration for a similar technology, the plasma drive.

- Plasma. Plasma is considered the fourth state of matter, after solid, liquid, and gas. It is, in fact, the result of heating gases to extraordinary temperatures—from 50,000 degrees Fahrenheit on up to millions of degrees. At those temperature levels, electrons are stripped out of the gas, creating a neutral miasma of charged particles. Estimates are that some 99 percent of our universe may be made up of plasma; visible manifestations include lightning, the Sun, and stars.

The extreme temperatures required to create plasma would destroy any of the materials we now work with that could conceivably be used to contain it (although that could change with the advent of nanotechnology materials). Yet due to its electrical state plasma is a good conductor, which makes it susceptible to magnetic fields, which can in turn be used to manipulate and guide the plasma. Generation can thus take place within carefully constructed magnetic cells, and those cells can be designed as engine components that would produce "plasma drive." Plasma may provide the next generation of propulsion for the space program. Unlike its chemical combustion forebears—but similar to ion propulsion—plasma engines will be able to control the relationship between thrust and exhaust. Current engines essentially burn fuel and spit out the exhaust in a relative flow, meaning the amount and release of exhaust is a direct function of fuel consumption. Plasma exhaust and thrust can be modulated independently, such that the thrust acceleration stage can be running at higher levels than the exhaust levels, and conversely, exhaust can increase even while thrust decreases. The end result is that the engine—and the vehicle in which it is used—takes on the characteristics of an automatic transmission and can shift into the appropriate gear.

This concept is being explored as a way to minimize interplanetary travel times, since the plasma drive uses less fuel and provides more efficiency than chemical rockets. On a trip to Mars, for instance, the estimated time of travel is currently eight months—a significant part of which is spent in unpowered drift to conserve energy and allow for course corrections. Plasma drives could reduce the time to as little as three months, which would have the added benefit of reducing passenger time spent in dangerous radiation belts. These drives would also provide more precise control over placement of objects in space, such as satellites and space stations. This could significantly reduce the time needed to get commercial ventures up and running.

Plans for use of plasma drives are already underway. In June 2000, NASA's Advanced Space Propulsion Laboratory at the Johnson Space Center (Houston, Texas) signed a collaboration contract with MSE Technology Applications (Butte, Montana) to work on the development of the Variable Specific Impulse Magnetoplasma Rocket (VASIMR). This vehicle will have three magnetic fuel cells that will heat hydrogen to a plasma state using radio waves that are created in a cyclotron (Source: http://spaceflight.nasa.gov/spacenews/releases/h00-91.html). NASA hopes to have a viable system ready for operation in the next decade.

- Nuclear fusion—the technology behind the hydrogen bomb. The conventional wisdom in the space community is that once we've mastered plasma drives, we'll have moved to a level of science where controlled nuclear fusion can be employed in rocket engines. Given careful consideration by two studies—Project Orion in the 1960s and Project Daedalus in the 1970s—nuclear fusion propulsion would involve creating an ongoing series of explosions that propel vehicles forward along the front of shock waves. Of course, the fusionable material in this case would have to be brought along and would ultimately expire. Suggestions for replenishing the nuclear core involved mining it from asteroids or planets encountered along the way. Additionally, researchers at Pennsylvania State University have written a paper on a form of nuclear drive fueled by antiproton-catalyzed microfission/microfusion, which uses pellets of uranium to create hydrogen fusion.

- Space sails. The construction of a light sail powered by the Sun or by onboard lasers has also been proposed. In this scenario, ultralight craft would use a sail (like a sailboat) or an array of panels to catch light that—in a high enough quantity—would push against it and carry it along. The sail would have to be monstrous in size in order to achieve the desired effects due to the very slight push that light exerts on objects. The structure itself would have to be durable and lightweight, which may be a perfect application for composites created using nanotechnology fabrication.

- Space scramjet. Modifying the scramjet concept for use in interstellar travel would involve the scooping up of some resource other than air. Ideas for this include having the craft "breathe in" protons from space to create nuclear fusion on board the craft. It would then be propelled as outlined above—on the shock waves of nuclear blasts.

- Using the strangeness of space and the concepts of quantum mechanics. Speculation about faster-than-light travel focuses on a means to negate the effects of gravity (which is a force we still don't fully understand). Additionally, it has been suggested that wormholes exist in space that allow objects to travel across space without our current regard for time. Such wormholes are thought to occur when space folds in on itself—yet another concept that defies our logic.

Each of these propulsion scenarios involves an increasingly better understanding of physics than we have now but which is sure to evolve in the decades to come. Given the growth of our body of scientific knowledge in the last few decades—and an accelerated application of that knowledge in the years to come—we may ultimately come to see concepts such as the "warp drive" as functional propulsion systems and not just the musings of science-fiction fans.

Final Thoughts

Consider the possibilities when any of the above categories of space business are combined. Using MEMS to operate a solar power space station or employing nanobots to keep the air clean in a space hotel or using solar power to run mining facilities on Mars all open up a world of possibilities not even hinted at by currently deployable technology. But it is all within our grasp because we have already begun work on it. Once the work has been done, all we need to do is make a good business out of it. That's the role of the private sector, and when we look to industry to undertake this—and not our government agencies—it will ultimately become a reality.

8

SPACE BUSINESSES AND PROFILES

Here are the top 100 players in the space-business game, presented in alphabetical order. The list includes companies previously noted and discussed as well as many more. If you're interested in how these companies represent themselves to the public and what information they make readily available, you can visit their websites. The material presented here was gathered from other sources.

Alcatel Space
 LOCATION: Toulouse, France
 HELD: Division of Alcatel (NYSE: ALA)
 REVENUES: $1.1 billion
 EMPLOYEES: 6,000
 WEBSITE: http://www.alcatel.com/space/
 BUSINESS: Alcatel Space is one of Europe's leading space contractors, involved in nearly every area of space business. It builds and operates satellites in domains ranging from observation and meteorology to broadcast and defense systems. It also serves as a provider of ground and support systems, including payload and production. The company has numerous

divisions located throughout Europe, including Alcatel Bell Space in Belgium and Indra Espacio in Spain. Customers and partners include Alenia, Boeing, ESA, Loral, Eutelsat, Intelsat, Globalstar, SkyBridge, TRW, and XM Satellite Radio.

Alcoa Industrial Components Group/Cordant

LOCATION: Salt Lake City, Utah
HELD: Subsidiary of Alcoa (NYSE: AA)
REVENUES: $2.5 billion
EMPLOYEES: 17,200
WEBSITE: http://www.alcoa.com
BUSINESS: Alcoa Industrial Components Group is a division of Alcoa, the number one producer of aluminum in the world (with sales of more than $22 billion). This particular group includes Cordant Technologies, acquired in 2000, which provides the solid rocket propulsion systems for the space shuttle. Alcoa formerly owned Thiokol Propulsion, maker of rocket motors for defense and commercial launches, which it sold to Alliant Techsystems.

Alenia Spazio SpA

LOCATION: Rome, Italy
HELD: A division of Finmeccanica (Italian: FNC)
REVENUES: $600 million +
EMPLOYEES: 2,800
WEBSITE: http://www.alespazio.it/
BUSINESS: Finmeccanica is Italy's leading aerospace company. Alenia Spazio is the prime contractor for all the programs managed through the Italian Space Agency (ASI) and participates in a majority of the projects organized by the European Space Agency (ESA). It produces satellites for all purposes and also develops ground control systems, as well as re-entry and launch components. It claims that its Small Satellite Center

is the space industry's first flexible assembly line, with output of one satellite per week. Alenia is building several modules and nodes on the ISS and is in discussions to take on construction of the Crew Return Vehicle.

Alliant Techsystems
LOCATION: Hopkins, Minnesota
HELD: Public (NYSE: ATK)
REVENUES: $1.1 billion
EMPLOYEES: 6,500
WEBSITE: http://www.atk.com
BUSINESS: A large government contractor, Alliant is the power—literally—behind rockets such as Boeing's Delta and Orbital Sciences' Pegasus, for which it builds engines. It also produces composite structures, including instrument benches, satellite assemblies, space-based antennae, and space launch vehicle structures as well as GPS systems. The company agreed in 2001 to buy rival Thiokol Propulsion from Alcoa.

Allied Aerospace Industries, Inc.
LOCATION: Greenbelt, Maryland
HELD: Joint venture (Dynamic Engineering, GASL, and Micro Craft)
EMPLOYEES: 1,000
REVENUES: NA
WEBSITE: http://www.alliedaerospace.com
BUSINESS: Alllied Aerospace Industries is an alliance of three companies (Dynamic Engineering, GASL, and Micro Craft) pooling their resources to provide a full spectrum of service to the aerospace and defense industries, primarily as a provider of test facilities and services. The company performs initial design and development, manufacturing, measurement, and analysis functions on aerospace hardware, notably new

planes, rockets, and engines. In addition, it builds mockups and prototypes and is the developer of the new hypersonic X-43 scramjet vehicle. Customers include NASA and defense agencies, as well as Lockheed and Boeing.

Analytical Graphics, Inc.

LOCATION:	Malvern, Pennsylvania
HELD:	Private
REVENUES:	$18.5 million
EMPLOYEES:	150
WEBSITE:	http://www.stk.com

BUSINESS: Analytical Graphics is one of the leading suppliers of a commercial off-the-shelf analysis software to the space industry called Satellite Tool Kit. The STK Software Suite provides tools that support the aerospace community applications such as system design and concept and real-time operations. Basic applications include calculating and visualizing a vehicle's position and attitude, determining acquisition times, and analyzing the vehicle's field of view. Interestingly, the basic software is free—it's the add-ons that generate revenue for the company.

Arianespace

LOCATION:	Paris, France
HELD:	Consortium
REVENUES:	$774 million
EMPLOYEES:	350
WEBSITE:	http://www.arianespace.com

BUSINESS: Arianespace, a consortium of more than 50 companies from 12 European countries (including 41 aerospace and engineering companies, 11 banks, and one space agency), currently holds more than 50 percent of the market for payloads launched to GEO. It has performed more than 130 commercial launches since 1984, and has signed launch contracts for 216 satellite payloads and nine ATV missions since the company's creation in 1980. Arianespace is responsible for the production, operation, and marketing of the Ariane 4 and 5 launchers and is a partner in the commercial operations of Russia's Starsem, which manufactures and markets the Soyuz launch vehicle.

Asia Cellular Satellite International (ACeS)

LOCATION: Hamilton, Bermuda (also Jakarta, Indonesia)
HELD: Joint venture
REVENUES: NA
EMPLOYEES: NA
WEBSITE: http://www.acesinternational.com
BUSINESS: ACeS offers global calling using small satellite phones and its geosynchronous Garuda satellite. Like Iridium, the company is offering anywhere in the world calling capability through its own Asian gateways and partnerships with operators on five continents. Unlike Iridium, it is using one satellite (to be joined eventually by a second one) instead of a large constellation in lower orbit. The company is co-owned by PT Pasifik Satelit Nusantara of Indonesia (NASDAQ: PSNRY), Lockheed Martin Global Telecommunications, the Philippine Long Distance Telephone Company, and Jasmine International of Thailand.

Asia Satellite Telecommunications Company Ltd.

LOCATION: Hong Kong
HELD: Public (NYSE: SAT)
WEBSITE: http://www.asiasat.com
BUSINESS: Asia Satellite Telecommunications Company leases transponder capacity and operates three AsiaSat satellites, which reach two-thirds of the world's population residing

in more than 50 countries and regional areas. The company's AsiaSats carry 100 television channels and 90 radio channels for 50 public and private customers. Public telephone networks, private VSAT networks, and high speed Internet are also available on the system. Société Européenne des Satellites (SES) and China International Trust and Investment own a combined total of nearly 70 percent of the company.

Assuresat, Inc.
LOCATION: El Segundo, California
HELD: Private
REVENUES: NA
EMPLOYEES: NA
WEBSITE: http://www.assuresat.com
BUSINESS: AssureSat is in the backup and restore business. It plans to launch two specially designed, high-powered satellites in 2002 to provide backup protection to GEO satellite operators by moving quickly to appropriate orbital slots to take over the communications tasks of malfunctioning spacecraft. It will also handle service for operators whose launches have failed, ensuring service for the operator's customers until the originals can be replaced. Shareholders include Securitas Capital, a global equity investment company funded by Swiss Reinsurance Company and Credit Suisse Group, and SpaceVest.

Astrium
LOCATION: Toulouse, France; Ottobrun, Germany; Portsmouth, England
HELD: Joint venture
REVENUES: $1.7 billion
EMPLOYEES: 7,500
WEBSITE: http://www.astrium-space.com
BUSINESS: Formed in 2000, Astrium bills itself as the

first tri-national space company. The company is owned 75 percent by EADS (the company that emerged from the merger of Matra Marconi Space and the space divisions of Daimler-Chrysler Aerospace) and 25 percent by BAE Systems of the U.K. The company provides total satellite communications system capability, from spacecraft design, manufacture, launch, and in-orbit operation to complete ground control and communications networks. It has built the Eurostar satellites and has contracts to build Intelsat and Inmarsat satellites in the future. Customers include Intelsat, EUTELSAT and Société Européenne de Satellites (SES), Singapore Telecom and Chunghwa Telecom Co. Ltd of Taiwan, WorldSpace Inc., and Egypt's Nilesat.

Astron Antenna Co.
LOCATION: Sterling, Virginia
HELD: Private
REVENUES: NA
EMPLOYEES: NA
WEBSITE: http://www.astronantennas.com
BUSINESS: Astron is a developer of custom antennas for both military and commercial applications. The company's products are used for a wide variety of communications needs including cellular telephone, personal communications, RF identification, and satellite reception.

AstroVision International, Inc.
LOCATION: Bethesda, Maryland
HELD: Private
REVENUES: NA
EMPLOYEES: 10
WEBSITE: http://www.astrovis.com
BUSINESS: AstroVision plans to provide the first live, color coverage of Earth. Its AVSTar Satellites, slated for launch

beginning in 2003, will carry hi-resolution cameras in GEO to offer around the clock, global observations of the Earth to customers. Its products based on this capability will enable a variety of specialized applications including news, weather, and crisis management, while engaging in traditional GIS and remote sensing activities for agriculture, forestry, land-use mapping, education, and scientific research. AstroVision will provide coverage of atmospheric and terrestrial events, including hurricanes, tornadoes, lightning, eclipses, and major catastrophic occurrences like fires and volcano eruptions. Funded by Canada's Sofinov and SpaceVest.

BAE Systems (formerly British Aerospace)
    LOCATION: Hampshire, England
    HELD: Public (OTC: BAESY)
    REVENUES: $18 billion
    EMPLOYEES: 83,400
    WEBSITE: http://www.baesystems.com
    BUSINESS: BAE Systems is the world's fourth largest aerospace company (after Boeing, Lockheed, and EADS) and Britain's largest defense contractor. The company provides turnkey satellite services as well as ground control stations and equipment, instrumentation, and communications systems. It is a 25 percent shareholder in the Astrium consortium and a 20 percent owner of Airbus.

Ball Aerospace & Technologies Corp. (BATC)
    LOCATION: Boulder, Colorado
    HELD: Public (NYSE: BLL)
    REVENUES: $383 million
    EMPLOYEES: 1,900
    WEBSITE: http://www.ball.com/
    BUSINESS: This division of the former glass jar maker—

they spun off that part of the business as Alltrista Corporation, a separate company, in 1993—develops and builds small to medium-sized spacecraft, civilian and defense payloads, science instruments, and a wide range of subsystems, components, software, guidance systems, and support services. Respected for its optics and engineering expertise, Ball was chosen to develop and build the Corrective Optics Space Telescope Axial Replacement (COSTAR) to correct the widely publicized flaws in the Hubble Space Telescope's primary mirror. Major customers are NASA and the defense community.

BF Goodrich Aerospace (formerly BF Goodrich)
  LOCATION: Charlotte, North Carolina
  HELD: Public (NYSE: GR)
  REVENUES: $4.4 billion
  EMPLOYEES: 22,136
  WEBSITE: http://www.bfgoodrich.com
  BUSINESS: Goodrich builds subsystems for satellites and launch vehicles that provide attitude control, thermal management, power management and distribution, command and data handling, digital signal processing, telemetry, and more. In 2000, it acquired Barnes Engineering, which makes Earth and Sun sensors that are employed by nearly every satellite currently in orbit. Goodrich also provides vehicle maintenance and overhaul services. The company's recent name change is designed to focus attention on its aerospace business and put to rest the image of its tire business, which it sold to Michelin.

Bigelow Aerospace
  LOCATION: Las Vegas, Nevada
  HELD: Private
  REVENUES: NA
  EMPLOYEES: NA

WEBSITE: http://www.bigelowaerospace.com

BUSINESS: Bigelow Aerospace currently engineers and manufactures tools and parts for the aerospace industry. It is the plan of company founder Robert Bigelow (owner of Budget Suites of America) to begin development on projects and applications that will promote space tourism, including launch vehicles and space habitats. Bigelow has committed to spending $500 million of his own money over 15 years to achieve this goal.

Boeing Co.

LOCATION: Chicago, Illinois

HELD: Public (NYSE: BA)

REVENUES: $51.3 billion

EMPLOYEES: 198,000

WEBSITE: http://www.boeing.com

BUSINESS: Boeing is the world's largest space and aerospace company. It is involved in nearly every aspect of space business, primarily in the areas of launch services, operations, and satellite and vehicle construction. A brief sampling of its endeavors will provide a sense of its scope: Boeing is a partner in United Space Alliance (with Lockheed), which manages the space shuttle and its operation; it is a prime contractor for the ISS; it is the lead partner in Sea Launch, a company that launches vehicles from a platform in the Pacific Ocean; its purchase of satellite pioneer Hughes Electronics (now Boeing Satellite Services) gives it a huge presence in the satellite manufacturing sector; it offers customers and competitors alike launch vehicles via its Delta rocket; it offers high-speed Internet access to travelers via its Connexion service; and it is the lead contractor on numerous NASA projects. This doesn't even include its acquisition of McDonnell Douglas or its GPS satellite contract with the U.S. Air Force. Indeed, it is almost impossible for a company to operate in the space business without coming into Boeing's sphere of influence, either through its subsidiaries, joint ventures, or numerous partnerships.

Canadian Space Agency (CSA)

LOCATION:	Quebec, Canada
HELD:	Government-owned
REVENUES:	NA
EMPLOYEES:	350
WEBSITE:	http://www.space.gc.ca/

BUSINESS: Formed in 1989, the Canadian Space Agency (CSA) oversees the development of the Canadian civil space industry by procuring business opportunities for local companies, primarily in the way of contracts from other space agencies such as the European Space Agency (ESA) and NASA. In addition to funding research missions, it is responsible for the robotic arm (the "Canadarm") used for construction on the ISS.

Celestis

LOCATION:	Houston, Texas
HELD:	Private
REVENUES:	NA
EMPLOYEES:	NA
WEBSITE:	http://www.celestis.com

BUSINESS: Celestis offers post-cremation memorial services whereby a "symbolic portion" of the cremated remains of people are sent into space. Roughly seven grams of ashes are encapsulated into a satellite and then launched by an Orbital Sciences launch vehicle. Destinations include near-Earth orbit, the Moon, and deep space. The company has launched three satellites, which have included the remains of Star Trek creator Gene Rodenberry and counterculture icon Timothy Leary. Celestis assisted NASA in launching the ashes of astronomer Dr. Eugene Shoemaker aboard the Lunar Prospector.

Centre National d'Etudes Spatiales (CNES)
>   LOCATION: Paris, France
>   HELD: Government-owned
>   REVENUES: NA
>   EMPLOYEES: NA
>   WEBSITE: http://www.cnes.fr/WEB_UK/index_v3.htm
>   BUSINESS: Like other national space agencies, Centre

National d'Etudes Spatiales (CNES) develops and administers French space efforts. It works closely with the government, research organizations, and commercial businesses to promote direct French participation in international space activity (through its participation in ESA). Its proposal for European-based launch vehicles and facilities resulted in the development of the Ariane rocket and the Kourou launch site.

China Great Wall Industries Corporation (CGWIC)
>   LOCATION: Beijing, China
>   HELD: Government-owned
>   REVENUES: $400 million
>   EMPLOYEES: 6,000 (estimated)
>   WEBSITE: http://www.cgwic.com/index1.html
>   BUSINESS: Established in 1980, China Great Wall Indus-

try Corporation (CGWIC) acts as the prime contractor of Chinese international commercial launch services and satellite technology. The organization developed and maintains the Long March launch vehicles, which are used by numerous international partners. Launch services are offered at three different centers across the Chinese mainland, located in Xichang, Taiyuan, and Jiuquan. In addition to serving the needs of the Chinese government (for which it is currently developing manned space

vehicles), the company has signed deals with high-profile organizations including Alenia and Intelsat. Although it is difficult to
untangle the exact structure of CGWIC and its various agency
partners (there are some 50 organizations that comprise the
China Aerospace Great Wall Enterprises Group), it is officially a
50/50 venture between two organizations: the China Aerospace
Science & Technology Corporation and the China Aerospace
Machinery and Electronics Corporation.

Com Dev International
    LOCATION: Ontario, Canada
    HELD: Public (Toronto: CDV)
    REVENUES: $134 million
    EMPLOYEES: 1,400
    WEBSITE: http://www.comdev.ca
    BUSINESS: Com Dev's space division has designed and
built equipment and instrumentation for more than 450 space
missions including communication and science satellites as well
as unmanned space probes. Its equipment is used for telecommunications, mapping, and remote sensing. Com Dev Space
also builds hardware for satellite transmission of high-speed
Internet signals. The company counts Boeing, Loral, Lockheed,
the Indian Space Research Organization, ESA, CSA, and Alcatel
Space among its customers. The space division accounts for
roughly half the parent company's revenues.

Computer Sciences Corp.
    LOCATION: El Segundo, California
    HELD: Public (NYSE: CSC)
    REVENUES: $10.5 billion
    EMPLOYEES: 58,000
    WEBSITE: http://www.csc.com
    BUSINESS: CSC has been a long-time provider of soft-

ware systems to NASA and other aerospace companies. In addition to design software, the company also creates administrative, operational, and management software and offers applications outsourcing and integration services. Clients include Raytheon, BAE Systems, General Dynamics, and United Technologies.

Comsat Corp. (Lockheed Martin Global Telecommunications)
LOCATION:	Bethesda, Maryland
HELD:	Wholly owned subsidiary of Lockheed Martin Global Communications (NYSE: LMT)
REVENUES:	$1 billion
EMPLOYEES:	4,000
WEBSITE:	http://www.lmgt.com
BUSINESS:	Originally created as the sales and market-

ing arm of Intelsat, Comsat was acquired by Lockheed in 2000. It is now at the heart of Lockheed's Global Telecommunications group (LMGT), which offers telecommunications, broadcast, and digital networking services between the U.S. and other countries via the 19-satellite Intelsat system. Satellite services also include the Comsat Mobile Communications system for mobile users at sea, in the air, and at remote land locations via the nine-satellite Inmarsat system. LMGT also offers personal satellite communications such as voice, fax, and data capabilities.

Comtech Mobile Datacom Corp.
LOCATION:	Germantown, Pennsylvania
HELD:	Subsidiary of Comtech Telecommunications Corporation (NASDAQ: CMTL)
REVENUES:	$66.4 million
EMPLOYEES:	689
WEBSITE:	http://www.comtechmobile.com/cmdc/news.html
BUSINESS:	Comtech Mobile Datacom provides data

communication services that connect mobile vehicles and fixed-site assets with each other, a headquarters facility, or with a mobile control station. The system employs an open architecture, enabling the use of commercial satellites around the world. Truckers, dispatchers, ship captains, and aircraft pilots can send and receive email and report their geographic position in real-time. The company's service is currently available in North America, the Caribbean, parts of South America, and Europe. Customers include Hughes Electronics, Northrop Grumman, DirecTV, and Litton.

Cronos Integrated Microsystems, Inc.
>   LOCATION: Research Triangle Park, North Carolina
>   HELD: Division of JDS Uniphase Corp. (NASDAQ: JDSU)
>   REVENUES: $1.4 billion (parent)
>   EMPLOYEES: 19,000 (parent)
>   WEBSITE: http://www.memsrus.com
>   BUSINESS: Cronos manufactures microelectrical mechanical systems (MEMS), primarily for fiber optic and communications applications. The company has created a standardized manufacturing platform for MEMS processes and components consisting of simple building blocks that comprise an entire application. It has over 50 MEMS patents and patents pending, and its initial products—microrelays, optical attenuators, and photonic switch components—are available at the chip-level as stand-alone components or in combined systems.

EchoStar Communications Corp.
>   LOCATION: Littleton, Colorado
>   HELD: Public (NASDAQ: DISH)
>   REVENUES: $2.7 billion
>   EMPLOYEES: 11,000

WEBSITE: http://www.echostar.com

BUSINESS: One of the two primary players in the U.S. market for direct-to-home satellite TV (along with DirecTV), EchoStar boasts more than five million subscribers. The company controls almost every aspect of its operations, from its six dedicated satellites to sales and installation of its products in consumers' homes. It is promoting its two-way Internet satellite service, known as StarBand, which it has developed with Microsoft and Gilat. The company is built around the personality of company founder CEO Charlie Ergin, who owns half the company, nearly all of the voting power, and conducts monthly chats online with subscribers.

Ellipso
    LOCATION: Washington, D.C.
    HELD: Private
    REVENUES: NA
    EMPLOYEES: NA
    WEBSITE: http://www.ellipso.com

BUSINESS: Ellipso is developing a satellite constellation for mobile phone users that relies on the company's unique orbital architecture. This architecture will concentrate 17 satellites in elliptical orbits (hence the company name) over the most populated and high-traffic communications of the globe. A partnership with New ICO to build a mobile satellite system could ultimately lead to acquisition of Ellipso by New ICO. The company's major equity holders include HarbourVest Partners, Israel Aircraft Industries, Boeing, L-3 Com, and Venture First II, LP. Additionally, Ellipso's sister company, VirtualGeo, will use a similar satellite configuration to provide broadband wireless Internet services.

EMS Technologies Inc.

LOCATION:	Atlanta, Georgia
HELD:	Public (NASDAQ: ELMG)
REVENUES:	$273 million
EMPLOYEES:	2,000
WEBSITE:	http://www.ems-t.com

BUSINESS: EMS is a communications company involved in wireless and satellite services. Half of EMS's sales come from its Space and Technologies Group, which supplies special purpose equipment to government and commercial projects. Primary products include antennas, digital command and control systems, spacecraft payloads and subsystems, and equipment for space science and research. SATCOM, a division of EMS, supplies customers with a broad array of satellite based terminals, antennas, and aeronautical applications for use in land mobile and emergency management environments.

Eurockot Launch Services GmbH

LOCATION:	Bremen, Germany
HELD:	Joint venture (Astrium and Khrunichev)
REVENUES:	NA
EMPLOYEES:	NA
WEBSITE:	http://www.eurockot.com

BUSINESS: Eurockot is a joint venture company founded by international consortium Astrium GmbH (51 percent) and Russia's Khrunichev State Research and Production Space Center (49 percent) designed to market launch services internationally. Astrium provides overall commercial and technical management expertise to Eurockot, while Khrunichev provides the Rockot launch vehicle to Eurockot and performs the mission analysis, payload integration, launch operations, and mission control. Launches are performed in the Russian city of Plesetsk.

European Aeronautic Defence and Space Co. (EADS N.V.)

LOCATION: Munich, Germany

HELD: Public (Euronext Paris: EAD)

REVENUES: $22.8 billion

EMPLOYEES: 100,600

WEBSITE: http://www.eads-nv.com

BUSINESS: EADS was founded on July 10, 2000 (the same day it went public) as a space consortium comprised of three aerospace partners: Aerospatiale Matra S.A. (France), Construcciones Aeronáuticas S.A. (Spain), and DaimlerChrysler Aerospace AG (Germany). This aggregation of assets puts it third on the list of the world's largest aerospace companies, after Boeing and Lockheed. The company has a complicated corporate structure (French and German co-CEOs) and dozens of space industry investments, ranging from 75 percent of Astrium and 25 percent of Arianespace to 80 percent of Airbus. In addition, through Astrium, it is a partner with Khrunichev in launch services company Eurockot and holds a position in the Soyuz company, Starsem. EADS' space division, which includes manufacturing and launch services, accounts for just approximately 11 percent of the company's total revenues. The company is also a satellite manufacturer, having produced satellites for numerous scientific missions as well as for Intelsat and INMARSAT, among others. For its launch services, the company uses the Ariane rocket for heavy-lift launches, Starsem for medium-lift launches, and Eurockot for small-lift launches.

European Space Agency (ESA)

LOCATION: Paris, France

HELD: Consortium

REVENUES: NA

EMPLOYEES: 1,700

WEBSITE: http://www.esa.int/export/esaCP/index.html

BUSINESS: The European Space Agency calls itself "Europe's gateway to space" and is responsible for the overall direction of Europe's space program. Working closely with national space agencies (such as CNES), ESA represents 15 member states: Austria, Belgium, Denmark, Finland, France, Germany, Ireland, Italy, the Netherlands, Norway, Portugal, Spain, Sweden, Switzerland, and the United Kingdom. Canada has special status and participates in some projects under a cooperation agreement. The group is independent of the European Union; not all member countries of the EU are members of ESA and not all ESA member states are members of the EU. ESA's mandatory activities (space science programs and the general budget) are funded by a financial contribution from all the Agency's members, calculated in accordance with each country's gross national product. In addition, ESA conducts a number of optional programs. Each country decides in which optional program it wishes to participate and the amount of its contribution. In addition, each country oversees specific aspects of space activity, such as astronaut training (Germany), ground stations (Sweden, Spain, Belgium), and Earth observation (Italy).

Eutelsat

LOCATION: Paris, France
HELD: Private
REVENUES: $500 million (approximately)
EMPLOYEES: NA
WEBSITE: http://www.eutelsat.com

BUSINESS: Eutelsat is comprised of 48 member countries in Europe, and it serves as a representative for the satellite interests of many of these countries. It operates a fleet of 18 GEO satellites, making it one of the world's leading satellite operators, with coverage of Europe, Africa, portions of Asia, and interconnectivity with the Americas. More than half of

Eutelsat's capacity is used for television broadcasting, with the remainder used for services that include high-speed Internet access and Internet backbone connections. The company is currently splitting itself in two, with one organization to emerge as a private company and the other to be maintained as an intergovernmental organization representing the public interests of each of the participating countries.

GenCorp—Aerojet

LOCATION: Rancho Cordova, California
HELD: Public (NYSE: GY)
REVENUES: $1 billion
EMPLOYEES: 7,895
WEBSITE: http://www.gencorp.com
BUSINESS: Aerojet is a major aerospace/defense contractor specializing in space electronics, missile and space propulsion, and smart munitions and armaments. The company builds the engines for a wide variety of rockets, ranging from Boeing's Delta and Lockheed's Atlas and Titan vehicles on to the reusable K-1 rocket from Kistler Aerospace and the orbiting subsystem rocket for the space shuttle. Aerojet accounts for more than half of parent company GenCorp's annual revenue.

General Dynamics Ordnance and Tactical Systems (GT-OTS)

LOCATION: Redmond, Washington
HELD: Division of General Dynamics (NYSE: GD)
REVENUES: $10.3 billion (parent)
EMPLOYEES: 43,300 (parent)
WEBSITE: http://www.primextech.com/
BUSINESS: General Dynamics Ordnance and Tactical Systems Aerospace Operations (built on the January 2001 acquisition of Primex Technologies) is one of the leading suppliers of liquid and electric propulsion products, providing full-service

capability to a wide variety of satellite, spacecraft, and launch chemical customers. The company's propulsion products are at the cutting edge of technology and include plasma thrusters and ion engines. Parent company is the leading builder of nuclear-powered submarines.

General Electric
LOCATION: Fairfield, Connecticut
HELD: Public (NYSE: GE)
REVENUES: $129.4 billion
EMPLOYEES: 313,000
WEBSITE: http://www.ge.com
BUSINESS: General Electric has vested interests in the space business, both from a communications (its NBC network) and defense contractor perspective. However, since 1998 it has been shifting that business around. It sold off Spacenet, a network solutions company, to satellite operator Gilat, and then sold GE Americom and its attendant satellite fleet (one of the largest in the world) to SES of France. At the same time, it announced plans to buy Honeywell, whose Aerospace business has revenues in excess of $10 billion, largely in manufacturing and avionics maintenance. However, it failed to obtain permission to buy Honeywell—a major disappointment for GE and its investors.

GER Holdings Corporation
LOCATION: Millbrook, New York
HELD: Private
REVENUES: NA
EMPLOYEES: NA
WEBSITE: http://www.ger.com
BUSINESS: GER is providing specialized airborne remote sensing systems and services for agribusiness, environmental

monitoring, and natural resource management. The company's planned GER Earth Resources Observation System (GEROS) will be a constellation of six, low-Earth-orbiting spacecraft and ground infrastructure designed to collect remotely-sensed data of interest to a wide variety of users. Customers are primarily governments and universities.

Gilat Satellite Networks Ltd.

LOCATION:	Petah Tikva, Israel
HELD:	Public (NASDAQ: GILTF)
REVENUES:	$504.6 million
EMPLOYEES:	NA
WEBSITE:	http://www.gilat.com
BUSINESS:	Gilat is an international provider of telecom-

munications solutions that use VSAT satellite network technology. The company delivers satellite-based, end-to-end enterprise networking and rural telephony solutions to customers across six continents and markets interactive broadband data services using its SkyBlaster and Skystar Advantage equipment and systems. Its Spacenet subsidiary (purchased from GE Americon—now SES—in 1998) provides two-way, satellite-based, broadband networking solutions for a wide range of organizations throughout North America. These solutions include provision of all equipment, bandwidth, implementation, and ongoing network and field support on a full turnkey, outsource basis. Additionally, Gilat is a partner—with Microsoft, EchoStar, and ING Furman Selz Investments—in StarBand Communications, the two-way, high-speed satellite broadband Internet service provider.

Harris Corp.

LOCATION:	Melbourne, Florida
HELD:	Public (NYSE: HRS)

REVENUES: $1.8 billion
EMPLOYEES: 10,000
WEBSITE: http://www.harris.com
BUSINESS: Harris has been a supplier of satellite and space-related communication systems for commercial and military customers for nearly 50 years. Its offerings are diverse and not easily categorized, as they range from satellite contracting to digital television transmission. The company can—and does—build satellites, antennas, computer subsystems, transmission equipment, and just about anything else related to high-end communications. Its space projects have included telemetry systems for Telstar, processors for the Hubble Space Telescope, deployable mesh antennas for Lockheed Martin Asia Cellular Satellite (ACeS), systems for the space shuttle, and the communications payloads for Ellipso, Inc. satellites. Despite its wide-ranging business endeavors, the government accounts for roughly half of the company's revenue.

Hughes Electronics Corp.
LOCATION: El Segundo, California
HELD: Public (NYSE: GMH)
REVENUES: $7.2 billion
EMPLOYEES: 9,800
WEBSITE: http://www.hughes.com
BUSINESS: One of the pioneers of the space business, Hughes Electronics is now a company in transition. Owned by General Motors, Hughes sold off its satellite business to Boeing (now called Boeing Satellite Services) in order to focus on its communications business, namely DirecTV and PanAmSat (of which it owns 81 percent). It also has Hughes Network Systems, which develops communications networks for commercial and government clients, ranging from VSATs to cellular and wireless systems. Despite Hughes' shift in focus, DirectTV is a hot

commodity—with nearly 10 million subscribers—and has attracted interest from Rupert Murdoch's News Corp. and rival EchoStar, both of whom have expressed interest in acquiring the division. If this occurs, Hughes Electronics will most likely cease to exist in anything resembling its current form.

Incredible Adventures

LOCATION:	Sarasota, Florida
HELD:	Private
REVENUES:	NA
EMPLOYEES:	NA
WEBSITE:	http://www.incredible-adventures.com
BUSINESS:	Travel company that is prebooking reserva-

tions for flights aboard suborbital vehicles in the next few years. While waiting, eager travelers can take advantage of offerings that include travel on a Russian MIG 25 fighter and a near-weightless experience aboard a specially equipped plane that flies in parabolic arcs.

Inmarsat Ltd.

LOCATION:	London, England
HELD:	Government consortium
REVENUES:	$290 million
EMPLOYEES:	400
WEBSITE:	http://www.inmarsat.org
BUSINESS:	Inmarsat was established in 1979 to

develop satellite communications for the maritime industry, with the goal of providing ship management and distress and safety applications. It has since expanded into land, mobile, and aeronautical communications and operates nine satellites. The Inmarsat satellite system consists of nine satellites in GEO, four of which serve dedicated functions for the company while the others are used as spares and for leasing purposes. In 1999,

Inmarsat became the first intergovernmental "treaty" organization to privatize and become a commercial entity.

Intelsat Ltd. (International Telecommunications Satellite
Organization)
    LOCATION: Washington, D.C.
    HELD: Private (formerly a consortium)
    REVENUES: $1.1 billion
    EMPLOYEES: 900
    WEBSITE: http://www.intelsat.com
    BUSINESS: Formed in 1964, Intelsat was the world's
first commercial satellite venture (despite its government affili-
ation). Its legacy is full of amazing achievements, including the
broadcast of the Apollo 11 Moon landing and the establishment
of a direct line between the White House and Kremlin. It has a
global fleet of 20 satellites which provide Internet, broadcast,
telephony, and corporate network services to companies in
more than 200 countries and territories worldwide. It provides
Internet, corporate network, broadcast, and carrier services. In
November 2000, Intelsat's 144 member governments formally
approved a plan to privatize the organization in 2001. Its initial
shareholders will include major telecommunications companies
from all the member countries (Lockheed Martin is the single
largest shareholder). An initial public offering is expected at
some point in the future.

International Launch Services (ILS)
    LOCATION: McLean, Virginia
    HELD: Joint venture
    REVENUES: NA
    EMPLOYEES: 80
    WEBSITE: http://www.ilslaunch.com
    BUSINESS: ILS is a dedicated launch services company

built on several related Lockheed Martin ventures. It was formed in June 1995 with the merger of Lockheed's Commercial Launch Services (the marketing and mission management division for the Atlas rocket) and Lockheed-Khrunichev-Energia International (which managed commercial Proton launches). The partners are Lockheed, which offers its Atlas vehicle, Russia's Energia, which builds fourth stage components, and Russia's Khrunichev, which supplies its Proton and Angara launch vehicles. The company provides launches from both Cape Canaveral in Florida and the Baikonur Cosmodrome in Kazakhstan. It led the industry with 14 launches in 2000 and claims to have a backlog of some $3 billion in launch services contracts. Customers include EchoStar, AsiaSat, Alcatel Space, PanAmSat, and SES. The company's structure and business model is similar to that of Sea Launch (see below).

Intersputnik

LOCATION: Moscow, Russia
HELD: Consortium
REVENUES: NA
EMPLOYEES: NA
WEBSITE: http://www.intersputnik.com
BUSINESS: Intersputnik is a Russian-led company formed in 1971 by members of the former Communist bloc (Bulgaria, Hungary, East Germany, Cuba, Mongolia, Poland, Romania, USSR, and Czechoslovakia) to coordinate the satellite communications needs of these countries. It began offering commercial services in 1992, and today it has more than 20 member nations. In 1997 it teamed with Lockheed Martin to form Lockheed Martin Intersputnik to offer a complete range of satellite services, from manufacture and launch to maintenance and operation.

Iridium Satellite LLC

LOCATION:	Tempe, Arizona
HELD:	Private (recovered assets from bankruptcy)
REVENUES:	NA
EMPLOYEES:	60
WEBSITE:	http://www.iridium.com

BUSINESS: The Iridium plan is simple: put 66 satellites into LEO and offer global communication from a single phone. Good idea, bad execution. Due to delays and high costs, the initial Iridium was shut down after only two years. After its initial failure, Motorola had planned on letting its satellites burn out, but investors from Brazil, Australia, and Saudi Arabia bought the $5 billion worth of assets for a paltry $25 million and formed Iridium Satellite LLC. The new Iridium has introduced products and services that are far less expensive than the fees that were being charged by its predecessor. It has already lined up a $72 million deal with the Pentagon to provide unlimited airtime for up to 20,000 subscribers, and the company is actively courting other federal agencies. Boeing is managing the Iridium satellite network.

Ishikawajima-Harima Heavy Industries Co. Ltd.

LOCATION:	Tokyo, Japan
HELD:	Public (Tokyo: 7013)
REVENUES:	$9.4 billion
EMPLOYEES:	12,800
WEBSITE:	http://www.ihi.co.jp/ihi/gaikyo/gaikyo-e.html

BUSINESS: IHI manufactures a wide range of equipment and machinery for use in industries ranging from shipbuilding to paper production. Its primary space development projects are rocket and satellite propulsion systems, altitude control systems, equipment for the ISS, and ground support facilities.

Israel Aircraft Industries Electronics Group (IAI)

LOCATION: Lod, Israel
HELD: Government-owned
REVENUES: $2 billion
EMPLOYEES: 14,000
WEBSITE: http://www.iai.co.il
BUSINESS: IAI is primarily a defense company and one
of Israel's largest corporations. Its Electronics Group builds
satellites, communications systems, and navigation and telemetry systems. It is a partner in West Indian Space (with ELOP
Electro Optics Industries, Ltd. of Israel and Core Software Technology of the U.S.), which plans to launch a constellation of
eight Earth Remote Observation Satellites (EROS). EROS will
provide global real-time high resolution imaging services for
commercial customers.

ITT Industries

LOCATION: White Plains, New York
HELD: Public (NYSE: ITT)
REVENUES: $4.8 billion
EMPLOYEES: 42,000
WEBSITE: http://www.ittind.com
BUSINESS: Not to be confused with ITT Corporation,
ITT Industries did initial development of much of the technology used on modern satellites. The company developed remote
sensing and imaging systems that are used for observation,
weather monitoring, and climate research, and it worked with
the U.S. Air Force to create its highly successful GPS system
(called NAVSTAR). ITT continues to develop systems for government and commercial satellite projects, including Internet
and communications systems. In April 1999, ITT made an investment in EarthWatch, which is launching a series of remote imag-

ing satellites for use by a wide variety of customers including community planners and insurance adjusters.

JSAT Corp. (formerly Japan Satellite Systems Inc.)
  LOCATION: Tokyo, Japan
  HELD: Public (Tokyo Stock Exchange: 9442)
  REVENUES: $320 million
  EMPLOYEES: 163
  WEBSITE: http://www.iijnet.or.jp/JSAT/e_index.html
  BUSINESS: JSAT is one of the primary satellite operators in the Asia-Pacific region. The company owns and operates eight satellites and provides communications and broadcasting services including network coverage, simultaneous content distribution, large content storage capacity, and strong damage resistance. The company has partnered with companies around the world, including SES and NTT DoCoMo. JSAT satellites are also used by Japan's first CS digital broadcaster SkyPerfecTV!, which has 3 million subscribers.

Kelly Space & Technology
  LOCATION: San Bernardino, California
  HELD: Private
  REVENUES: NA
  EMPLOYEES: NA
  WEBSITE: http://www.kellyspace.com/
  BUSINESS: Kelly Space has developed a unique reusable launch vehicle (RLV) based on its Eclipse system. Eclipse involves towing a vehicle (called the Astroliner) into space behind a modified Boeing 747. Once airborne, the Astroliner separates from the plane to deliver satellite payloads into orbit and returns to Earth. Since its inception in 1993, Kelly Space has successfully demonstrated the technique and under-

taken several feasibility studies for NASA. The company is actively looking for financing to continue its program.

Kistler Aerospace

LOCATION: Kirkland, Washington
HELD: Private
REVENUES: NA
EMPLOYEES: NA
WEBSITE: http://www.kistleraerospace.com/
BUSINESS: Kistler is the acknowledged "startup" leader among companies developing reusable launch vehicles (RLVs). Having secured a half billion dollars in investment since its formation in 1993, Kistler's development of its K-1 rocket has attracted numerous partners (Lockheed Martin, Northrop Grumman, Aerojet, Draper Labs) who are involved in the project. Its RLV concept involves returning empty rocket stages to Earth using parachutes and airbags (which is how the Russians land their manned vehicles). To the surprise of many in the space community, Kistler received a contract from NASA in May 2001 for $135 million to provide launch data and perform test flights as part of NASA's Strategic Launch Initiative. This money will certainly aid the company in continuing the development of its RLVs, which it hopes to have in use by 2003.

Khrunichev State Research and Space Production Center

LOCATION: Moscow, Russia
HELD: Government-owned
REVENUES: NA
EMPLOYEES: NA
WEBSITE: http://www.khrunichev.ru/internet.www/
               eng/i.htm
BUSINESS: Khrunichev is a formidable presence in the space industry due to its long history of developing launch

vehicles and manned spacecraft. Khrunichev manufactured all the Russian manned orbital stations, including Mir, all the heavy modules that dock to the orbital stations, and Russia's three-seater recoverable manned spacecrafts. It currently markets its Proton, Rockot, and Angara rockets to international customers. A major participant in the International Space Station, it developed the first components to be deployed on the ISS: the Functional Cargo Module (FCM), Service Module, and Universal docking module. The company is a partner in International Launch Services (with Lockheed and Energia) and a partner in Eurockot (with Astrium, part of EADS). It is also part of an international consortium to develop remote-sensing spacecraft.

L-3 Communications

LOCATION:	New York, New York
HELD:	Public (NYSE: LLL)
REVENUES:	$1.9 billion
EMPLOYEES:	14,000
WEBSITE:	http://www.L-3com.com/

BUSINESS: L-3 is an electronics and communications company that provides products and customized services to the defense, aerospace, and marine industries. In space, its products are used for guidance, navigation, positioning, and control of satellites and launch vehicles and are found on Delta rockets and on the ISS. Its Satellite Networks division is a manufacturer of satellite communications products and systems for use in satellite Internet service, traditional transmission, very small aperture terminals (VSATs), and digital video broadcasting. Much of the company's space expertise was gained through acquisition of assets from companies including Bendix, Allied Signal, and Gilat.

Litton Industries Inc.

LOCATION:	Woodland Hills, California
HELD:	Public (NYSE: LIT) Subsidiary of Northrop Grumman
REVENUES:	$5.6 billion
EMPLOYEES:	40,300
WEBSITE:	http://www.litton.com
BUSINESS:	Litton is a large electronics-based company

with manufacturing capabilities (it also builds ships) and numerous government contracts. The company is a primary supplier of electronics systems to the aerospace and satellite industry with products ranging from navigation and motion control systems to oxygen-generating equipment and data recorders. The company is likely to undergo a fair degree of transition in the immediate future as it was purchased by aerospace and defense firm Northrop Grumman in April 2001.

Lockheed Martin Corp.

LOCATION:	Bethesda, Maryland
HELD:	Public (NYSE: LMT)
REVENUES:	$23.5 billion
EMPLOYEES:	126,000
WEBSITE:	http://www.lockheedmartin.com
BUSINESS:	The world's number two aerospace com-

pany, Lockheed Martin's presence in the space industry is nearly as pervasive as the number one company, Boeing. As an international entity, its core business areas are systems integration, aeronautics, space, technology services, and global telecommunications. Its activity in the space industry is nothing less than comprehensive; through its numerous divisions it builds satellites, offers launch services and vehicles (the Atlas and Titan series), and manages satellite operations (it owns Comsat and is a majority shareholder in Inmarsat). It oversees the operation of the space shuttle as a partner in United Space Alliance with Boeing; it has partnered with Russia's Khrunichev and Energia to form the launch company International Launch Services; it is the satellite provider for Intersputnik (part of a joint venture called Lockheed Martin Intersputnik); and it is part owner of the Asia Cellular Satellite International. In short, there is little that Lockheed isn't involved in when it comes to space. NASA and other government agencies account for 22 percent of its business.

Loral Space & Communications
> LOCATION: New York, New York
> HELD: Public (NYSE: LOR)
> REVENUES: $1.2 billion
> EMPLOYEES: 3,700
> WEBSITE: http://www.loral.com
> BUSINESS: Loral is one of the largest satellite manu-

facturers in the world and one of the only companies that derives the bulk of its revenue (three-quarters) from building satellites. To reflect the level to which it serves the satellite industry, its business is stratified into specific satellite businesses: Space Systems/Loral, which has received contracts to build more than 210 satellites in the last four decades; fixed satellite services, which includes ten satellites and attendant services (as well as its partnerships); broadband data services, provided through its Loral CyberStar group; and global telephone services, which oversees Iridium rival Globalstar. Loral is a partner with Alcatel Space in Europe*Star, a company that delivers satellite services to Europe, South Africa, the Middle East, India, and Southeast Asia.

MAN Technologie AG
> LOCATION: Augsburg, Germany
> HELD: Public (German: MAN)

REVENUES: $13.8 billion
EMPLOYEES: 71,000
WEBSITE: http://www.ag.man.de/
BUSINESS: MAN Aktiengesellschaft is one of the oldest heavy equipment manufacturers on the planet, founded in 1845. Its MAN Technologie division is a major supplier to the European space industry and builds components for launch and space vehicles, including structural and propulsion systems. It built and maintains the Arianespace launch facility in Kourou, French Guyana.

MicroCHIPs, Inc.
LOCATION: Cambridge, Massachusetts
HELD: Private
REVENUES: NA
EMPLOYEES: NA
WEBSITE: http://www.mchips.com/
BUSINESS: MicroCHIPS develops MicroElectroMechanical Systems (MEMS) for delivery and sensing systems for use in the areas of pharmaceuticals, diagnostics, and consumer products. MicroCHIPS' technology is based on tiny silicon or polymeric microchips containing up to thousands of micro-reservoirs, each of which can be filled with any combination of drugs, reagents, or other chemicals. Complex chemical release patterns can be achieved by opening the micro-reservoirs on demand. The company is currently developing external and implantable MEMS for the delivery of proteins, hormones, pain medications, and other pharmaceutical compounds.

MirCorp
LOCATION: Amsterdam, Netherlands
HELD: Joint Venture (Gold & Appel Transfer S.A. and RSC Energia)

REVENUES: NA
EMPLOYEES: NA
WEBSITE: http://www.mirstation.com/
BUSINESS: With money from Gold & Appel Transfer
S.A. and expertise from RSC Energia, MirCorp's goal is to open
up space to any and all commercial possibilities. The company
made a name for itself when it took over the operation of Mir in
early 2000 and then reached agreements with Dennis Tito and
the producers of the TV show *Survivor* to provide them with
tourist travel to the now gone but not forgotten Mir. The Russian station's instability, however, put an end to those plans. In
the wake of Tito's successful trip to the ISS, it is now focused on
other possibilities within the Russian space community, such as
Soyuz flights to the ISS. Its international investors have committed funding for commercial operations in space—first on Mir
and then on the International Space Station—and MirCorp is
tasked with raising additional funds that will support the Russian operations on the ISS for the medium term. Tourism may
play a big role in these plans.

Mitsubishi Electric Corp.
LOCATION: Tokyo, Japan
HELD: Public (OTC: MIELY)
REVENUES: $35.7 billion
EMPLOYEES: 116,600
WEBSITE: http://www.mitsubishielectric.com
BUSINESS: Mitsubishi Electric builds both industrial
and consumer electronic products, ranging from elevators to
refrigerators. Since 1960, it has also been building electronic
space equipment, notably satellites and satellite components.
The company has contributed to the production of more than
half the satellites currently in use by Japan (science and commercial). In addition to the construction of satellites like the

Superbird series for Space Communications Corporation, Mitsubishi Electric also manufactures satellite communications equipment and manages Earth stations and tracking operations.

Mitsubishi Heavy Industries Ltd.
>   LOCATION: Tokyo, Japan
>   HELD: Public (Tokyo: 7011)
>   REVENUES: $27.2 billion
>   EMPLOYEES: 40,300
>   WEBSITE: http://www.mhi.co.jp/indexe.html
>   BUSINESS: Known for its work on massive projects such

as building ships, nuclear power plants, and water treatment systems, Mitsubishi Heavy Industries has a significant presence in the space industry. It provides satellite launch integration services, is developing a new low-temperature rocket engine with Boeing for a next-generation launch vehicle, is overseeing construction of the Japanese Experiment Module (JEM) and transfer module for the ISS, and is working on rocket and experimental shuttle projects for NASDA, Japan's space agency.

Mobile Satellite Services Corp.
>   LOCATION: Gaithersburg, Maryland
>   HELD: Private
>   REVENUES: NA
>   EMPLOYEES: NA
>   WEBSITE: http://www.mobile-sat.com/
>   BUSINESS: Founded in 1993, Mobile Satellite Services

provides design services and supplies satellite communication products to various industries. Its products include a satellite-based car radio receiver (which it has developed with Sirius Satellite Radio), satellite modems, and hubs and gateways to connect satellite networks to terrestrial telephone and data networks.

Mobile Telesystems Inc.

LOCATION: Gaithersburg, Maryland

HELD: Division of Optical Scientific Inc.

REVENUES: NA

EMPLOYEES: NA

WEBSITE: http://mti-usa.com/

BUSINESS: Mobile Telesystems (MTI) is the largest U.S. manufacturer of Inmarsat terminals with an installed base of over 5,000 terminals. The company was founded in 1975 as a group within Comsat Corporation and was spun off in 1988 as a private company. It was one of the early developers of transportable satellite communication devices for land, marine, and fixed-base-station satellite facilities. Not to be confused with Russian wireless carrier Mobile TeleSystems (MTS).

MSE Technology Applications

LOCATION: Butte, Montana

HELD: Private

REVENUES: NA

EMPLOYEES: 230

WEBSITE: http://www.mse-ta.com

BUSINESS: MSE is an engineering company that applies technology to a number of problems, namely hazardous waste management, including plasma, mine, industrial, and offgas waste. Founded in 1974, it was originally an arm of the Department of Energy until it was spun off as a private company in 1996. From that unlikely business start MSE gained a knowledge of fuel and power generation technologies that the company has since used to develop new propellants, engines, and space vehicles. Primary among these is the Hypersonic X-43 vehicle, a NASA prototype that uses an air-breathing scramjet engine. In addition, MSE is developing plasma and ion drives, electromagnetic propulsion, and pulse generation engines. The bulk of this work is funded by NASA research centers.

National Aeronautics and Space Administration (NASA)
LOCATION: Washington, D.C.
HELD: Government-owned
REVENUES: NA
EMPLOYEES: 18,000
WEBSITE: http://www.nasa.gov
BUSINESS: NASA is the agency responsible for all of the U.S. government ventures involving space. Created in 1958 from the National Advisory Committee for Aeronautics (formed in 1915), NASA's role in space exploration—from manned lunar landing to exploring the surface of Mars—is unmatched by any other agency on Earth. It oversees numerous labs and research facilities (Jet Propulsion Laboratory, Ames Research Center, Goddard Space Flight Center, Johnson and Kennedy Space Centers), vehicle and satellite development, and launch operations. Its budget is $14 billion, much of which goes to the space shuttle and ISS; it's also used for research projects, hard science, satellite missions, space exploration, and education. NASA is not considered a viable agency for the promotion of space commercialization, and its opposition to Dennis Tito's trip to the ISS further cemented the agency's role as one not interested in space business.

National Space Development Agency of Japan (NASDA)
LOCATION: Tokyo, Japan
HELD: Government-owned
REVENUES: NA
EMPLOYEES: 1,088
WEBSITE: http://www.nasda.go.jp/index_e.html

BUSINESS: The National Space Development Agency of Japan (NASDA) was established in October 1969 to act as the nucleus for the Japanese development of space. By law, it is responsible for the development of satellites (including space experiments and the space station), launch vehicles and services, and the development of methods, facilities, and equipment required for these activities. Like all national space agencies, NASDA promotes research, exploration, and education and awards projects to industry contractors. It has a budget of approximately $1.5 billion and is aggressively pursuing its own manned flight program.

NEC Toshiba Space Systems

LOCATION: Yokohama, Japan
HELD: Joint venture
REVENUES: NA
EMPLOYEES: 1,200
WEBSITE: http://www.nec.com
BUSINESS: Japanese electronics giants NEC and Toshiba decided to merge their space-based businesses together in late 2000 and formalized the deal in April 2001. The plan came about in order for the companies to garner a larger share of their domestic business while creating a larger company to pursue international business (dominated by companies like TRW, Litton, and Loral). NEC owns 60 percent and Toshiba 40 percent of the new entity, which will be involved in all aspects of the space business except launch vehicles. It will design and manufacture satellites and satellite components such as transponders, sensors, solar array panels, and deployable reflectors. It will also provide consultation and develop products for manned flights, including onboard electrical equipment and ground systems.

New ICO

LOCATION: London, England
HELD: Private (formerly ICO Global Communica-
                tions
REVENUES: NA
EMPLOYEES: NA
WEBSITE: http://www.ico.com
BUSINESS: Built on the assets of the former ICO Global
Communications, which went bankrupt in 1999, New ICO is
targeting markets that are underserved by terrestrial communications services using a network of 12 satellites. Its initial strategy is to provide Internet access and other wireless services to
serve markets such as the maritime, transportation, oil and gas,
and construction industries and governmental agencies where
there is an established demand for satellite communications
services. The company plans to eventually extend its focus to
broader markets such as small and medium-sized businesses,
small office, and residential users. New ICO was resurrected by
cellular pioneer Craig McCaw, who led a group of international
investors to provide $1.2 billion to acquire the New ICO busi-
ness in May 2000.

New Skies Satellites NV

LOCATION: The Hague, Netherlands
HELD: Public (NYSE: NSK)
REVENUES: $198 million
EMPLOYEES: 103
WEBSITE: http://www.newskies.com
BUSINESS: New Skies Satellites was spun off from Intel-
sat during that company's privatization in 1998. In the process,
it got five GEO satellites with global coverage, and now offers
direct-to-home TV broadcasting, Internet access, and data and
voice transmission services. Building on its Intelsat roots, New

Skies has more than 100 customers, including broadcasters (CNN, the BBC), corporate networks, and telecommunications companies. The company has three new satellites on order and claims to be one of the only satellite companies with global coverage (the others being the original Intelsat, PanAmSat, and SES).

Northrop Grumman Corp.
LOCATION: Los Angeles, California
HELD: Public (NYSE: NOC)
REVENUES: $7.6 billion
EMPLOYEES: 39,300
WEBSITE: http://www.northgrum.com
BUSINESS: Northrop Grumman is best known for its military aircraft, but it also provides electronics and software to the space industry. Its Logicon division (which accounts for about $1 billion in revenue) is responsible for managing ground operations at NASA's Kennedy Space Center and the Cape Canaveral Air Station, along with providing technical services to various NASA facilities. Northrop Grumman acquired Litton Industries in 2001 (see above), which is a leading supplier of electronics systems to the aerospace business.

Orbital Sciences Corp.
LOCATION: Dulles, Virginia
HELD: Public (NYSE: ORB)
REVENUES: $725 million
EMPLOYEES: 4,200
WEBSITE: http://www.orbital.com
BUSINESS: Founded in 1982, Orbital Sciences is one of the more prominent non-aerospace companies in the space industry. Primarily because it targets "small space" applications. Nonetheless, it has several groups that serve the needs of specific markets. Its Launch Systems Group features the air-launched

Pegasus and ground-launched Taurus and Minotaur rockets for boosting small satellites into LEO. The company's Space Systems Group manufactures small, low-cost satellites for scientific research, remote imaging, and communications. Through its Magellan subsidiary, Orbital offers a line of GPS navigation, positioning, and guidance products for outdoor recreation, industrial surveying, and automotive navigation. Its ORBCOMM affiliate was designed to provide global wireless communications but has been put up for sale after declaring bankruptcy.

PanAmSat Corp.

LOCATION: Greenwich, Connecticut
HELD: Public (NASDAQ: SPOT)
REVENUES: $1 billion
EMPLOYEES: 800
WEBSITE: http://www.panamsat.com
BUSINESS: PanAmSat is owner of one of the largest fleets of global satellites in the world. Formed in 1984 by Rene Anselmo, who saw a huge potential market for satellite service in Latin and South America, the company overcame huge resistance to become the predominant player in the marketplace with 21 satellites in GEO. The company builds, owns, and operates networks that deliver entertainment and information to cable television systems, TV broadcast affiliates, direct-to-home TV operators, Internet service providers, telecommunications companies, and corporations. Major clients include broadcasters and news organizations such as the BBC, China Central Television, Discovery, Disney, NHK, Reuters, AOL Time-Warner, Bloomberg, Viacom, and others. More than 45 Internet service providers receive their Internet backbone connection over PanAmSat's satellites worldwide in countries such as Argentina, Australia, Chile, Colombia, Japan, Korea, New Zealand, Peru, and Taiwan. The company is 81 percent owned by Hughes Electronics, which

is the subject of an acquisition by either News Corp or EchoStar. If either of these companies bought Hughes, it is likely they would spin PanAmSat off.

Raytheon Co.

LOCATION:	Lexington, Massachusetts
HELD:	Public (NYSE: RTN)
REVENUES:	$16.9 billion
EMPLOYEES:	93,700
WEBSITE:	http://www.raytheon.com/

BUSINESS: Known primarily for its electronics products, Raytheon is actually the third largest aerospace company in the U.S. after Boeing and Lockheed. The company's space business activity is varied and ranges from satellite components to ground tracking stations. In the latter category, Raytheon has more than 40 satellite ground stations worldwide. It has also developed ECLIPSE, satellite command and control software that provides command and control for management of satellites, including orbit determination ground equipment status and control, spacecraft payload control, data archiving and analysis, and fleet or constellation management. Raytheon is responsible for designing the Optical Telescope Assembly (a deployable mirror) for the successor to the Hubble Telescope, NASA's Next Generation Space Telescope (NGST). A substantial amount of the company's revenue comes from government contractors, although it has a significant amount of domestic and international commercial business.

Rocket Space Corporation Energia (RSCE)

LOCATION:	Korolev, Russia
HELD:	Private (formerly government-owned)
REVENUES:	6,011,941 in thousands of rubles
EMPLOYEES:	20,000

WEBSITE: http://www.energialtd.com

BUSINESS: Energia has the distinction of being the organization that launched the first satellite (Sputnik) and first man (Yuri Gagarin) into space. Privatized in 1994, the company has traditionally been viewed as an organization of the Russian state that performs much of the launch and maintenance of spacecraft, especially those involving manned flight, such as Mir and the ISS. In some cases, its expertise and experience matches and even exceeds that of its western counterparts. It manages the Baikonur Cosmodrome launch facilities and is a partner with Lockheed Martin in International Launch Services (ILS), a company that provides launches from both Cape Canaveral in Florida and the Baikonur Cosmodrome in Kazakhstan. Energia is also a 25 percent partner with Boeing in Sea Launch.

Rockwell Collins
    LOCATION: Cedar Rapids, Iowa
    HELD: Public (NYSE: COL)
    REVENUES: $7.2 billion
    EMPLOYEES: 41,200
    WEBSITE: http://www.collins.rockwell.com
    BUSINESS: Rockwell has been divesting itself of its former aerospace and defense holdings to focus on its automation and electronics business, now called Rockwell Collins. Its offerings in this area will now be comprised of navigation, communication, and sensing equipment. Its Precision Lightweight GPS Receiver (PLGR) family of hand-held and vehicular devices is the U.S. military's standard for GPS equipment. This division (formed after much of the aerospace group was sold to Boeing) may ultimately be spun off as a separate public entity with some 16,000 employees.

Sea Launch
LOCATION: Long Beach, California
HELD: Joint venture
REVENUES: NA
EMPLOYEES: NA
WEBSITE: http://www.sea-launch.com
BUSINESS: Sea Launch provides launch services to clients from its home port in Long Beach and its marine launch facility in the Pacific Ocean. Formed in 1995 with its first launch in 1999, the partnership is held by Boeing (payload fairing, integration, and operations), RSC Energia (upper stages of launch vehicles), Anglo-Norwegian Kvaener Group (platform construction and operations), and Yuzhnoe/Yuzhmash (first stage of launch vehicles). The company offers low-cost heavy payload launches by combining the strengths of its various partners and has performed more than 20 launches to date for customers ranging from PanAmSat to XM Satellite Radio. Its mandate and corporate structure is very similar to that of International Launch Services (see above).

Sirius Satellite Radio
LOCATION: New York, New York
HELD: Public (NASDAQ: SIRI)
REVENUES: NA
EMPLOYEES: 180
WEBSITE: http://www.siriusradio.com
BUSINESS: Sirius is offering subscription-based satellite radio services to users. Founded in 1990, it is initially targeting the automotive market, offering drivers 100 channels of uninterrupted digital radio across the United States. The cost for the service will be about $10 per month and will require dedicated radio hardware. The company has already formed partnerships with Ford, DaimlerChrysler, BMW, Mercedes, Mazda,

Jaguar, and Volvo. Content providers include C-Span, Fox News Network, Bloomberg, CNBC, and National Public Radio. Its competitor in this space is XM Satellite Radio.

SkyBridge Satellite
LOCATION: New York, New York
HELD: Partnership (Alcatel, Boeing, ComDev, CNES, others)
REVENUES: NA
EMPLOYEES: NA
WEBSITE: http://www.skybridgesatellite.com/
BUSINESS: SkyBridge was formed in 1997 by Alcatel with the intention of creating a partnership that will provide broadband services to homes and offices in less-densely-populated areas. The company plans to launch a constellation of 80 LEO satellites and two GEO satellites that will reach users anywhere in the world, offering high-speed local access to the Internet and multimedia broadcasts. Service is slated to begin in 2003. Its full complement of international partners includes Boeing, Loral Space & Communication, EMS Technologies, ComDev, Mitsubishi Electric, Sharp, Toshiba, Thomson Multimedia, CNES, SNECMA, Belgium's SRIW, Litton, and L-3 Communications.

Sky Global Networks
LOCATION: New York, New York
HELD: Subsidiary of News Corp, IPO planned (NASDAQ: SGN)
REVENUES: $793 million
EMPLOYEES: 2,400
WEBSITE: http://www.newscorp.com
BUSINESS: Sky Global is the satellite broadcasting arm of Rupert Murdoch's News Corporation. It includes British Sky Broadcasting (BSkyB), Asia's STAR TV, and Latin American

operations. Together, the various holdings reach approximately 85 million subscribers. Sky Global also owns just over 21 percent of Gemstar-TV Guide International, the programming and viewer listing company. Murdoch hopes to add Hughes Electronics' DirecTV to this group—an acquisition he is proposing with partners Microsoft and Liberty Media.

Société Européenne des Satellites SA (SES)

LOCATION: Betzdorf, Luxembourg
HELD: Public (Luxembourg Exchange: SES)
REVENUES: $787 million
EMPLOYEES: 420
WEBSITE: http://www.ses-astra.com
BUSINESS: SES operates Europe's Astra satellite system, which carries more than 1,000 digital and analogue TV and radio services to 22 countries and some 87 million subscribers via its 11 European satellites. The company has holdings all over the globe, including 34.3 percent of Asia Satellite Telecommunications Company (AsiaSat), 50 percent of the Nordic Satellite Company NSAB, and nearly 20 percent of Star One/BrasilSat. It also acquired GE Americom for $5 billion in 2001, which already had one of the largest satellite fleets in the world (17), and the single largest North American fleet (12). All told, SES now has a global reach with 28 satellites and 13 partner satellites (three AsiaSat, three SIRIUS, five Brasilsat, and two more through Americom's interests in Latin America and Asia). The Luxembourg government owns 20 percent of SES, while Deutsche Telekom has a 21 percent stake in the company.

Société Nationale d'Etude et de Construction de Moteurs d'Avion (Snecma)

LOCATION: Paris, France
HELD: Government-owned

REVENUES: $4.8 billion
EMPLOYEES: 35,000
WEBSITE: http://www.snecma.com
BUSINESS   Snecma is one of the oldest and largest propulsion companies in the world, with roots extending back to 1905. Engines developed by its Snecma Moteurs group are used by Boeing and Arianespace for launch vehicles, including the Delta and Ariane rockets, as well as for satellite maneuvering. The company is working on plasma thrusters for satellite propulsion and is a partner in SkyBridge.

SPACE.com
LOCATION: New York, New York
HELD: Private
REVENUES: NA
EMPLOYEES: 80
WEBSITE: http://www.space.com
BUSINESS: Space.com is an Internet site that offers space content featuring daily news, information, education, entertainment, science fiction, and games. The company also sells astronomy software and has a magazine publishing group.

Space Adventures
LOCATION: Arlington, Virginia
HELD: Joint venture
REVENUES: NA
EMPLOYEES: NA
WEBSITE: http://www.spaceadventures.com/
BUSINESS: Space Adventures is offering to fly people into space for $98,000 as soon as the first flight is available, which it hopes will be between 2003 and 2005. The company assisted Dennis Tito in contacting the Russians for his historic trip to the ISS and has been offering trips on MIG 25s and near-

weightless parabolic flights for several years. It has several astronauts on its board of advisors, including Buzz Aldrin and half a dozen space shuttle veterans. Space Adventures is a partnership between several travel organizations.

Space Communications Corp.

LOCATION:	Tokyo, Japan
HELD:	Private (nearly 75% owned by various Mitsubishi companies)
REVENUES:	NA
EMPLOYEES:	200
WEBSITE:	http://www.superbird.co.jp/english/index.htm

BUSINESS: Space Communications Corporation (SCC) is a Japanese communications company established in 1985 by Mitsubishi Corporation and Mitsubishi Electric Corporation. It controls the Superbird fleet of satellites, which provides telecom and broadcasting services in Japan, including DirecPC. Much of the company's revenue comes from news gathering and cable TV companies, as well as business transmission of seminars, conferences, and training programs.

SpaceDev

LOCATION:	Poway, California
HELD:	Public (OTC BB: SPDV.OB)
REVENUES:	$3.9 million
EMPLOYEES:	25
WEBSITE:	http://www.spacedev.com

BUSINESS: Calling itself "the world's first publicly traded commercial space exploration and development company," SpaceDev's stated mission is to provide low-cost entry to space and eventually undertake deep space missions. Formed in 1996, it is developing hybrid rocket/motor-based spacecraft, ranging from a micro-launch vehicle to a small maneuverable craft that can perform orbital operations such as satellite inspection, repair, and parts replacement. To date, much of its work has been in conducting research studies for government labs, although it shuns the government-contractor tag. It is building the CHIPSat exploration satellite for the University of California at Berkeley and is organizing its own Near-Earth Asteroid Prospector (NEAP), with a fixed fee for payloads ranging from $2.5 million to $12 million. It hopes to launch this project by 2006.

SPACEHAB

LOCATION: Washington, D.C.
HELD: Public (NASDAQ: SPAB)
REVENUES: $105.7 million
EMPLOYEES: 776
WEBSITE: http://www.spacehab.com
BUSINESS: Founded in 1984, SPACEHAB develops pressurized modules for use in space research aboard the Space Shuttle. Spacehab builds and owns three of these modules, which it then leases out to NASA for onboard use as self-contained research labs or cargo-holding areas. With Russia's Energia, SPACEHAB is designing and producing the Enterprise module for the ISS, which will be an area for performing commercial work in space. Its Astrotech subsidiary offers payload planning and packing skills to commercial businesses, while its Johnson Engineering division manages the Neutral Buoyancy Pool, a facility that trains astronauts for space flight by submerging them in water. SPACEHAB also builds trainer mockups of the space shuttle and the ISS through its Space Vehicle Mockup Facility. NASA accounts for more than 80 percent of the company's revenues.

Space Island Group

LOCATION:	West Covina, California
HELD:	Private
REVENUES:	NA
EMPLOYEES:	NA
WEBSITE:	http://www.spaceislandgroup.com

BUSINESS: Founded by former TRW engineer and entrepreneur Gene Myers in 1997, Space Island Group wants to utilize discarded space shuttle external fuel tanks (which are about the size of a Boeing 747) and link them together in a circle, creating a "space island." The resulting vacation destination would rotate in order to provide artificial gravity for guests and small manufacturers. Estimating that it will cost roughly a billion dollars per year over the next few years to get operations underway, the company expects to be open for business in 2007.

Starsem

LOCATION:	Paris, France
HELD:	Joint venture
REVENUES:	NA
EMPLOYEES:	40
WEBSITE:	http://www.starsem.com/starsem/starsem.html

BUSINESS: Starsem is the company that provides commercial launch services using the Soyuz family of launch vehicles (it calls itself "The Soyuz Company"). Created in 1996, the European-Russian organization brings together all key players involved in the production and operation of Soyuz and is responsible for international sales of the vehicle for launches involving satellite systems, scientific spacecraft, and observation and meteorological platforms. Founding partners include EADS (35 percent), Arianespace (15 percent), the Russian Space

Agency (25 percent), and Russia's Samara Space Center (25 percent). Starsem has been contracted to provide launch services for the European Space Agency and for at least 32 of the planned 80 SkyBridge satellites. It is worth noting that there have been more than 1,660 successful Soyuz launches to date.

Swales Aerospace
> LOCATION: Beltsville, Maryland
> HELD: Private (employee-owned)
> REVENUES: $95 million
> EMPLOYEES: 900
> WEBSITE: http://www.swales.com
> BUSINESS: Swales provides support services to space

missions, ranging from ground support and payload management to development of vehicle electronic and thermal systems. Formed in 1978, the company also has a long history of instrument design and analysis for use on spacecraft, as well as production capabilities. The company is providing space shuttle and ISS payload support and was the prime contractor for NASA's New Millennium Program Earth Orbiter-1 (EO-1) spacecraft (launched in 2000), which is designed to develop new technologies that will enhance satellite performance. Customers include NASA, Goddard Space Flight Center, Johns Hopkins University, Jet Propulsion Laboratory, and the European Space Agency.

Telesat Canada
> LOCATION: Ottawa, Canada
> HELD: Wholly owned subsidiary of BCE, Inc. (NYSE: BCE)
> REVENUES: $272.4 million
> EMPLOYEES: NA
> WEBSITE: http://www.telesat.ca/index_e.html

BUSINESS: Serving Canada, parts of North America, and South America, Telesat has launched more than a dozen satellites since its founding in 1969, including the world's first domestic communications satellite launched into geostationary orbit by a commercial company in 1972. As part of Bell Canada, the company offers a wide array of services to customers, including TV and business telecommunications. It also specializes in satellite consulting, notably in the area of launch vehicle services, ground systems services, and insurance procurement and risk assessment. The company provides operational services as well; it won a 15-year contract with XM Satellite Radio to manage the satellite operations and associated infrastructure of XM's radio service. Other clients include Ford (for which it manages 5,500 VSAT-equipped dealerships), WildBlue, and Arabsat.

Thales Group
    LOCATION: Paris, France
    HELD: Public (Euronext Paris: HO)
    REVENUES: $8 billion
    EMPLOYEES: 65,000
    WEBSITE: http://www.thalesgroup.com
    BUSINESS: Formerly Thomson-CSF, Thales is an aerospace, electronics, and communications company with businesses throughout Europe. Much of its space business is in GPS solutions, an area in which it has staked out a leadership position in Europe via its Thales Navigation, Thales Geosolutions, and Global Telematics subsidiaries. It upped its space ante with the May 2001 announcement that it would purchase two of Orbital Sciences' satellite businesses: Magellan, a satellite navigation and positioning business, and NavSol, a joint venture with car-rental giant Hertz that provides satellite-based car navigation services.

Trimble Navigation Ltd.

LOCATION: Sunnyvale, California
HELD: Public (NASDAQ: TRMB)
REVENUES: $369 million
EMPLOYEES: 2,300
WEBSITE: http://www.trimble.com/
BUSINESS: Trimble is a little known company that ultimately wants to become synonymous with GPS services and
products. Founded in 1978, the company offers more than 100
products for a variety of industries and applications, including
road surveying, emergency vehicle dispatch, earthquake damage mapping, individual locators, fleet tracking, et al. Trimble
claims that its devices can be found in cars, boats, airplanes,
construction equipment, movie-making gear, farm machinery,
laptop computers, and eventually in personal digital assistants.
Trimble's technology is also used for precision timing for weather
radar systems, cellular companies, paging networks, investment
banks, and electrical utilities. It owns more than 200 GPS-
related patents, which gives it more than any other organization in the world, including the U.S. government, whose GPS
satellite system it uses.

TRW

LOCATION: Cleveland, Ohio
HELD: Public (NYSE: TRW)
REVENUES: $17.2 billion
EMPLOYEES: 103,000
WEBSITE: http://www.trw.com
BUSINESS: TRW's electronics are nearly ubiquitous
throughout the space industry. It works closely with both satel-
lite and launch services companies, and its technology has
been used on missions ranging from Pioneer 10 to the Chandra
X-ray telescope to the Next Generation Space Telescope. The com-

pany develops products and offers services in space communications and surveillance, observation and remote sensing, meteorology and test equipment, and command and control systems. It is also active in researching and developing MEMS technology and has successfully demonstrated a MEMS-based microthruster for use by small (50 pounds and less) satellites. The company has also been an entrepreneurial breeding ground for space industry startups, with its executives founding or participating in a large number of space companies. TRW's Aerospace & Information Systems (which includes space systems) accounts for about 40 percent of the company's revenues; its automotive group accounts for the rest.

United Space Alliance (USA)
    LOCATION: Houston, Texas
    HELD: Joint venture (Boeing and Lockheed)
    REVENUES: NA
    EMPLOYEES: NA
    WEBSITE: http://www.unitedspacealliance.com
    BUSINESS: Contrary to popular belief, NASA does not operate and maintain the space shuttle. That responsibility falls to the United Space Alliance, which was established in 1996 as a joint venture between Rockwell and Lockheed Martin, after NASA decided to consolidate its operations under a single prime contractor. USA won the contract to "manage and conduct space operations work involving the operation and maintenance of multi-purpose space systems, including systems associated with NASA's human space flight program, Space Shuttle applications beyond those of NASA, and other reusable launch and orbital systems beyond the Space Shuttle and Space Station." In essence, USA handles just about everything NASA does when it comes to manned missions. Rockwell's share of USA became part of Boeing following its acquisition of Rock-

well's aerospace and defense businesses in December 1996, making aerospace rivals Boeing and Lockheed close partners when it comes to servicing their biggest space client.

United Technologies Corporation – Aerospace Division

LOCATION: Hartford, Connecticut
HELD: Public (NYSE: UTX)
REVENUES: $12.3 billion
EMPLOYEES: 75,000
WEBSITE: http://www.utc.com/index.htm
BUSINESS: United Technologies is one of the largest companies in America, with divisions that include Pratt & Whitney and Sikorsky. In space, it literally provides the means by which astronauts are able to live and work aboard the shuttle and ISS. Via its Hamilton Sundstrand division, UTC is the prime contractor for NASA's space suit/life support system and produces environmental control, life support (oxygen and water systems), mechanical systems, and thermal control systems for international space programs. The company also makes launch vehicle hydraulic power units, engine control systems, pumps, filters, gearboxes, and a host of other components.

WildBlue Communications

LOCATION: Denver, Colorado
HELD: Private
REVENUES: NA
EMPLOYEES: 40
WEBSITE: http://www.wildblue.com
BUSINESS: Founded in 1995 as KaSTAR Satellite Communications, WildBlue plans to deliver high-speed Internet access services via satellite to homes and small offices in the U.S. and Canada. Its target market is anyone interested in simple, reliable, and inexpensive access to broadband services.

Scheduled for takeoff in 2002, WildBlue's service will provide the full range of Internet features including e-mail, shopping channels, instant messaging, web hosting, and news and information. Investors include Gemstar-TV Guide International (22 percent), Liberty Satellite (20 percent), and EchoStar (13 percent).

WorldSpace Inc.

LOCATION:	Washington, D.C.
HELD:	Private
REVENUES:	NA
EMPLOYEES:	NA
WEBSITE:	http://www.worldspace.com
BUSINESS:	WorldSpace was founded in 1990 to pro-

vide satellite delivery of digital audio communications and multimedia services to the emerging markets of the world, including Africa, the Middle East, Asia, Latin America, and the Caribbean. The company views its mission as one of providing "affluent information" to underserved markets, which will in turn open those markets to more commerce. Its direct-to-person communications and multimedia services (but not TV) are accessible to WorldSpace users via a specially designed portable receiver. The company's satellite network currently consists of two geostationary satellites, AfriStar and AsiaStar, with a third—AmeriStar—planned. It debuted its service in Africa in October 1999 and in Asia in September 2000. The company has alliances with Arianespace, Alcatel, Sanyo, JVC, Matsushita, and Hitachi for development and distribution of its system.

XM Satellite Radio

LOCATION:	Washington, D.C.
HELD:	Public (NASDAQ: XMSR)
REVENUES:	NA

EMPLOYEES: 250

WEBSITE: http://www.xmradio.com

BUSINESS: XM Satellite Radio will be offering CD-quality radio to listeners in North America via its two satellites, named "Rock" and "Roll." The company claims that these Boeing-made satellites are the most powerful communications satellites ever built. Along with investor General Motors (which holds approximately 22 percent of the company and will install the requisite radios in its cars), XM has lined up the BBC, USA Today, CNN, C-Span, The Weather Channel, BET, NASCAR, and others to provide content for its planned 100 channels. It has agreements from manufacturers including Alpine, Pioneer, Clarion, Blaupunkt, Delphi-Delco, Visteon, Panasonic, and Sanyo to build radio receivers. Like competitor Sirius Satellite Radio, XM is offering its service for about $10 per month.

AFTERWORD

As these pages have shown, "space business" is much more than space shuttles and satellite launches. With hundreds of corporate players—including some of the world's largest organizations—generating billions of dollars in revenue, the business of space is headed toward a commercial revolution. The low profile that space has had within the investment community will transform into higher visibility in the near future due to our increasing reliance on space for communications and media transmission. In addition, Dennis Tito's trip has provided us with an indication of how large the interest in space as a "destination" truly is.

Investment opportunities already abound in this environment, and they will continue to present themselves in the months and years to come. Interested investors have to follow the field, educate themselves about the potential of the various types of space businesses, and understand the way the industry works—just as they would investigate any industry in which they planned on investing. Following this industry is also no different from following any others. Watching the companies profiled in these pages, monitoring Internet sites like Space.com, and paying attention to the increasingly frequent events in the business (such as rocket tests, partnerships, and political maneuvering) are all part and parcel of becoming familiar with the space business. Space, while more exciting and potentially mysterious than many market segments, still adheres to the basic tenets of business and investing: there needs to be a revenue flow, a profit potential, and a strong business plan.

In the coming years, there will be a myriad of new and emerging technologies and industries in which to invest, including genomics, nanotechnology, biomedicine, and artificial intelligence. Space will compete with these businesses for investment dollars and investment bandwidth. One of the advantages that space will have over these other technologies and nascent industries—at least at the outset—is that it is largely unencumbered by profound moral and ethical issues. Businesses built on the success of the Human Genome Project will one day be able to prevent and cure diseases for which we currently have no successful treatment. Nanotechnology companies will ultimately create machines so small that they can work unfettered within the tissue of our bodies. In both cases, however, these technologies will not come to market until they have run a gauntlet of moral and ethical scrutiny, indignation and evaluation, and have been tried in the court of public opinion.

The business of space is free of these immediate concerns and potential dilemmas. There is no ethical or moral issue about flying into space, nor is there a new set of business concepts that have to be put into place. After all, what we intend to do in space is largely a reflection of what we already do on Earth, from mining and manufacturing to transportation and energy generation. Most of the competitive political baggage that accompanied the world's space programs in their infancy is gone, as is much of the danger of space flight. Several thousand satellites have been launched in the last four decades, and each new launch hardly raises an eyebrow. The fact that we have made traveling into space a routine endeavor—and are now considering the more frequent flying of paying customers—should signal that its risks have been brought in line with that of many other businesses. Thus, investing in space business should elicit a similar degree of safety and comfort.

As we get more of our Internet access via satellite, send parcels around the world in a matter of hours, listen to satellite radio in our cars, and watch as more and more people take personal trips to the International Space Station or make orbital flights around the Earth, the vast potential of space will literally be closer to our grasp. Once these undertakings become routine, the next steps are easier to envision—indeed, they will even be expected. Trips to the Moon and other planets, the mining of precious metals from asteroids, and the harnessing of unlimited solar energy will be obvious business pursuits, as common in the future as space shuttle flights are today (note that there have now been more than 100 shuttle launches). Once we are at that stage of doing business in space, we will see benefits back on Earth—for those of us who choose to remain here. Energy and transportation will be changed forever; we can even imagine solar-powered personal space vehicles jetting around orbital cities in the next hundred years. It has been predicted before, but now the technology, and the business, is catching up to the dreams of science-fiction writers.

Beyond that, as they say, the sky is the limit. Yet in this case, the sky isn't the limit. The only constraints are those of our imaginations and the wherewithal to make it work.

ABOUT THE AUTHORS

L ou Dobbs is the anchor and managing editor of CNN's *Lou Dobbs Money-line*. A founding member of the network in 1980 as well as CNN's financial news division, Dobbs spent 19 years with CNN before leaving in 1999 to launch Space.com, the first multimedia company dedicated to space and space-related content. He returned to CNN in 2001 to his current position. Dobbs also anchors a financial news radio report, which is syndicated by United Stations Radio Networks, Inc. to 750 stations nationwide.

Dobbs became anchor of *Moneyline* the year he joined CNN. During his tenure at the network, he helped develop CNN financial news to the award-winning leader in television business journalism and oversaw the launch of CNNfn in December 1995. He managed the network as president of CNNfn and executive vice president of CNN until June 1999. Dobbs has won nearly every major award for television journalism. He received the George Foster Peabody Award for his coverage of the 1987 stock market crash. In 1990, he was given the Luminary Award by the Business Journalism Review for his "visionary work which changed the landscape of business journalism in the 1980s." His other honors include CableACE, Front Page, Janus, and Emmy awards. In 1999, he won the Horatio Alger Association Award for Distinguished Americans and, in 2000, the National Space Club Media Award.

HP Newquist is the author of more than a dozen books, including *The Brain Makers* (Macmillan), *Virtual Reality* (Scholastic), *Artificial Intelligence* (Lafferty), and *Yahoo! The Ultimate Desk Reference to the Web* (Harper Collins). He has written hundreds of articles on the business of technology, and his work has been cited in publications ranging from the *Wall Street Journal* and *The New York Times* to *Newsweek* and *USA Today*. His website is www.newquist.net.